Effective Reading

Improving Reading Rates and Comprehension

McGRAW-HILL COMMUNICATION SKILLS SERIES

Dr. Alton L. Raygor, Consulting Editor

Spelling
Lewick-Wallace: SPELLING

Vocabulary
Lewick-Wallace: VOCABULARY BUILDING AND WORD STUDY

Writing
Lewick-Wallace: PUNCTUATION AND MECHANICS
Lewick-Wallace: GRAMMAR AND SENTENCE STRUCTURE

Reading
Raygor and Raygor: EFFECTIVE READING: IMPROVING READING RATES
AND COMPREHENSION

Study Skills
Kagan: COPING WITH COLLEGE: The Efficient Learner

Effective Reading

Improving Reading Rates and Comprehension

Alton L. Raygor, Ph.D.
University of Minnesota

Robin D. Raygor, Ph.D.
Anoka-Ramsey Community College

105187

McGraw-Hill Book Company

New York ■ St. Louis ■ San Francisco ■ Auckland ■ Bogotá ■ Hamburg
Johannesburg ■ London ■ Madrid ■ Mexico ■ Montreal ■ New Delhi
Panama ■ Paris ■ São Paulo ■ Singapore ■ Sydney ■ Tokyo ■ Toronto

Library of Congress Cataloging in Publication Data

Raygor, Alton Lamon, date
    Effective reading.

    (McGraw-Hill communication skills series)
    1. Reading (Higher education)—Programmed instruction.
2. Reading comprehension—Programmed instruction.
3. Rapid reading—Programmed instruction.   I. Raygor,
Robin D.   II. Title.   III. Series.
LB2395.R377   1985   428.4′3′077   83-22232
ISBN 0-07-051262-0

EFFECTIVE READING
Improving Reading Rates and Comprehension

1 2 3 4 5 6 7 8 9 0   DOCDOC   8 9 8 7 6 5 4

See Acknowledgments on page 321. Copyrights included on this page by reference.

ISBN 0-07-051262-0

This book was set in Times Roman by A Graphic Method Inc. The editors were
Jim Dodd and James R. Belser; the designer was Joseph Gillians; the production
supervisor was Phil Galea. The drawings were done by Fine Line Illustrations,
Inc.
R. R. Donnelley & Sons Company was printer and binder.

CONTENTS

PREFACE

Effective Reading is part of a series designed to improve the basic skills of students in college and other postsecondary educational institutions. Reading, writing, spelling, vocabulary, and study skills are important elements in school success and need to be given special attention.

The main focus of this book is the improvement of reading skills. It includes all the necessary materials, exercises, and answer keys for a self-study program. It will be helpful to most students in reading programs and can be used in classroom settings as well as in clinics or individualized programs.

The skills emphasized are those that are important to school success and that cause trouble for students most often. The readings included have been especially selected for their relation to everday life, including topics that have interest and utility for the average person.

The book is organized into four parts. Parts One, Two, and Three deal with various aspects of reading speed: rapid reading rates, skimming and scanning skills, and reading-rate flexibility. Part Four focuses on reading comprehension skills. Some students and teachers will want to use the parts of the book in sequence. Others may wish to work on the two kinds of reading skills at the same time by doing alternating units.

Like most authors, we have been influenced by many people. Outstanding among them are the professional colleagues and the graduate students that we have worked with over a period of many years. In addition, special appreciation is due to Michelle Patraw and Betty Ruth Raygor for their assistance in the development of the book.

Alton L. Raygor
Robin D. Raygor

INTRODUCTION

What Are Reading Skills?

The purpose of this book is to improve your reading skills. Let's stop first and think a few moments about what we mean by "reading skills."

Since the word "reading" can mean a lot of things, it is not easy to offer a simple definition. *A Dictionary of Reading and Related Terms* lists 4780 terms, all associated with reading.

In spite of the fact that we have many technical terms for the scientific study of reading, most of us have a good idea of what we mean when we use the word "read." We mean a process in which we look at words printed on a page and derive some meaning from them. However, to understand how to improve reading, we must look at it in more detail. Reading is really a set of skills. The efficient reader must be able to do many things:

1 Understand the author's main ideas.

2 Recognize how the material is organized.

3 Recognize and use the detailed, factual information given.

4 Retain the information gained in reading.

5 Recognize the author's purpose and tone.

6 Locate needed information in reference materials.

7 Distinguish between reliable, valid information based on good authority and unreliable opinions.

8 Apply different concepts and skills, depending on the area of study.

9 Skim over unimportant or unnecessary material when total comprehension is not necessary.

10 Vary the reading speed and approach, depending on the purpose for reading and the difficulty of the material.

11 Draw inferences and conclusions from the author's presentation.

12 Have a broad knowledge of the meaning of words.

In addition to being able to do the things listed above, the good reader operates in an efficient manner, doing all of these things quickly and effectively. This brings up the topic of reading speed. It is important to be able to read rapidly when it is appropriate to do so, but difficult, complicated material needs to be studied carefully, not skimmed. One of the most important reading skills is knowing *when* to read rapidly and when to read slowly and carefully.

If you wish to improve your reading rate, the way to do so is to practice reading rapidly. If you want to improve comprehension, then you need to focus on the reading skills that are involved in comprehension. This book will enable you to do both. It focuses on rapid reading, skimming and scanning, reading for main ideas, important facts, or details, and the organization of materials. In addition there are sections devoted to using reference materials, critical reading, and reading in particular content areas. There are many subskills in reading; a much longer book would result if a section were devoted to each. However, we have chosen to emphasize the skills that are most useful for studying because we see so many students who need help in this area.

Are You a Good Reader?

It is sometimes hard to evaluate your own reading skills. One way is to look for some of the symptoms of poor reading in the following list. You can make some of these observations yourself, but items 2 and 3 are best observed by someone else when you are unaware of it.

1 Do you read very slowly and cautiously, uncertain of your ability to get the full meaning?

2 Do you move your lips and tongue as your read?

3 Do you move your head back and forth along the line as you read?

4 Do you constantly go back over material you have already read?

5 Do you read everything at the same rate?

6 Do you have trouble with the meanings of many of the words you read?

If the answer to any of the above questions is yes, then the chances are good that you do need to improve your reading quite a bit. If you answered yes to more than one or two items, it would be wise to seek help in finding out more about your reading. Most schools have someone who can give you a standardized reading test that will give you good, reliable information about where you stand. The person in the reading program can probably also give you suggestions about where to get remedial help if your problems require serious attention.

The materials in this book are designed to help people who wish to improve their reading skills. They are not designed to be the total answer for people who have major reading problems or severe learning disabilities. Such people need special, personal, expert help.

Developing a Reading Vocabulary

One of the most important skills in reading is the knowledge of words. Since "Vocabulary Building and Word Study," another book in this series, is devoted to vocabulary development, we are not going to deal with this skill directly, but you should be aware of some basic facts. The number of words you know determines the difficulty and complexity of the material you can read and understand. If you have an extremely limited reading vocabulary, you will be able to read only very simple material. For example, children just beginning to read in first grade must use books that only have a few dozen words in them. As they progress through school their reading vocabulary keeps increasing until they are adults. Adults typically have reading vocabularies of over 50,000 words.

Failure to develop an extensive reading vocabulary will definitely hold you back in your efforts to improve comprehension. Most people learn new words by encountering them in reading or conservation, where the meaning is usually clear from the context. A few words are learned by looking them up in the dictionary.

A good way to expand your vocabulary is to read a lot, especially in different areas. That way you will find many new words, which are often explained by the author. One of the main purposes of a beginning textbook is to explain the language of the field about which it is written. Thus you can expect to increase your vocabulary a lot if you read a textbook in a field that is new to you.

If you feel that vocabulary is a problem for you, you may wish to do something systematic about it. There are many good books designed to help develop vocabulary, including the one in this series.

How to Use This Book

This book can be used as a textbook in a course or it can be used individually for personal improvement. If you are using it in a course, it is a good idea to have periodic conferences with the instructor to be sure that you are getting the maximum benefit from it. You or your instructor may find that there are certain types of errors that you often make, or some parts of the book may give you special difficulty. A teacher can be a great help when special problems come up.

Each part of the book focuses on a specific skill area, and each part has an answer key in the back of the book to enable you to check the correctness of your work. If you are in a class, the teacher will probably tell you how fast to move through the book. If not, we suggest that you spread out your efforts over at least a month. Learning that is spaced out in time is more effective in producing long-term results.

How Much Time Will It Take?

There are 33 Units in this book. Each one will probably take you about half an hour to complete. Thus the total time spent on this book will be about 10 to 20 hours, depending on how you read now and how much you improve. The total amount of time you spend improving your reading will depend on how much you read beyond the material in this book. Actually, almost all the reading you do in the future could be thought of as part of your reading improvement plan. You will continue to improve long after you finish this book if you put into practice the things you learn. Most people do improve their general reading skills over a lifetime, if for no other reason than that they constantly learn the meanings of new words.

It is useful to schedule times to do the work in this book if you are not doing it in a class. Consistent, spaced practice is best. It also helps to develop good habits if you can have a regular place to practice where you are not likely to be disturbed.

Effective Reading

Improving
Reading Rates
and Comprehension

PART ONE

RAPID READING

Introduction

The purpose of this part of the book is to help you become more efficient in reading by speeding up the process generally. Most people can learn to cover material much faster than they do now while maintaining a high level of comprehension.

Improvement in reading efficiency has several major benefits. We need reading skills to benefit from the wealth of information that is now available in printed form. Most people get the rough outlines of their daily news from television and radio. However, the printed word still provides the in-depth coverage of topics that really produces well-informed people. Reading is also a great source of entertainment for many people. For students, it is the primary method of studying.

The time you now spend reading can be made much more productive by increasing your reading rate. For some people this will mean that they can obtain more information in the same length of time. For others it will mean that time now devoted to reading can be used in other more interesting and profitable ways.

Determining Your Reading Rate

To determine how fast you are reading material that is not in this book, you first have to get some idea of the number of words in a given passage. Then you simply divide the number of words by the number of minutes it took to read. That will give your rate in words per minute.

If you are reading a short selection, you might want to actually count the words. Usually, however, you can make an excellent estimate of word length by counting the number of words in a ten-line segment of the passage, then dividing by 10. This will give you a good idea of the average number of words per line. Then you simply count the lines in a short selection and multiply by the average number of words per line to get the total length in words. For example, if the average number of words per line is eleven and there are sixty lines in the article, the estimated number of words in the article is calculated as follows:

Average number of words per line $= 11$
Number of lines in article $= 60$
Estimated number of words in article $= 11 \times 60$
$= 660$

If you are reading a long selection or a book, you can estimate the number of words per page, then count the number of pages read in a given span of time, and divide the total estimated number of words by the number of minutes. For example, you are reading a paperback novel. Using the method described above, you find that there is an average of eleven words per line. The book has forty lines per page. This gives the following calculation:

Average number of words per line $= 11$
Number of lines per page $= 40$
Estimated words per page $= 11 \times 40$
$= 440$

If it takes you twenty-five minutes to read twenty pages, you can calculate your reading rate by multiplying the number of words per page by the number of pages read, then dividing the total by the number of minutes.

Number of words per page $= 440$
Number of pages $= 20$
Total number of words $= 440 \times 20$
$= 8800$
Reading rate $= 8800 \div 25$
$= 352$

This technique can be used on any reading material. If the book or publication contains a lot of pictures, charts, or diagrams, you may have to estimate the number of pages of reading material. In a typical paperback there are usually about 350 to 450 words per page. If your estimate is not in that general range, you have a book with unusual pages or you have made an error in estimating.

Each unit in Part 1 covers a particular aspect of reading speed and contains a practice reading selection that is designed to develop your ability to read easy, interesting material at high rates. Use these practice selections to calculate your reading speed. Simply record the time you start to read and the time you finish in the space provided, then subtract the starting time from the finishing time to find out how long it took you to read the passage. Look up your time on the chart that accompanies each reading selection for your reading rate in words per minute, then record the time on the progress chart at the back of the book.

Each reading selection is followed by a comprehension check, consisting of ten questions. Use the key at the back of the book to check your answers. Calculate your comprehension score by multiplying each correct answer by 10. For example, if you get seven answers right, your comprehension score would be 70 percent. Record your comprehension score on the progress chart at the back of the book.

Let's go on to the next unit to find out how fast you are reading right now.

How Fast Do You Read?

The first thing we want to do is to get some idea of how fast you are reading now. To do that, you should read the practice selection, "Prospecting for Gold," in the same way that you usually read easy, interesting material. Do not try to read it any faster or slower than you normally do. You will want this first practice session to be as typical as possible so that you can compare future results with it. Then you will know that you have really improved.

Before you start to read, record your starting time in the space provided. If you don't have a stop watch, the easiest way to do this is to look at a clock or watch with a second hand and record the time it will be at the start of the next minute. Then when the time reaches the minute that you have recorded, start reading. As soon as you finish reading, record your finishing time. Go on to the comprehension check immediately. You can look up the reading rate after you answer the questions.

Compute your reading time and obtain your reading rate from the chart that follows the selection. Record your reading rate on the progress chart that appears on page 320 at the back of the book. Use the answer key at the back of the book to calculate your comprehension score, and record your score on the progress chart. This is the format you will follow for the rest of the book unless otherwise indicated.

Now, if you are ready, record your starting time and begin reading.

finishing time _____

starting time _____

reading time _____

Prospecting for Gold

Michelle Patraw

The rugged old prospectors and their mules have long ago turned to dust, but there's still gold in them thar hills! Of course, the most renowned of the gold rushes took place in the west in the mid to late 1800s, but there were other gold booms. The pioneers located the majority of the gold mines that were again put to use during the depression of the 1930s. Throngs of people hoping to strike it rich swarmed into the areas that echoed of the forty-niners. Unfortunately, too many met with little or no success. It has been estimated that fewer than one out of every thousand people who prospected in the west ever made a strike. The lack of success during the depression confirmed the theory held by many people at the time that more research needed to be done. The most outstanding finds occurred in areas that were already known to have yielded gold; no systematic search for new areas was made.

Post-World War II mining efforts were directed mainly toward locating base-metal ores rather than panning for placer deposits. A placer deposit is a concentration of mineral that has accumulated along with the sediment in a stream. Because of the length of time needed for gold to corrode and its relatively heavy weight in comparison to the sediment in the stream, gold tends to accumulate in placer deposits close to the rocks from which it came.

Since World War II placers have been rapidly declining. It is estimated that of all the gold mined in the United States today only about 1 percent comes from placers, while slightly less than half (about 47 percent) comes from base-metal ores, and the remainder (approximately 52 percent) comes from lode mining. As with the gradual disappearance of placers, small mining operations are also on the decline in the United States. More than 90 percent of the domestic lode gold produced comes from one of three mines: the Homestake Mine in South Dakota; the Cortez Mine in Nevada; and the Carlin Mine, also in Nevada. The Carlin Mine was opened only after numerous scientific and technological advances had been made.

What are the prospects for today's adventurers and fortune seekers? There still may be a chance for financial advancement, though only after a careful study of the mining records and geology of the area has taken place. There are other considerations as well. Serious prospecting should be avoided by those who don't have sufficient money to see them through several long and discouraging weeks (and possibly months) of hard work. Just like the miners of old, today's prospectors must have some type of reliable vehicle capable of covering a lot of rough terrain. Once all of these things have been taken into consideration modern-day prospectors will be ready to start out for the area of their choice—that is, as soon as they have obtained the necessary permission from the owner of the land.

Panning for gold is likely to be the simplest and least expensive form of prospecting. Panning is often the most rewarding in areas where placer deposits are known to exist.

Placer deposits in the United States are widely scattered. However, California is most closely associated with panning for gold and is, by no strange coincidence, the leading gold-producing state. Rivers that became synonymous with the gold rush of the 1840s and the 1850s, such as the Mother Lode, the Mokelumne, American, Calaveras, Yuba, and Trinity, continue to yield small amounts of gold. Following the California gold rush, a wilderness known as Alaska came on the scene with a rush all of its own. As in California, the Alaskan gold rush began with the panning of placer deposits. The principal regions of this sort were and still are found in the Yukon River basin which crosses central Alaska. Many of the richest deposits are located near Fairbanks, where dredging has produced more gold than in any other part of Alaska. Other large placer deposits have been found on beaches in the Nome district.

Placers were found and still exist in lesser-known areas around the country too. The Missouri River in Montana continues to yield placer deposits near Helena and Virginia City. Idaho was once a principal placer mining state but now is yielding primarily fine-grained "flour gold" along the Snake River in the southern part of the state. Highly productive placers have been located in the Fairplay district in Park County, Colorado, and also in the Breckenridge district in Summit County, Colorado. Both of these areas underwent vast amounts of dredging during their peak period of activity in the 1930s. Minor deposits have also been located in South Dakota (particularly around the Deadwood area), in Washington on the Snake and Columbia rivers, and in intermittent streams in the arid regions of Nevada, Arizona, New Mexico, and southern California. Although more difficult to find, limited amounts of gold have been discovered in parts of Maryland, Virginia, North Carolina, South Carolina, Georgia, and Alabama in the streams that drain the Appalachians. It should be noted, however, that this gold is usually of a lower grade than that found in the west.

Panning for placer deposits are not the only kind of mining, but the inexperienced prospector without ample capital has little chance of discovering a lode rich enough to be worth developing. Lode gold is gold that is encased in solid rock and requires rather advanced mining and processing techniques for extraction. As a result, most future discoveries of lode gold will probably be made after extensive investigation and new advances in mining have taken place in those areas already known to be productive. Some possibilities for discoveries of this nature are Grass Valley, Nevada City, districts of San Juan, Cripple Creek, Lead in South Dakota, and Juneau in Alaska.

For additional information on geological surveys modern prospectors may contact the geological agencies of the principal gold-producing states.

Record your finishing time. Then answer the comprehension questions.

Comprehension Exercise for Unit 2

1   It has been estimated that fewer than one out of every _____ prospectors ever made a strike in the west.
   a   50
   b   100
   c   500
   d   1000

2   Out of all the gold mined in the United States, approximately 52 percent comes from
   a   Placers
   b   Lode mining
   c   Base-metal ores
   d   Panning

3   A placer deposit is a mineral deposit that
   a   Is located several miles underground
   b   Must be extracted from the rock around it
   c   Has accumulated along with the sediment in a stream
   d   Is mixed together with several other types of minerals

4   The leading gold-producing state in the United States is
   a   Alaska
   b   California
   c   Montana
   d   Idaho

5   Many of the richest deposits in Alaska have been located near Fairbanks and are a result of _____ .
   a   Dredging
   b   Panning
   c   Lode mining
   d   Mining for base-metal ores

6   "Flour gold" is gold that is
   a   Primarily coarse-grained gold
   b   Primarily fine-grained gold

    c   Another name for gold that is panned
    d   Another name for gold that has already been processed

7   Lode gold is gold that
    a   Has accumulated along with the sediment in a stream
    b   Is encased in solid rock
    c   Must be panned
    d   Is discovered by dredging

8   Future discoveries of lode gold will probably be
    a   Of lower grade than earlier finds
    b   Made in areas not known to have deposits
    c   Made after extensive investigations and new advances in mining have taken place
    d   Found by experienced prospectors

9   This passage is mainly about
    a   The techniques and history of gold mining
    b   The personalities of famous gold miners
    c   How modern law affects gold mining
    d   The value of gold today as opposed to its value in past years

10   This passage is mainly concerned with
    a   Selling gold
    b   Refining gold
    c   Making gold jewelry
    d   Finding gold

Check your answers using the key on page 314.
Refer to the chart on the next page to get your reading rate. Then plot your rate and comprehension on the progress chart on page 320.

Time-Rate Table for Unit 2

"PROSPECTING FOR GOLD" (988 words)
Time in seconds converted to rate in words per minute

Time	Rate		Time	Rate
:30	1976		8:00	123
:40	1481		:10	120
:50	1185		:20	118
1:00	988		:30	116
:10	846		:40	113
:20	740		:50	111
:30	658		9:00	109
:40	592		:10	107
:50	538		:20	105
2:00	494		:30	104
:10	455		:40	102
:20	423		:50	100
:30	395		10:00	98
:40	370		:10	97
:50	348		:20	95
3:00	329		:30	94
:10	311		:40	92
:20	296		:50	91
:30	282		11:00	89
:40	269		:10	88
:50	257		:20	87
4:00	247		:30	85
:10	237		:40	84
:20	227		:50	83
:30	219		12:00	82
:40	211			
:50	204			
5:00	197			
:10	191			
:20	185			
:30	179			
:40	174			
:50	169			
6:00	164			
:10	160			
:20	155			
:30	152			
:40	148			
:50	144			
7:00	141			
:10	137			
:20	134			
:30	131			
:40	128			
:50	126			

UNIT 3

How Well Do You Read?

In Unit 2 you read a selection at your usual reading rate, and you answered some comprehension questions. We can use the results of that unit to give you a general idea where you stand. First, however, let's look at some of the things we know about how people read.

There are wide differences in reading skills. If you take a typical group of 100 people who graduated from high school in the United States, you would find reading abilities representing almost every possible level. You might find some people who could barely read at all. At the other extreme you would find a few people with extremely high reading ability.

If you consider the fact that most human abilities vary greatly, it isn't surprising that such differences exist. If we looked at tennis playing, high jumping, mathematical skills, or any other ability, we would find the same thing; some would have very little aptitude and others would be highly competent.

To a certain extent such differences are a matter of training. If you are not taught mathematics, for example, you would not be good at it, regardless of any native ability. On the other hand, some people have special talents and aptitudes that make it easier for them to develop a high level of skill. They benefit more from training in that special skill and sometimes even develop high-level aptitudes with little or no formal training.

Reading, like other skills, is subject to influence by factors inside and outside the person. The internal factors are such things as general verbal aptitudes, interests, and motivation to learn. The person is also influenced by factors such as environment, available training, family background, and opportunity to take advantage of education.

Your current level of reading ability is the result of a variety of influences, some of which are in your physical and mental makeup. Others are factors outside your control, such as quality of schools, family background and attitudes, frequent changes in schools, and a multitude of others.

We can get a general idea of your current reading skills by making some comparisons with other people. Table 3-1 shows approximate reading rates of beginning students in community colleges. They read material of about the same type as you read in Unit 1. These results are an extremely general estimate. They should not be assumed to be an accurate placement of your reading skills in a group. However, they will give you some idea where you stand.

When it comes to comparing your comprehension score with those of other people, we must be even more cautious. One brief ten-question exercise is simply not enough to tell us what your typical score might be. As you continue through this book, you will get a better idea of your average scores. We will be discussing the topic of reading comprehension at greater length in Unit 7.

Why Don't I Read Faster?

As we discussed earlier, your reading skills are the result of many influences. In many people, the slow reading rates they show are simply the result of lack of training. Perhaps you were never encouraged to read rapidly. Many of the techniques used to teach reading to young children do not emphasize a fast reading process. Instead, the emphasis is on very careful, accurate reading. While it is important to learn to be careful and accurate, it is true that if all reading instruction slows down the learner, that pattern will become a habit. The student may never become a rapid reader.

TABLE 3-1   READING RATES OF FIRST-YEAR COMMUNITY-COLLEGE STUDENTS

Group	% in group	Words per minute
Top	10	over 360
Upper-middle	40	250–360
Lower-middle	40	150–250
Bottom	10	under 150

You may have to change reading habits that you have had for a long time. That is one of the reasons for spreading the work in this book over a longer period. Just as it takes a while to develop slow habits, it takes a while to change them.

Now a Practice Exercise

As we go through the units in this book we will be working on the improvement of various reading skills. Lots of discussions of topics and techniques will take place. However, one of the main ways of improving reading rates is simply to practice trying to read faster. That is what we are going to do in this unit. Read the selection which follows as rapidly as you can while still understanding what you read. You may be surprised to find that it is quite easy to increase your reading rate this way.

One way to increase your reading rate is to put a lot more energy into the process. Sit up straight in your chair, put your feet flat on the floor, and generally get into an "action" attitude.

Now apply that eager, action-oriented approach to the selection on the next page. Don't forget to record your starting time before reading. When you finish, record your finishing time, and go on to answering the questions. Then compute your reading time and check your answers to the questions. Finally, record both your rate and your comprehension score on the progress chart.

finishing time _____

starting time _____

reading time _____

Okay, So How Fast Does a Chipmunk Run?

Robert Kraske

A white-tail deer bounding through the trees. A hooked pike streaking toward green lake depths. A ruby-throated hummingbird darting between flowers. Mammals, fish, and birds. How fast do they run, swim, fly?

Wildlife watchers the world over ask these questions, but soon learn, once they delve into the matter, that accurate figures are hard to come by. The reason? Animals simply don't cooperate when it comes to speed trials over a measured course.

However, one fairly reliable way to time mammals and birds is to follow in a car while you watch the speedometer.

Roy Chapman Andrews, the famous naturalist, once trailed a herd of Mongolian gazelles in the Gobi Desert. "They ran so fast," he said, "that we could not see their legs any more than you can see the blades of an electric fan. We found they could leg it at sixty miles an hour for about half a mile and then slow down to forty or fifty."

Animals charging fleeing cars provide other figures. Lion, 50 mph; elephant, 25 mph; grizzly bear, 30 mph. The horn of one black rhinoceros prodded the tailgate of a truck traveling 35 mph.

The fastest mammal in North America? Naturalists agree on the pronghorn antelope. When paced by a car, one pronghorn ran 60 mph for two miles, then slacked off to 50 mph, and finally slowed to 40 mph.

Sixty miles-per-hour for one-half to two miles seems to be the highest sustained speed of any mammal, but it isn't the fastest. That honor belongs to the cheetah.

The London Times once reported on speed trials for these fleet cats. One cheetah accelerated to 45 mph in *two* seconds from a standing start. A few strides later, it was sprinting 103 feet per second, or 70-plus mph. No wonder rajahs in India once used these speedsters to hunt game.

Other animals have been timed on closed courses—the race horse and greyhound are two—and this is where stopwatch times come in.

Man o' War, perhaps the greatest American racehorse, winner of 20 of 21 races, once ran a quarter-mile at 43 mph. For the longer mile, though, most racehorses run 35 mph. Champion quarter horses—a breed especially raised to sprint 440 yards—hit 47.5 mph.

Fast animals like a horse or deer get an assist from long, lower-leg bones which provide a limber snap-kick to propel these animals in swift, leaping strides.

Winning greyhounds at West Flagler Dog Track in Miami chase a mechanical rabbit at speeds up to 40 mph. Aided in full stride by a flexing spine, these fastest of all dogs run off the ground half the time, twice during each complete stride.

Speedy Fish/Birds

Calibrating the speed of fish is difficult at best. However, one fisherman found a unique way to measure the speed of a bluefin tuna. To his fishing rod he affixed a motorcycle speedometer and ran the line from the reel over a drive pulley. Taking the lure, a 60-pound bluefin pulled 200 yards of 36-thread linen line through the water at a top speed of 44 mph!

An engineer, the fisherman later figured that the tuna, in pulling this length and weight of linen line at 44 mph, was towing the equivalent of 78 deadweight pounds. By extension, the tuna's feat is equivalent to a 150-pound man or woman running flat out while hauling a 200-pound sack of cement.

One reason for the tuna's high speed is its tail which beats an incredible 10 to 20 times per second, as efficient, fisheries biologists say, as a rotating propeller on a boat. Another reason is special muscles under the tuna's skin that automatically adjust to slight changes in water pressure. These continuous muscle alterations create a smooth, non-turbulent flow of water along the tuna's flanks. In contrast, a turbulent flow robs fish—and boats—of speed.

The speediest animals of all are birds. The reasons are many: lightweight, hollow bones—the skeleton of a pigeon, for example, makes up only 4.4 percent of its body weight—well-developed lungs and circulatory systems; feathers shaping the body into streamlined contours; legs retracting in flight. All these features combine to produce smooth, swift passage through the air.

Among the fastest fliers are homing pigeons which have been clocked at 94.3 mph. Over an 80-mile route, pigeons have averaged 90 mph. One covered 182 miles at 73 mph.

Topping the pigeon though is the red-breasted merganser. One merganser was reported ahead of an airplane flying 80 mph into a 20 mph headwind—a ground speed calculated at 100 mph.

Most observers claim the fastest bird is the peregrine falcon. In level flight, its speed has been estimated at 66-75 mph. However, in a dive after prey, one European peregrine was timed with a stopwatch at 165–180 mph.

Many ducks and geese fly 65-70 mph; mourning doves, 55 mph; starlings, 45-50 mph; wading birds (sandpiper, curlew, etc.) 45-50 mph; crows, 40-45 mph; English sparrow, 35-40 mph; blue jay, 25-30 mph. A special radar once timed a quail at 44.5 mph and a pheasant at 38.2 mph.

Fastest Man

Among his fellow creatures on this planet, where does man fit as a speedster?

The fastest speed for competition runners has been recorded for 100 yards. In June 1963, Bob Hayes—"The World's Fastest Human"—set a world record of 9.1 seconds, a speed of 22.48 mph from a standing start. However, his top speed came between 60 and 75 yards. He covered those 15 yards in 1.1 seconds, 27.89 mph.

This speed capability puts man slightly behind wart hogs, emperor penguins, and domestic cats (30 mph), just ahead of galloping moose (25 mph), road runners (22 mph), and mountain goats (20 mph), but far in advance of running quail (15.5 mph), pigs (11 mph), and chickens (9 mph).

For sheer running ability among mammals, though, the nod has to go to the common squirrel. This furry speedster can run *up* a tree as fast as it runs on level ground—12 mph.

Scientists who have studied this phenomenon claim that, to provide the spurt of energy necessary for its vertical dash, the squirrel increases its oxygen consumption. However, since the squirrel lifts only a pound or so, its oxygen increase is modest. In contrast, for a horse to run its 1,000-1,400 pound frame up a tree would require an oxygen increase of 630 percent.

Speed Ain't Everything

Far down the list of animal speedsters is the giant tortoise who, in an all-out effort, can achieve 0.17 mph—back and forth along the length of a football field three times in one hour. The garden snail—0.03 mph—would make it only to the 50-yard line.

Question is: If the tortoise and snail could go faster, would they? Speed, after all, isn't everything. Take the three-toed sloth, for example.

As a speedster—0.15 mph—the sloth might challenge the tortoise. But it's not likely. Sloths avoid speed; they don't even like to move. A resident of South American forests, the sloth lives in trees and sleeps by hanging from a branch with one hook-like claw. So little does the sloth move that algae grows on its long, coarse fur.

Yet the sloth, for all its avoidance of speed, loves to feed on grasshoppers. How does this slowest of mammals capture the fleet grasshopper, an insect capable in a twinkling of leaping 20 times its own length?

Other animals that prey on grasshoppers rely on speed and dash, right? But not the sloth. Oh, no. The sloth uses what its admirers, and they are legion, claim is pure talent.

When a sloth spies a grasshopper on a branch, it cups its paws and ever so slowly places them on either side of its prey. Slow as a shifting shadow the paws come together. If the grasshopper notices anything, it is only a gradual dimming of light, like an eclipse at high noon. Then—*plink!*—off goes the light and grasshopper finds itself enfolded.

No rush. No fuss. Yet the sloth never starves. Like I said, it (*yawn*) takes talent.

Record your finishing time. Then answer the comprehension questions.

Comprehension Exercise for Unit 3

1　This passage is mainly about
   a　Chipmunks
   b　Chipmunks and squirrels
   c　Land animals
   d　Animals in general

2　Cheetahs were once kept as hunters by
   a　English sportsmen
   b　Rajahs in India
   c　Speedsters
   d　Naturalists

3　Cheetahs have been known to sprint at 45 mph in two seconds, or over _____ miles per hour.
   a　30
   b　40
   c　55
   d　70

4　Fast animals like horses or deer have _____ which help them to run in swift, leaping strides.
   a　Long lower leg bones
   b　Limber snap-kicks

c   Long upper leg bones
d   Flexing spines

5   The speed of fish has been measured by
a   Speed boats with special equipment
b   Swimmers with special gauges
c   A fishing rod with a speedometer attached
d   A pulley

6   The passage is mainly concerned with
a   How fast animals can travel
b   How animals get their food
c   Where different animals are found
d   The mating habits of animals

7   The tuna is able to swim fast because of
a   Its propellerlike tail
b   Its special skin
c   Muscles that adjust to slight changes in water pressure
d   Its hollow bones

8   Over an 80-mile route pigeons have averaged
a   94.3 mph
b   90 mph
c   73 mph
d   80 mph

9   The European peregrine has been timed with a stopwatch going after its
prey in dives of
a   66 mph
b   75 mph
c   66–75 mph
d   165–180 mph

10   Although they are not the fastest animal, squirrels are remarkable
because
a   They are the fastest animal for their size
b   They are the fastest animal for their body weight
c   They can run faster than animals three times their size
d   They can run up a tree at the same speed they can run on land

Check your answers using the key on page 314.
Refer to the chart on the next page to get your reading rate. Then plot your
rate and comprehension on the progress chart on page 320.

Time-Rate Table for Unit 3

"OKAY, SO HOW FAST DOES A CHIPMUNK RUN?" (1418 words)

Time in seconds converted to rate in words per minute

Time	Rate		Time	Rate
:30	2836		8:00	177
:40	2127		:10	174
:50	1702		:20	170
1:00	1418		:30	167
:10	1215		:40	164
:20	1064		:50	161
:30	945		9:00	158
:40	851		:10	155
:50	773		:20	152
2:00	709		:30	149
:10	654		:40	147
:20	608		:50	144
:30	567		10:00	142
:40	532		:10	139
:50	500		:20	137
3:00	457		:30	135
:10	448		:40	133
:20	425		:50	131
:30	405		11:00	129
:40	387		:10	127
:50	370		:20	137
4:00	355		:30	135
:10	340		:40	112
:20	327		:50	110
:30	315		13:00	109
:40	404		:10	108
:50	292		:20	106
5:00	284		:30	105
:10	274		:40	104
:20	266		:50	103
:30	258		14:00	101
:40	250		:10	100
:50	243		:20	99
6:00	236		:30	98
:10	230		:40	97
:20	224		:50	96
:30	218		14:00	95
:40	213		:10	93
:50	208		:20	92
7:00	203		:30	91
:10	198		:40	91
:20	193		:50	90
:30	189		15:00	89
:40	185			
:50	181			

What Improvement Can You Expect?

Fortunately, reading rate is quite easy for most people to improve. In fact, if you really tried to read the selection in Unit 2 as rapidly as you could, you have already demonstrated to yourself that you can read faster. And we have hardly started on the process at this point. You will have much more time to improve!

Most people who take courses in reading improvement find that they can greatly improve their rate of reading without any negative effect on comprehension. In fact, comprehension very often improves.

The amount of improvement you experience will depend on a number of factors. Your current level of skill, your school history, your reading vocabulary, and your general background will all play a part. However, the most important factor is your motivation. You have to be eager to improve and be willing to try new ways to read faster. And you need to practice what you learn in this book on other reading material.

Like most skills, reading about improving reading is not enough. You have to actually *do* the improving, practicing new, higher reading rates until they become easy for you. If you do practice enough at higher rates, you will soon find that you read faster without even having to think about it.

It is difficult to predict what any one person will do. However, we do have a great deal of evidence that, on average, people more than double their rate of reading in working though a course like this. If they try especially hard they will do better. Some will improve much more than others. Typical results show rate increases of from 40 percent to over 300 percent.

Set Goals

One way of increasing your improvement is to set specific goals for each practice session, It has been shown that goal setting really helps by giving you something to aim for. Changing reading habits will be easier if you have small-step goals to reach, one at a time.

Begin with the rate you recorded for Unit 2. That was the first time in this improvement program that you tried to read faster. You probably could read at least twenty-five words per minute faster than that now if you really tried. That would be a good goal for each practice session: an improvement of *at least* twenty-five words per minute. You may find that it will be possible to set higher goals. If so, keep moving them up whenever you can.

Work in Surroundings that Encourage Improvement

The work you will be doing in this book will require a great deal of mental effort and concentration. It should be done in an environment that is free from distractions. If you are not doing the work in a classroom it would be wise to seek a location that is quiet: no operating television or radio and no other people. The best location would be one associated with work, that is, one with an straight-backed chair, good lighting, and available work tools such as pencils, paper, and reference books.

Will I Make Constant Improvement?

The typical results of a course like this are somewhat irregular. A few people do show a regular pattern of constant rate increase. However, the more frequent pattern is one in which the rate goes up unevenly. Sometimes no improvement will take place for a while, and then a big jump will occur. It seems that some people need to practice at a rate for a while before they can go on to the next step. Don't be discouraged if you don't always achieve the goals you set on each unit. Keep moving up your goals, and you will get there eventually.

What are the Lasting Effects of Reading-Rate Improvement?

The long-term effects of efforts to improve reading rate vary a lot from person to person. They depend on whether or not you continue to practice the skills learned as you improve. Studies of long-term results show a great deal of variation, but the average person will maintain between 60 and 100 percent of the gains made. Some people who keep working at it will never stop improving.

Why Practice on Easy Material?

You will notice that the material in this first part of the book is easy reading. The reason is that it is easier to improve if the practice material is simple. It is much harder to improve your rate on difficult, technical material. Fortunately, reading-rate improvement on easy material tends to transfer to difficult material. If you learn to read easy material faster, you will find that while you read difficult material more slowly than easy material, your rate will still be much higher than it was before on both kinds of reading.

Could I Be Too Old to Improve?

No. Often the best results are obtained by people who are older. They have more experience, more opportunity to develop an adequate vocabulary, and often they are mature enough to make the commitment that it takes to put a serious effort into improving.

Can I Learn To Read 20,000 Words Per Minute?

Not if you mean "read" as most reading experts use the term. It is possible, using techniques that most people call skimming or scanning, to cover material at almost any speed. However, comprehension will be limited to what can be obtained by seeing only part of the material. We will cover this topic in more detail in Units 5 and 6.

Even though astronomical rates aren't possible with complete comprehension, there is still a great deal of room for valuable rate improvement. The typical reader, perhaps reading 200 or 250 words per minute on easy material, can probably at least double reading speed. That would mean a saving of half the time spent reading. Over a period of years, hundreds of hours of reading and study time would be saved.

A Practice Exercise

Now it is time for more speed practice. Read the passage which begins on the next page as rapidly as you can. On this passage, try not to worry about comprehension at all! (You can always go back and read it again if you decide it is that important to you.) Our purpose here is to have you break loose from your habitual patterns of reading by moving over the material at a very high rate. You will find when you answer the comprehension questions that you probably have gained more information than you thought. Remember, you goal is to read *at least* twenty-five words per minute faster than you did in Unit 3.

Now, record your starting time, and begin reading.

finishing time _____

starting time _____

reading time _____

Getting the Hang of It

Remember when you were a kid and used to climb to the top of the tallest tree in the neighborhood and dream you could fly away like a bird? Those long-ago yearnings deep in all of us must be the reason for the popularity of that exciting sport usually known as hang gliding. (We say usually because in some parts of the country it's called sky surfing, kiting, or self-soaring.)

Sailing through the air, suspended from a big, kite-like wing, provides the exhilarating sense of unpowered flight that has fascinated human beings through the ages.

The Glider

The most popular type of hang glider is the Rogallo design, also known as a delta wing because of its roughly triangular shape. Francis Rogallo of NASA wasn't thinking of fun when he developed it. He visualized it as a means of carrying parachuting fighter pilots safely away from enemy territory.

The Rogallo design has rigid nose poles flaring out at an angle of about 90°. Slung below the wing is a simple framework from which the pilot hangs, supported in a harness similar to those used on parachutes.

The sail wing glider is similar to the Rogallo but flares out to a broader angle at the nose—from 90° to as much as 180°. This design provides more lift but makes pitch control more difficult. It also results in wider wingspans and increased structural weight.

The swing wing, invented by an engineer named Volmer Jensen, resembles a conventional glider, having a cantilevered wing with a separate tail assembly on the end of a boom. It also features a three-axis control stick that determines pitch, roll and yaw. This is too sophisticated for a beginner, of course.

There are many versions of these basic designs around, plus other styles such as bi-wings, but most people begin with the delta wing because it is simple and stable.

The typical glider is constructed of aircraft aluminum tubing, aircraft bolts, stainless steel cable, and dacron sail. Dacron is preferred to rip-stop nylon because the nylon tends to stretch and sag, messing up the aerodynamics.

The true hang glider is carried and launched by the pilot. If it requires any type of towing device, it's a different sport.

Techniques

The pilot's body does the work in hang gliding. Moving the body forward or backward changes pitch of the wing, tilting it up or down to gain maximum lift. Swinging the body sideways controls lateral direction, banking the wing for turns.

Winds are important to hang gliding and techniques vary according to the terrain and the strength of prevailing winds. Usually, the beginner learns to take off by running down a slope into a slight headwind, holding the kite level and then pushing out on the frame to raise the nose until the glider begins to lift off by itself. It takes a wind of five to 12 mph to become airborne and an average airspeed of 20 mph to remain aloft.

The beginner will probably stay in the air only about five to 10 seconds, although it will seem longer. After he gains some experience, he will be able to take off from bigger slopes and flights will extend to several minutes. Of course, it is possible to stay aloft for much longer but this depends on winds, skill of the pilot and his knowledge of air currents plus the ability to concentrate intently for long periods. Most people who enjoy the sport don't aim toward extremely long flights.

Landing is relatively simple. As the flight nears its end, the technique is to pull down the nose to pick up extra airspeed. This increased speed assures good stability and control during the final approach and avoids the danger of premature stalling. As the glider nears the ground, the pilot levels off to reduce speed, then pulls the nose up into a stall for a gentle touchdown.

Some places have installed tows similar to the type used by snow skiers to make it a little easier to return after short flights. After longer flights, the pilot must land, disassemble the kite, attach it to the roof of a vehicle, transport it up the slope, then reassemble and preflight. A two or three minute flight can involve an hour and a half of preparation time and some pretty hard work.

Assembling the glider involves attaching the A-frame (the part one hangs on to), spreading the wing tubes, and raising the king post (the vertical post on top to which the cables are attached). The cables attached to this post simply hold the sail up while not in flight. They will slacken somewhat when the weight is off them in flight. In the air it is the cables underneath that are critical since they are under tension then. Cables on top and bottom must be attached and tightened.

The preflight is an absolute must before each flight. It includes an inspection of all cable fittings and turnbuckles, cotter pins, cables themselves, self-locking nuts on the bolts, and exposed tubing. The hidden tubes inside the edges of the sail are inspected by "feel-up." The fingers are run along the tube for any dimples or bends that might weaken it.

Instruction

As with any other sport or hobby, people approach hang gliding in different ways. There are the types who first time out dive off a cliff strapped to a plastic and bamboo rig wearing nothing but their cut-offs. Not only are they taking dumb risks but they are denying themselves the chance to gain the skills that will make them really good at the sport.

Then there are the ones who look for a good instructor, are fussy about the quality of their gliders, use harness and helmet properly, and are fully clothed to protect their skin. These are the ones who return to the slopes weekend after weekend and rarely worry about whether they are carrying their Blue Cross card.

The helmet, incidentally, is not just to save your head in case of a crash. When a kite is being moved around at the take-off area, people frequently get rapped on the noggin with wing tubes. A helmet makes this a minor matter.

If you want to try some hang gliding, by all means look for a good instructor. If you have friends who are experienced at the sport, whose judgment you trust, who have proper equipment and are honestly willing to spend the necessary time with you, that's fine. But the very best thing to do is to pay for instruction from a school or individual whose qualifications you can check out in advance.

Remember that you need to know not just about the actual flying but also how to put the kite together correctly and how to preflight it.

A good instructor will impress you with the need to use a glider made of the finest quality materials. Steer well clear of people who think bamboo poles covered with patched polyethylene plastic are good enough. A good glider can set you back a month's pay. Purchasing the materials separately and building it yourself would probably bring the price down about 40%. But you don't need to own one yourself. Gliders can be rented from schools or clubs. Some schools also will let you apply the rental fee toward the purchase price later if you decide you like the sport.

How dangerous?

Make no mistake about it— hang gliding can be a dangerous sport. Jump off into the unknown, maybe from too steep a cliff into turbulent air, and you're in trouble. Be careless about your equipment, sloppy about your preflight, and your luck will run out. Let your concentration waver or forget what the instructor told you about hanging on to the frame during a bad landing and that loud snap you hear is likely to be your arm bones.

It's no secret that people get killed hang gliding. It's a sport that is highly unforgiving of errors. As in any other risky endeavor, danger can be minimized by the basic four: Good equipment. Good training. Good physical condition. Good sense.

Record your finishing time. Then answer the comprehension questions.

Comprehension Exercise for Unit 4

1 The Rogallo glider was originally designed to
   a Test air currents
   b Get parachuting fighter pilots to safety
   c Teach new pilots about wind currents
   d Be used strictly for recreational purposes

2 The sail wing glider provides more lift, but also results in more
   a Weight
   b Height
   c Expense
   d Speed

3 Most beginners start with the
   a Swing wing glider
   b Rogallo glider
   c Sail wing glider
   d Delta wing glider

4 Dacron is preferred to
   a Sail cloth
   b Rip-stop nylon
   c Rayon
   d Cotton

5 It takes an average airspeed of _____ to remain aloft.
   a 12 mph
   b 20 mph
   c 22 mph
   d 32 mph

6 This passage is mainly about
   a Flying jet fighters
   b Flying commercial airplanes
   c Flying private airplanes
   d Hang gliding

7 It is a good idea for a beginner to get
   a A well-built glider
   b Protective clothing and a helmet
   c A good instructor
   d All of the above

8 Besides learning how to fly a hang glider it is essential to know how to
   a Land
   b Make repairs
   c Build a glider
   d Put a glider together

9 This passage does *not* discuss
    a Techniques of hang gliding
    b Types of hang gliders
    c The dangers of hang gliding
    d Banning hang gliding

10 Mountainous areas may appear to be ideal for hang gliding but may prove to be
    a Unpredictable because of air currents
    b Too cool
    c Too rocky for safe landings
    d Difficult because of numerous trees

Check your answers using the key on page 314.
Refer to the chart on the next page to get your reading rate. Then plot your rate and comprehension on the progress chart on page 320.

Time-Rate Table for Unit 4

"GETTING THE HANG OF IT" (1345 words)
Time in seconds converted to rate in words per minute

Time	Rate		Time	Rate
:30	2690		8:00	168
:40	2017		:10	164
:50	1614		:20	161
1:00	1345		:30	158
:10	1152		:40	155
:20	1008		:50	152
:30	896		9:00	149
:40	807		:10	146
:50	733		:20	144
2:00	672		:30	141
:10	620		:40	139
:20	576		:50	136
:30	538		10:00	134
:40	504		:10	132
:50	474		:20	130
3:00	448		:30	128
:10	424		:40	126
:20	403		:50	124
:30	384		11:00	122
:40	366		:10	120
:50	350		:20	118
4:00	336		:30	116
:10	322		:40	115
:20	310		:50	113
:30	298		12:00	112
:40	288		:10	110
:50	278		:20	109
5:00	269		:30	107
:10	260		:40	106
:20	252		:50	104
:30	244		13:00	103
:40	237		:10	102
:50	230		:20	100
6:00	224		:30	99
:10	218		:40	98
:20	212		:50	97
:30	206		14:00	96
:40	201		:10	94
:50	196		:20	93
7:00	192		:30	92
:10	187		:40	91
:20	183		:50	90
:30	179		15:00	89
:40	175			
:50	171			

Variety Is the Spice of Reading

You get up in the morning and get dressed. At breakfast you read the back of the cereal box, the milk carton, and perhaps the morning newspaper. You read the bus schedule and go out to catch the bus. On the bus you read the advertising inside the bus and street signs to know where you are. You get to school and notice an interesting art exhibit in the lobby. You read a bit about the artist and the titles on the art works and go on. In the elevator you read and punch your floor number. Out of the elevator you read classroom numbers to find your classroom. In the classroom you skim over the material you read (or should have read) to prepare for the class. During the class you read and perhaps copy the material written on the blackboard.

After class you may go the library and read textbooks, workbooks, the school paper, and several posted notices of meetings, interesting programs or concerts, and perhaps other material.

We could go on, but you have the idea by now. All of our lives in a civilized society are filled with reading of many types. The material we read varies over an infinity of possible contents. Our purposes for reading and the situations in which we read are also extremely varied.

With all this variety in mind, let's consider the question, What is a good reader? When we say, for example, "Sarah is a good reader," what exactly do we mean? What do we need to know about Sarah to be sure that we have accurately described her?

Consider what Sarah had to be able to do to be the person we were referring to earlier. She had to recognize the words on the cereal box, in the paper, on the advertising, etc. In addition she had to be able to refer those words to her own experience so that they had meaning for her. She had to take the simple, literal meaning of what she read and translate it into useful information by interpreting it for her own purposes. For example, she had to not only recognize the numbers on the bus schedule but also put that information together with several other things: how long she needed to get to school, what time it was then, and what time her class started.

It should be clear from the example above that it is very difficult to determine where "reading" stops and "thinking" starts. Actually they are parts of the same information-processing event, and we really do not have to distinguish between them. We will be discussing the relationship between reading and thinking some more later in this book.

Since in this part of the book we are interested in improving rates of reading, let's look at how different materials and purposes influence how fast we read. Most good readers have many different rates at which they read, but they can be broken down into the general ones below.

1 A *skimming and scanning rate* (usually over 1000 words per minute) should be used for
    a Locating a reference or identifying material to be read more carefully
    b Answering a specific question
    c Getting a general idea of a selection

2 A *very rapid reading rate* (about 500 to 800 words per minute) should be used for
    a Reviewing familiar material
    b Reading a light novel or story for its plot

3 A *rapid reading rate* (about 350 to 500 words per minute) should be used for
    a Reading fiction of moderate difficulty to enjoy the story or anticipate the outcome
    b Reading easy descriptive or nonfiction material for information

4 An *average reading rate* (about 250 to 350 words per minute for most people) should be used for
    a Reading complex fiction for characterization or plot analysis
    b Reading nonfiction material of moderate difficulty to note details, grasp relationships, or to evaluate the author's ideas

5 A *slow reading rate* (about 100 to 250 words per minute) should be used for
    a Study-type reading and mastering content
    b Reading highly technical, difficult material
    c Evaluating quality and literary merit
    d Solving a problem or following directions

This general breakdown of typical reading rates will give you some idea of the variety of reading approaches. Good readers often use several of these rates in the course of reading a single passage. We will be working most in this unit on rapid reading rates. When you get to the point where you can cover easy, interesting material with a high rate, then we will go further. We will begin working on skimming and scanning skills.

Now let's go on with some speed practice. Read the passage which begins on the next page as rapidly as you can while maintaining enough comprehension to understand the article. We are still trying to get you to read faster—to change your slow habits to fast habits. Remember, your goal is to read *at least* twenty-five words per minute faster than you did on the last exercise.

Now turn the page, record your starting time, and begin reading. When you finish, record your finishing time, then answer the questions which follow. Finally, look up your rate on the rate table, check your answers with the key on page 314, and record your rate and comprehension on the progress chart on page 320.

finishing time _____

starting time _____

reading time _____

Women and the Vote

Sgt. Maj. Bruce N. Bant

Ask any high school boy who the 10th President of the United States was and he'll probably tell you John Tyler. Ask the girl sitting next to him the same question and she just might tell you Jimmy Carter.

Technically of course, she'd be wrong, but from the standpoint of women voters in this country, she'd be correct. Women have only had the right to vote in presidential elections for 60 years, making Carter the tenth president they've had a say in electing. Men, on the other hand, have voted for 38 presidents.

Women got their voting rights when the 19th Amendment to the U.S. Constitution was ratified. The amendment was proposed by Congress on June 4, 1919, and certified as being ratified by the States on August 26, 1920. It reads in part, "The right of citizens of the United States to vote shall not be denied or abridged by the United States or by any State on account of sex."

But the Women's Suffrage Amendment, as it's known, involved a lot more than voting rights, and the struggle for its ratification took a lot longer than the 15 months indicated on the official record.

The uphill struggle for women's suffrage began quietly in 1848 at a rights convention at Seneca Falls, N.Y. At the time, women had virtually no rights under the law. Men had complete control of children, complete and sole ownership of property and, if a wife worked, the employer was bound by law to pay her wages to her husband. Women were also denied the rights of survivorship. A man could, and often did, ignore his wife in his will leaving his possessions to a male heir. The purpose of the convention was to balance the scales by gaining rights for women equal to those of men.

The convention's organizer, Elizabeth Cady Stanton, startled some delegates by proclaiming that among other rights, women should also have the right to vote. In fact, she believed that if women were to be assured any rights, they must first have the right to vote.

Stanton's idea, although taken for granted today, was radical, even revolutionary in 1848. Nowhere in the "civilized" world did women have the vote at that time. It was truly a man's world. Anyone who challenged that was considered a radical and against motherhood, God and country.

But Stanton's ideas did attract some followers and supporters. Among the best known were Susan B. Anthony, Lucy Stone and Julia Ward Howe.

The women's suffrage movement began to grow but lost some momentum and support during the Civil War. Following the war, both interest and support began to increase. At the same time opposition to the movement became more vocal.

Women in the movement came under constant ridicule and public abuse. They were called trouble makers, malcontents, unAmerican and unwomanly. Many had to endure personal attacks on their character, morals and motives.

One publication of that era editorialized: "... But it is now obvious to impartial observers that these rights are in reality demanded by only a very small group of women—mostly mannish women, too, belonging to what has been aptly called the third sex; and that to grant them the rights demanded would in reality be to inflict a grievous wrong on the vast majority of women—the womanly women—as well as on children, on men, and on society in general."

As the debate continued, the women's movement began to gain ground. But in 1869 it received a major setback. That year Congress approved the 15th Amendment granting the vote to citizens regardless of "race, color, or previous conditions of servitude." Suffragists tried to have the word "sex" included but Congress refused.

A Representative from New York said, "Women are well represented by their husbands and fathers. Once women were given the vote the sexes would be at war."

A Senator from Missouri added, "It will unsex our mothers, wives and sisters, who are today influencing by their gentle caress the action of their husbands toward the good and pure. It will turn our blessed country's domestic peace into ward assemblyrooms."

But the true mood and fears of Congress may have been best expressed by Senator Charles Sumner of Massachusetts when he said, "We know how the negro will vote, but we are not sure of the women."

As disappointing as the defeat in Congress was, it didn't discourage the suffragists. In fact, it had the opposite effect. Members of the movement increased their efforts to get the vote for women.

Later that same year their determination began to pay off when the Territory of Wyoming, followed closely by Utah, gave women the vote. After that, it was 24 years before another victory was achieved. In 1893, Colorado extended the franchise to women.

In the years between 1869 and 1893, women's suffrage became an international movement. New Zealand became the first country to grant women electoral equality with men in 1893. By the end of World War I, 12 other countries had followed suit.

But in the States, women were still struggling. They got the vote in Idaho in 1896 but they had to wait until 1910 before their next victory in Washington. California joined the bandwagon in 1911, followed by Arizona, Kansas and Oregon in 1912. Montana and Nevada joined in 1914.

The bitter struggle of almost seven decades was paying off and seemed finally at an end when both party platforms in 1916 advocated the granting of voting rights to women. But the lack of action by Congress led women to resort to more aggressive tactics in 1917. They picketed the White House, burned copies of the President's speeches and when arrested, they went on hunger strikes.

The new tactics were successful. New York, Michigan, Oklahoma and South Dakota gave the vote to women that same year and Congress finally took the women's movement seriously.

Whether the Congress acted with conviction and belief in the women's suffrage cause, or whether it acted with the knowledge that two-thirds of the women in the country already had the vote is debatable. But the fact is, after 71 years of struggle, the women's movement finally convinced them to act.

In 1919 the Women's Suffrage Amendment was submitted to the states by Congress for ratification as the 19th Amendment.

The disaster predicted by the doom-sayers never came to pass. Neither did the improvements in the morality of the political system promised by the supporters of the 19th Amendment. In 1920, Senator John S. Williams of Mississippi probably came closest to predicting the effect women voters would have on the political system. He said, "The practical results of the adoption or defeat of the women's suffrage amendment will amount to nothing."

Almost any measurement or poll result you use seems to prove the senator right. There really doesn't seem to be a "women's vote" as such. Women vote for issues and personalities in much the same way men do.

If a husband is against gun control, his wife is likely to be against gun control. If a wife is anti-abortion, the husband probably will be, too.

If a woman is married, she's more likely to vote than if she is single. If she's married to a Republican, she'll vote more than she would if she were married to a Democrat. And, if her husband doesn't vote, chances are pretty good that she won't vote either. The same is true for men in almost every category.

White urban, affluent and well educated women are more likely to vote than black rural, poor or poorly educated women. The same is true for men.

The differences between men and women voters appear to be few. The difference in how they got the vote is significant. For men it was a birth right but for women it was a battle that included 56 state referendum campaigns and 277 state party convention campaigns.

It was a continuous and seemingly endless chain of activity. Young suffragists who helped forge the last links of that chain weren't born when it began. Suffragists who helped forge the first links were not alive when it ended.

For women like Susan B. Anthony the battle never ended. Having the right to vote was only the beginning. She believed that "exercising that right is the difference between freedom and slavery." Anthony died in 1906 without ever enjoying the freedom that she and others fought so hard to get.

Women today have the right to vote. They have the right to select their representatives. They've come a long way ... maybe. The trip will have been in vain if they don't exercise their right to vote.

Record your finishing time. Then answer the comprehension questions.

Comprehension Exercise for Unit 5

1 This passage is mainly about
a How women vote
b How men vote
c How women got the right to vote
d Who women vote for

2 The first convention for women's rights was organized by _____.
a Susan B. Anthony
b Elizabeth Cady Stanton
c Lucy Stone
d Julia Ward Howe

3 In 1869 Congress passed the Fifteenth Amendment granting the right to vote to citizens regardless of
a Sex
b Race
c Religion
d National origin

4 Women first received the right to vote in
a Utah
b The Territory of Wyoming
c Colorado
d New York

5 The first country to grant full equality to women was
a The United States
b Canada
c New Zealand
d Mexico

6 This passage would probably best be described as coming under the topic of
a Sports
b Advertising
c History
d Medicine

7 Women were finally given the right to vote in 1919 with the ratification of the _____ Amendment.
a Fifteenth
b Eighteenth
c Nineteenth
d Twenty-first

8 Since 1919 certain trends have developed in the female vote:
   a   Married women are more likely to vote than single women
   b   Married women are less likely to vote if their husbands vote
   c   Well-educated women are less likely to vote
   d   All of the above

9 _____ women are most likely to vote.
   a   Poor
   b   Rural
   c   Well educated
   d   Black

10 Not all of the original suffragists lived to see women gain the right to vote; _____ died in 1906.
   a   Lucy Stone
   b   Elizabeth Cady Stanton
   c   Susan B. Anthony
   d   Julia Ward Howe

Check your answers using the key on page 314.
Refer to the chart on the next page to get your reading rate. Then plot your rate and comprehension on the progress chart on page 320.

Time-Rate Table for Unit 5

"WOMAN AND THE VOTE" (1464 words)
Time in seconds converted to rate in words per minute

Time	Rate		Time	Rate
:30	2928		8:00	183
:40	2195		:10	179
:50	1756		:20	175
1:00	1464		:30	172
:10	1254		:40	168
:20	1097		:50	165
:30	976		9:00	162
:40	878		:10	159
:50	798		:20	156
2:00	732		:30	154
:10	675		:40	151
:20	627		:50	148
:30	585		10:00	146
:40	548		:10	143
:50	516		:20	141
3:00	488		:30	139
:10	462		:40	137
:20	439		:50	135
:30	418		11:00	133
:40	399		:10	131
:50	381		:20	129
4:00	366		:30	127
.10	351		:40	125
:20	337		:50	123
:30	325		12:00	122
:40	313		:10	120
:50	302		:20	118
5:00	292		:30	117
:10	283		:40	115
:20	274		:50	114
:30	266		13:00	112
:40	258		:10	111
:50	250		:20	109
6:00	244		:30	108
:10	237		:40	107
:20	231		:50	105
:30	225		14:00	104
:40	219		:10	103
:50	214		:20	102
7:00	209		:30	100
:10	204		:40	99
:20	199		:50	98
:30	195		15:00	97
:40	190			
:50	186			

Understanding the Reading Process

Some people think that reading is a very simple matter. You move your eyes along the lines and the author's message appears somehow in your mind.

When a person is highly skilled as a reader, it does seem that something like that takes place. However, the actual process is quite complicated. Try to think back when you were first learning to read. Or observe a young child just learning to read. It is a very difficult, complex, sometimes painful process.

As a child you come to school with a well-developed oral language. You can speak the language fluently, but you have to learn how to relate that oral language to the printed one. Early reading instruction deals mostly with techniques for identifying words and simple sentences. (Remember "Run, Spot, run"?) The vocabulary is very limited because you can only recognize a small number of words at first.

As rapidly as possible, the teacher tries to get you to know more words and more word-recognition techniques. This involves teaching you to sound out words using phonetic clues, recognizing words using the word structure (prefixes, suffixes, and roots), and other word-recognition strategies. The teacher also teaches you to use the context to get the meaning and begins to help you develop the comprehension skills necessary to be a good reader.

We will be discussing comprehension in more detail in a later unit, but for the moment, consider the many things we mean when we speak of effective reading. The following is only a partial list.

1 Recognize the main ideas the author presents.

2 Distinguish between main ideas and details.

3 Recognize and retain the most important facts.

4 Understand the sequence and organization of the ideas presented.

5 Use reading material to prepare for examinations.

6 Skim over some material quickly to save time (also know *when* to skim instead of study).

7 Recognize the reliability and authority of the author as a source of information.

8 Recognize the author's point of view, intentions, style, and, perhaps, biases.

We could go on with this list, but it should be clear by now that reading comprehension is not a simple process.

Other aspects of the reading process are also complex. As you learn to read you sometimes develop habits that can interfere with efficient reading. For example, some people have a tendency to mumble the words as they read. Young children do a certain amount of reading aloud, and it is easy to form the habit of saying the words. This process is called "vocalization" because it involves vocal behavior. If the reader does not actually say the words but moves lips, tongue, or throat muscles, the process is called "subvocalization." Both vocalization and subvocalization are not bad in themselves, but they do tend to slow the reading process. Normal speech is only 140 to 160 words per minute, and a good reader should read much faster than that. If you have to go slowly enough to say each word, it will almost certainly slow you down.

Another part of your behavior in reading is important to understand. It is a process called "verbalization." As you read, think, or talk, you somehow "hear" words passing through your mind. Stop reading this for a moment and think about some object; your desk, chair, or pencil. Notice that you do it with words. That verbalization process is a necessary part of reading or thinking. Sometimes people think that to get rid of a vocalizing habit, they should try to read without verbalizing. It simply cannot be done. The way to get rid of vocalizing, if you do it, is to practice reading faster than you can physically say the words. The habit will soon drop out, and you will become much more efficient.

One last comment should be made about this part of the process. Sometimes when you are reading very carefully, or reading very difficult material, you will begin to vocalize. It seems to help the comprehension process in some cases. For example, reading very difficult and confusing directions aloud may help make them clear. There is nothing wrong with using vocalization as an aid to very difficult reading. Just don't make a habit of it when you want to read rapidly.

Does Faster Reading Interfere with Comprehension?

Probably not. Most people can considerably increase rate of reading without a drop in comprehension. In fact, in many cases in which people have been reading very slowly, comprehension increases when they speed up. Good readers are generally faster readers, but there are lots of fast careless readers and slow efficient readers. The speed at which a person reads tells you very little about that person's general reading ability.

However, it is important to recognize that while increasing reading rate usually does not change comprehension, there are some limits to that statement. If you try to read *very* rapidly, beyond that rate at which you can see all of the words on the page, obviously comprehension will suffer. We will discuss this further when we get into the matter of eye movements in the next unit. For the moment it is enough to say that you can probably double or even triple your current reading rate without losing comprehension.

Some Very Important Directions

We are now ready to make a big improvement in your reading rate. You know enough about the process and have done four practice exercises. This time you should be able to make big gains.

We have not yet talked about one of the most important ways to speed up. You have been reading the practice exercises without any warm-up. Reading is like many other activities. If you want to improve, you need to do more than perform as you habitually do. One element in good practice is a good warm-up. We are going to try warming up to a high rate before reading the next selection.

One thing that slows readers down is the fear that they will miss something as they read. A good way to speed up in practice is to read something that you have already read and understood. That way you do not have to worry about comprehension and can focus all of your attention on reading faster.

We are going to "warm you up" by having you do just that. You have now finished reading this unit and have probably understood it quite well. Before you do the practice exercise which follows, go back and read this unit again *as rapidly as you possibly can*. Then go on to the next page and time yourself on the passage. Try to read as fast as you did on your second reading of this unit.

Don't forget to record your starting time before you begin to read the passage. Then after you read, record your finishing time, answer the questions which follow, and check and record your rate and comprehension on the progress chart on page 320.

Hiking the Appalachian Trail

Branley Owen shouldered into his pack, then paused to inspect the starless, pre-dawn sky. "There's bad weather brewin'," he said. "Hope you all remembered to bring your ponchos. We're probably gonna need 'em today."

Owen switched on his flashlight and pointed it along the foot trail that led off into the woods. The beam seemed tiny and weak in the vast blackness of the night. "We might as well get started," Owen said. "The way it feels, the weather's not gonna get any better." He moved off up the trail with a loose, ground-eating stride. Steve Shugars and I fell in step behind him.

You didn't need a barometer to assess the accuracy of Owen's forecast about the ponchos. The air had that wet wintry smell that often precedes foul weather. Overhead, the wind moaned lonesomely through the trees. The leaves that covered the trail were damp and noiseless underfoot. It made you feel uneasy, listening to the wind and smelling the air and knowing full well that the elements were getting set to serve up some kind of unpleasantness.

Earlier, we had been optimistic about the weather. We had seen stars glimmering in the dark sky as we drove the 70 miles from our homes in Knoxville, Tennessee, to Davenport Gap at the extreme northern edge of the Great Smoky Mountains National Park. But when we parked our car at the gap and stepped out into the night, our optimism vanished. The stars were gone. The wind and the raw dampness of the air left little doubt about what kind of day it was going to be.

We were starting on a five-day backpacking trip over the length of the Appalachian Trail in the Smokies—68 rugged, up-and-down miles from Davenport Gap near Cosby, Tennessee, to Fontana Dam at the south end of the park in North Carolina. The threatening weather signs didn't make for a very enheartening start. But we didn't consider turning back. One of our reasons for the trip was to photograph the famous fall colors of the Smokies, and we had already made one postponement to await the color peak. Any further delay and the best of the foliage would be gone. All we could do was strike out and hope that the bad weather wouldn't last long.

The trail was easy enough at first, but it grew steeper as we progressed along it. Despite the chilliness of the damp air, we soon had to stop and shed our jackets. By the time we had covered the first mile, I was down to my T-shirt, soaked with sweat and panting for breath. I began to wonder if I could keep up with my two companions, both of whom were younger and far more experienced at hiking than I.

Owen, who runs a backpacking specialty shop for a Knoxville sporting goods firm, had hiked the entire 2,000 miles of the Appalachian Trail in the summer of 1970. Shugars, a Knoxville securities salesman, had never undertaken anything as ambitious as the whole trail, but he had built up his endurance with numerous weekend excursions. By contrast, it had been several years since I had done any hiking with a heavy pack, and now it was plain that the inactivity had taken its toll.

Daybreak found us about halfway up the side of Mt. Cammerer, the first peak the Appalachian Trail ascends after it enters the northern end of the park. Shortly after it became light, a fine drizzle of rain began to fall. It brought with it a blanket of fog that completely enveloped the mountain and cut visibility to not much more than a hundred yards.

The wind grew stronger as we continued to climb. It tore at the treetops like a dog worrying a bone, blustering so strongly at times that it was difficult to carry on conversation. We escaped the full force of it, walking down among the trees. But once when we stopped for a breather on an exposed point, it whipped at us with such keenness that we had to dig into our packs and don our jackets again.

"If we had a sail and a set of wheels, we wouldn't have to walk," Owen quipped. "We could just let this wind blow us along."

We reached the crest of Mt. Cammerer shortly after 8 a.m., having made the five miles and the 3,250-foot ascent from Davenport Gap in about two-and-a-half hours. It was not bad time for such a rugged climb, but I felt as if I had a separate ache for every step I had taken. We took a long break to recuperate, then pushed on at a somewhat more leisurely pace. Once when we came to a sort of natural overlook along the trail, the fog dissolved briefly to the east of us. We stopped to marvel at a striking panorama of autumn color, delicately muted by the mist and rain. Then a sharp gust brought the fog boiling in again, blotting out the scene.

About 11 a.m. we stopped for lunch at the trail shelter on Crosby Knob, some eight miles from our starting point. We were in the process of polishing off the last crumbs of our food when another hiker came down the side trail to the shelter and cheerfully greeted us. He was young—in his early 20's—and slender-framed, with pale blond hair and friendly blue eyes.

"You don't mind if I join you while I fix my lunch, do you?" he asked.

"Heck no," Owen replied. "Come on in."

The new arrival pulled an alcohol stove from his pack and set a small kettle of water on it to boil. "That's for tea," he explained. "I've gotten so I can't do without tea at lunch." He dug into his pack again and came out with a plastic container of peanut butter and part of a loaf of bread. "I'm gettin' terribly tired of peanut butter, though."

"Well heck, why don't you try some of our grub?" Owen offered.

"Oh no. I'm used to peanut butter now. It's no trouble to fix, and it has a lot of energy in it."

"Where you headin' for?" Owen asked.

"Springer Mountain," was the reply. Springer Mountain, near Ellijay, Georgia, is the southern terminus of the Appalachian Trail.

"Hey, you're doin' the whole trail then?"

"Yeah. Or trying to at least," the young man answered, grinning sheepishly. "It's taking me a lot longer than I had counted on. I've loafed a lot. Whenever I came to a place where I felt like stopping and laying over for a day or two, I just did it. I also got a bad case of poison ivy and had to come off the trail and go into the hospital. That delayed me for several weeks."

"Why'd you decide to do the whole trail?" I asked.

"Oh, I don't know. I was in school, but I was getting fed up with it. Everything seemed so pointless. I thought if I took some time off and did the AT, I could think about things and maybe find some answers for myself. I don't know that I've solved anything, but I've really had fun doing it. Say, I suppose I should introduce myself. I'm Jim Rutter from Foxboro, Massachusetts."

We returned the introduction. When he heard Owen's name, Rutter's mouth fell open in surprise.

"Branley Owen!" he said. "You don't mean it? Man, I've been hearing about you ever since I started this trip!"

Rutter probably was not exaggerating. Owen's name has become a byword along the Appalachian Trail as a result of his 1970 hike over the long footpath. He started his journey at Springer Mountain on the first of April. On the 12th of June, a scant 73 days later, he reached the northern end of the trail at Mt. Katahdin in Baxter State Park, Maine. No one had ever walked the trail that fast before, and Owen's feat is yet to be surpassed.

We invited Rutter to throw in with us for the portion of his trip that lay within the park. He readily accepted. It had been quite a spell since he had encountered any other hikers, and he was hungry for company. We gathered up the scraps of paper left over from our lunch, hitched up our packs, and pushed on.

The morning had been a painful one for my flabby, unused muscles, but the afternoon was pure agony. There were no climbs to match the grueling pull up Mt. Cammerer. But I had been fresh, then, and eager. By afternoon my legs had turned to jello, and my lungs were functioning like an ancient leather bellows that rats have gnawed full of holes. When we finally pulled into Tri-Corner Knob shelter—our stopping place for the night—I was utterly exhausted. But after a supper of fresh beef steak and baked potatoes, I felt greatly rested and restored.

Just before nightfall, the rain that had been coming down as a misty drizzle most of the day turned into a slashing downpour. The balsam trees turned gray and blurry behind a thick curtain of raindrops, and dirty water ran in sheets across the bare earth in front of the shelter. But despite its ferocity, there was something comforting about the rain. And the shelter—which was dank and uninviting when we first walked into it—now seemed cozy and pleasant with our cooking fire flickering in the fireplace and the rain rattling upon the tin roof.

A great many Appalachian Trail hikers have probably experienced much the same sense of comfort and security after taking refuge from the elements in one of the shelters along their route. There are some 225 shelters between Springer and Katahdin, an average of one for each nine miles of trail. Most of them are small and simple log lean-tos. In the Smokies, however, and on other intensively used portions of the trail, the shelters are of more elaborate construction and of larger size. Some of the shelters have been erected by government agencies such as the National Park Service, the U.S. Forest Service and the old Civilian Conservation Corps. But many of them were built by private hiking clubs.

Maintenance of the trail is a cooperative enterprise involving government agencies, hiking clubs and individuals. The efforts of the clubs and individuals are coordinated by the Appalachian Trail Conference, headquartered in Washington, D.C. The conference also publishes pamphlets, a newsletter and highly detailed guidebooks to the trail.

The creation of the Appalachian Trail was proposed in 1921 by forester, philosopher, planner and nature lover Benton MacKaye of Shirley Center, Massachusetts. MacKaye, who worked as a planner for TVA during the 1930s, set forth his idea for a wilderness footpath in an article in *The Journal of the American Institute of Architects*. Now 93 years old, MacKaye saw the trail get off to a modest start in 1922, the year after his article appeared. Construction was completed in 1937.

The Appalachian Trail, which was declared a National Scenic Trail by Congress in 1968, passes through eight national forests, two national parks and portions of 14 states. Some 470 miles of the trail—nearly a fourth of its total length—lie within the Tennessee Valley watershed. Its beginning at Springer Mountain (or end, depending on whether one is going north or south) is on the Tennessee Valley Divide. The trail follows the Divide through northern Georgia and then goes altogether into the Valley just across the North Carolina line. After it crosses Fontana Dam and enters the Smokies, the trail ascends to the Tennessee-North Carolina border, which lies along the lofty backbone of the park. It follows the border through the park and for another 135 miles to a point near Roan Mountain, Tennessee. It then cuts through the extreme northeastern corner of Tennessee and crosses into Virginia near the little town of Damascus. The trail leaves the Tennessee Valley watershed on Iron Mountain a few miles south of Marion, Virginia.

The rain was still coming down on Tri-Corner Knob the next morning when we awoke. It had diminished to a persistent drizzle, but each little wrinkle in the face of the mountain was full of water rushing to find its way downhill. We puttered over breakfast, dreading to go out in the wet. When the rain showed no signs of ending, we finally draped ourselves in ponchos and struck out.

The trail was like a miniature brook. Our feet were soon squishing miserably inside our boots. Our ponchos kept the rain off, but we sweated so profusely underneath them that it became a choice of whether we wanted to get wet from the outside-in or the inside-out. We finally stopped and pulled them off, deciding it was better to be soaked in the rain than to stew in our own juices.

"This reminds me of when I was doin' the whole trail," Owen remarked as he stuffed his poncho inside his pack. "There was one stretch when I had nothing but rain for eight solid days. I had to sleep wet every night. I finally got to the point where I was actually considerin' goin' off the trail and restin' until the weather got better. But about that time, it finally cleared off. That blue sky looked the prettiest of anything I've ever seen."

We kept hoping to see a bit of blue sky as we wound our way along the trail but to no avail. About mid-morning the rain did cease, and the fog dissipated somewhat. But the visibility remained too poor for us to really see the scenery or to make the kind of photographs that we had planned. We were tired, aching and thoroughly disgusted when we pulled into Ice Water Springs shelter about four in the afternoon of our second day out.

When the third day dawned as wet and bleak and sodden as the previous two, we decided to say goodbye to Rutter, quit the trail at Newfound Gap—the halfway point—and come back and finish our trip when the weather cleared. But other commitments arose to interfere with our plans, and seven months passed before Owen and I finally got around to completing our walk through the Smokies. Since we only had two days to do the second half, we decided to skip the rather uninteresting portion of the trail that parallels the highway between Newfound Gap and Clingman's Dome. That left us with 30 miles to walk from Clingman's to Fontana Dam.

We left the parking lot at Clingman's at sunrise one morning in the last week of May. Spring had come more than a month earlier down at the foot of the mountains. But up on top it was just arriving. Trilliums were still in bloom, and bluets were bursting forth in bright clumps of color all along the trail. The leaves on the trees were just beginning to unfold. As we tramped through the dew-wet grass of Silers Bald, we heard a bob-white calling. We stopped and listened and wondered what in the world that bird of the lowlands was doing up at an elevation of more than 5,000 feet.

"You know, it's a funny thing," Owen said. "Out for just a short trip like this you'll stop and listen to birds or to look at flowers and such. You just sort of push along, takin' your time and enjoyin' things, and it seems like a day out like this just lasts forever. But when you're doin' the whole trail and tryin' to do it as fast as I was, it gets to be like any other job. All you think about is puttin' those miles behind you, and a day just seems to fly by."

We pushed on across Silers Bald, through Buckeye Gap and up Cold Spring Knob. One couldn't have asked for a better day for hiking. The sky was clean and blue, and the air was so clear that the hollows and wrinkles of far distant mountains stood out in sharp relief. A cool breeze played with the tiny new leaves on the trees. We paused for lunch at Derrick Knob, 10 miles from our starting point, then continued on the backbreaking slopes of Brier Knob and Thunderhead. On Rocky Top, a mile or so beyond Thunderhead, we stopped for a long time to rest and admire the scenery. Then we dropped down to Spence Field, shucked out of our packs, spread our sleeping bags and prepared for the night.

Owen fired up his pack stove and placed a kettle of water on the flame. He opened two plastic packages of freeze-dried beef stew. When the water began to boil, he poured a generous dollop of it into each package, and the dry lumpy material inside changed miraculously into savory beef stew. I picked up a spoon and dug in.

"Man oh man, Branley," I said. "Is that ever good."

"It's the best thing I've found yet for backpackin'. No cookin' and no mess to clean up afterwards. And it's just as good as fresh. I would've thought I was livin' like a king if I had had food like this when I was doin' the whole trail. I did start out with a full pack of good freeze-dried food, and I had some more cached just across the Virginia line. That got me through the first five weeks. But I couldn't afford to buy any more freeze-dried food after that. It's pretty high priced, and I just had $60 to do the whole trail on. So I just about lived on peanut butter and loaf bread the rest of the way.

"Whenever I came to a little country store where the trail crossed a road, why I'd buy me a can of pork and beans and eat them on the spot. Then I'd buy a jar of peanut butter and a loaf of bread to carry with me. And I'd pick greens and mushrooms and stuff like that that I found along the trail and eat them. I could go for three days on a six-ounce jar of peanut butter and a loaf of bread and what I could pick along the way. There was one week there towards the end when I didn't eat anything but fried flour and water and wild greens. But I was burnin' up more than I was takin' in, and the farther I went, the weaker I got. I weighed 217 pounds when I left Springer, and when I got to Katahdin, I was down to 178. If I had had another 100 miles to go, I don't think I would've ever made it."

We rose at daybreak the next morning and ate a quick breakfast of freeze-dried beef and rice. Shortly after the sun topped the rim of the mountains, we were on the trail. The dew glistened like jewelry on the lush grass of Spence Field. We walked through the field and entered the cool, dark woods. We hadn't covered more than half a mile when Owen suddenly stopped in front of me and held up his hand. He pointed to a laurel thicket a few yards down under the crest of the ridge. There was a wiggling in the laurel, and then a black snout popped out of the foliage. It was followed by about 200 pounds of evil-looking wild boar. The boar stared at us defiantly for perhaps 10 or 15 seconds. Then he wheeled and trotted off down the ridge.

Later in the morning we were both startled out of our wits when a grouse flushed almost from under our feet. The bird flew only a few yards before it lit and began dragging its wings and making piteous whickering sounds. It was a hen trying to lure us away from her chicks. We looked carefully around our feet but saw nothing except sticks and dead leaves. I took a step, and a grouse chick materialized from nowhere and began running along the ground. Owen scooped it up and held it in his hand while I broke out the camera to make photographs. The outraged mother rushed at us, her neck ruffles up, her wings held out in a threatening attitude. Then her courage broke, and she flew off out the ridge. I hurried with the photographs, and we placed the chick where the distressed mother would find it when she came back for the rest of her unseen brood.

The miles weren't rolling off as easily now as they had been the day before. We made the hard climb up Mollies Ridge, dropped down to Ekaneetlee Gap, then climbed again to the crest of Powell Knob. We stopped to rest. What I thought was a wrinkle in my sock upon examination turned out to be the angry red beginnings of a big blister. It grew worse as the day wore on. By the time we reached the top of Shuckstack and the start of the long descent down to Fontana Lake, I had full-fledged blisters on both feet.

"Well, she's all downhill from here," Owen announced as we started down the last four-mile leg of our trip.

"Yeah, and I wish it was up. These downhill grades are what's killing my dogs." But it wasn't just my feet that were aching. My knees were as stiff as rusty hinges as a result of my using them to ease the impact on my feet on the downhill portions of the trail. I made Owen stop twice going down

Shuckstack, but it didn't help much. By the time the waters of Fontana Lake finally appeared before us through the trees, it felt as if both my boots were lined with hot coals.

Just before we crossed Fontana Dam—our journey's end—we met an elderly hiker coming towards us up the road. He waved and grinned and asked us how far it was to Birch Spring shelter, the first shelter on the trail going into the park from the south.

"Five miles," said Owen, "and it's uphill nearly all the way."

"Oh me," said the old man. "There was a time when I could've made it. But I'm 67 years old now, and I don't believe I can do five more miles before dark. I'll probably just have to camp beside the trail."

"Where'd you start from?" Owen asked.

"Springer," the old man announced proudly. "I've been out nearly two weeks. I was just about pooped out this afternoon until I stopped down at the dam and took a shower. That made me feel a lot better."

The old man was speaking of a shower room that TVA installed last spring as part of the visitor facilities at Fontana Dam. It was intended primarily for the benefit of people hiking the Appalachian Trail, and it has received a great deal of use.

"Are you goin' all the way to Katahdin?" Owen asked.

"No. I wish I was, though. I'm just going to Davenport Gap. That's all I have time for. Maybe someday I'll get to do it all. Well, I'd better be getting on up the mountain. Nice to talk to you."

After we were out of earshot, Owen turned and looked back at the old man. "You know, seein' somebody like that just does my heart good," he said. "Too many people think they ought to have a road into everything worth seein'. They say they're not able to walk. Well, that old man proves there are a lot of people who could walk if they'd simply try it. They might get a whole new outlook on life if they'd just get out of their cars and use their feet for a change."

Record your finishing time. Then answer the comprehension questions.

Comprehension Exercise for Unit 6

1   One of the purposes of the author's trip was to
   a   Try out some backpacking equipment
   b   Observe weather conditions in the Smokies
   c   Photograph the famous fall colors
   d   Observe the wildlife

2   The author's party met a young hiker who had to have _____ with his lunch.

    a   Coffee
    b   Cheese
    c   Beef jerky
    d   Tea

3   This passage is mainly about
    a   Men hiking together on a trail
    b   U.S. history
    c   Wilderness medicine
    d   American wildlife

4   The author of this passage went hiking
    a   Alone
    b   With three other hikers
    c   With two other hikers
    d   With a large party of hikers

5   The Appalachian Trail is maintained by
    a   The United States government
    b   The Sierra Club
    c   The state of North Carolina
    d   Individuals, hiking clubs, and government agencies

6   The author's party quit the trail at the halfway point, which is known as
_____ .
    a   Newfound Gap
    b   Cold Spring Knob
    c   Buckeye Gap
    d   Clingman's Dome

7   The Appalachian Trail was proposed by
    a   Branley Owen
    b   Benton MacKaye
    c   Edmund Hillary
    d   John Muir

8 When the author and Branley Owen resumed their hike on the Appalachian Trail it was
    a   Spring
    b   Fall
    c   Winter
    d   Summer

9 When Owen first hiked the Appalachian Trail he stopped eating freeze-dried food after the first five weeks because
    a   He got tired of it
    b   It didn't provide enough nourishment
    c   It was too expensive
    d   There was no place to buy it

10 During the last part of his trip the author encountered a _____.
    a Deer
    b Moose
    c Bear
    d Wild boar

Check your answers using the key on page 314.
Refer to the chart on the next page to get your reading rate. Then plot your rate and comprehension on the progress chart on page 320.

Time-Rate Table for Unit 6

"HIKING THE APPALACHIAN TRAIL" (3989 words)

Time in seconds converted to rate in words per minute

Time	Rate	Time	Rate	Time	Rate
6:00	665	13:00	307	20:00	199
:10	647	:10	303	:30	195
:20	630	:20	299	21:00	190
:30	614	:30	295	:30	186
:40	598	:40	292	22:00	181
:50	584	:50	288	:30	177
7:00	570	14:00	285	23:00	173
:10	557	:10	282	:30	170
:20	544	:20	278	24:00	166
:30	532	:30	275	:30	163
:40	520	:40	272	25:00	160
:50	509	:50	269	:30	153
8:00	498	15:00	266	26:00	153
:10	488	:10	263	:30	151
:20	479	:20	260	27:00	148
:30	469	:30	257	:30	145
:40	460	:40	252	28:00	142
:50	452	:50	245	:30	140
9:00	443	16:00	249	29:00	138
:10	435	:10	247	:30	135
:20	427	:20	244	30:00	133
:30	420	:30	242	:30	131
:40	413	:40	239	31:00	129
:50	406	:50	237	:30	127
10:00	399	17:00	235	32:00	125
:10	392	:10	232	:30	123
:20	386	:20	230	33:00	121
:30	380	:30	228	:30	119
:40	374	:40	226	34:00	117
:50	368	:50	224	35:00	114
11:00	363	18:00	222	36:00	111
:10	357	:10	220	37:00	108
:20	352	:20	218	38:00	105
:30	347	:30	216	39:00	102
:40	342	:40	214	40:00	100
:50	337	:50	212	41:00	97
12:00	332	19:00	210		
:10	328	:10	208		
:20	323	:20	206		
:30	319	:30	205		
:40	314	:40	203		
:50	311	:50	201		

Your Eyes and the Reading Process

In this unit we will discuss vision and the way it works in reading. It is important to understand vision, how to avoid visual difficulties, and what your eyes are doing when you read.

It is unusual for vision problems to be undiscovered causes of reading problems with the good screening and testing programs that exist in most schools. However, it does happen, even when schools do have vision testing. Unfortunately, many vision screening tests involve having a person read a vision chart on a wall 20 feet away. That will give some good information about distance vision for driving a car or other tasks, but it tells us nothing about how well the person sees a book 15 or 16 inches away. This means that even if you have no difficulty seeing objects clearly at a distance, you could still have vision problems that will interfere with reading.

There are two general types of vision problems. One type is due to the way the eyes are formed. The other is due to the way the eyes function together, that is, the way they are controlled by the muscles around them.

There are three common problems that are due to improper structure of the eye. The human eye is like a camera, with the lens in front and the film in the back. The lens is called the "cornea" and the film is called the "retina." If the eyeball is too long, the light coming through the cornea tends to focus in front of the retina instead of on it. The person will then have good vision for things close to the eye but not for distant things. This condition, called nearsightedness (or "myopia," if you like the medical term) does not usually cause reading problems.

The second structural problem occurs when the eyeball is too short. The light rays tend to focus behind the retina, and the person has good vision at distances but not up close. This condition, called far-sightedness (or "hyperopia"), does cause problems, since vision is blurred at reading distances.

The third kind of structural problem is caused by an eyeball that is distorted, with curves or bulges that make the image fuzzy. It is called "astigmatism."

To summarize, the vision problems that occur because of the structure of the eye happen when the eyeball is too long (nearsightedness), too short (farsightedness), or distorted (astigmatism). All these conditions can be corrected with glasses or contact lenses.

The other major type of vision problem is caused by a lack of proper coordination of the muscles that control the eye. The normal person has no problem making both eyes focus on the same spot. However, some people are cross-eyed or wall-eyed. These conditions result in great difficulty in directing both eyes to the same spot. While it is very obvious to the observer when a person is seriously cross-eyed, minor amounts of this problem are not noticeable. As a result, not all coordination problems are discovered.

If you find that you have headaches or other evidence of eye strain after reading a while, you could be suffering from a coordination problem. Other symptoms are redness, excess tearing, blurred vision, and double images after reading a while. If you suspect that you could have problems be sure to see an eye doctor and make sure that you are checked for coordination problems as well as for clarity of vision.

If you do not have any serious vision problems, you still need to be concerned about your eyes. There are some simple rules you can follow in order to maintain healthy vision.

1   Be sure to have adequate lighting when you read.

2   Try to avoid reading in a situation where the book is brightly illuminated and the background is dark. It leads to eyestrain.

3   Avoid glare. Try to have the light come from the side or over your shoulder. It should not bounce off a shiny desk or book into your eyes. Try to face away from bright window scenes.

4   Move around. Periodically looking at objects far away will tend to rest your eyes as you read. Also moving from a single body position now and then will help prevent fatigue.

5   Use glasses if you have them, especially if they are designed for reading.

6   Be careful of the general health of your eyes. Stop reading or other close work if you begin to experience any of the symptoms of eyestrain. Have

your eyes checked periodically for diseases, and be especially careful in removing foreign objects from your eyes.

What Your Eyes Are Doing When You Read

Think about what your eyes seem to be doing as you read this line of print. You move along one line from left to right until you get to the end of the line. Then you return to the left side of the page and start on the next line. It seems that your eyes are moving smoothly along the line, but they actually are not. If you watch the eyes of another reader you will see that the eyes move along in jumps. These jumps are called "saccades"—from a French word *saquer,* "to pull"; the movements were discovered by a French scientist. Strange as it may seem, your eyes are stopped about 94 percent of the time and move only about 6 percent of the time. Each stop, or fixation, usually lasts about one-fourth of a second in normal reading.

During each eye fixation you see a small part of the line of print you are reading. Young children see about one-half of a word per fixation. They stop about two times for each word. The average college student sees 1.1 words per fixation. A really outstanding reader (the best reader in a highly selective college, for example) might average as many as two and a half words per fixation.

You sometimes hear of people who claim to be able to read at extremely high rates—thousands of words per minute. Don't believe it! It is true that you or anyone else can cover material at a high rate and perhaps get some meaning from it. However, if you do, you will not be seeing all of the words and will be doing what most reading experts call skimming or scanning.

Skimming and scanning are extremely useful skills, and we will be working on developing them later in this book. However, it is important in many reading tasks to actually see every word on the page. It simply is not possible to see all of the words on a page at a rate of reading above the physical limits set by the vision process. We might imagine someone able to see as many as three words per fixation. The shortest duration of a fixation ever measured is about one-fifth of a second. This superreader would then see three words in each of five fixations per second, or fifteen words per second. That comes to a reading rate of 900 words per minute. Most people. when pushed to go faster and faster, break into a skimming process, skipping whole lines and sometimes paragraphs, when they get to rates above 600 or 700 words per minute.

Even though there is no miraculous process by which you can see whole paragraphs at a time, as some claim, you can make great gains in reading. Most people can at least double their rate, and many have done much more than that with practice.

One last point should be made about eye movements in reading. It is useful to know what your eyes are doing and what is possible and impossible. However, it is *not* a good idea to focus your attention on your eye movements as you read. It will serve no useful purpose and will distract your attention. Comprehension will suffer, and you will not have gained anything.

Now let's move on to a practice exercise. You may want to warm up by reading this or something else that you have already read and understood. Read as fast as you can! Be sure to raise your rate at least twenty-five words per minute above the rate on the last unit.

finishing time _____

starting time _____

reading time _____

Cost-Conscious Vacations:
Pick One Close to Home

Tent Camping

One simple, inexpensive vacation is a family camping trip. Tent camping is simplicity itself; it refreshes both body and mind. It also affords millions of Americans a visit into our natural heritage. Many families live only a short distance from a mountain valley or seaside beach where they can pitch their tents.

At first glance, camping equipment might seem expensive but it's one of the best vacation buys around today. Good outdoor equipment has a usable lifespan of about 10 years. A family of four can purchase a camping outfit for less than what they would spend in two days at a motel for bed and board.

For the novice campers, renting equipment offers an economical way of finding out whether or not a camping vacation is for them. Most recreational services rent camping equipment at reasonable fees as do local outdoor equipment shops.

"Bring your own" is the essence of camping. The basic equipment required for a camping trip is—a tent, sleeping bags, a camping stove, a fuel container and fuel, a camping lantern, cots or mattress bedrolls, a cooler, water container, matches, and a first-aid kit. Other items to consider for an outdoor excursion into nature's domain are an ax, a shovel, metal buckets, a flashlight with extra batteries, and several yards of rope. In the wild, children seldom find time for boredom but it's a good idea to bring along some games, books, and a deck of playing cards. Also bring along the family bicycles to tour the park or forest.

Food supplies for your camping trip can be found on your family's kitchen shelves along with the necessary cooking utensils. No special menus are needed; the meals a family enjoys in the confines of their home can be enjoyed in the wilderness. An extra benefit is that fresh mountain air sharpens appetites. Even though most developed campgrounds have "good" water available, it's wise to carry an emergency water jug.

In many campgrounds, especially the heavily used ones, firewood is scarce and seldom supplied. Cutting forest and seaside vegetation in or near a campground is usually prohibited. Thus, camp cooking requires a camping stove. The barbeque-type pits often provided at campgrounds are fine for an occasional cookout or weenie roast. Charcoal cooking is just the thing for those summertime backyard cookouts. But, in general, both are inconvenient for cooking every meal while you're camping.

Choice of proper clothing can make or break a camping trip, especially in early summer when a chill can set in after dark. So, it's important to match clothing to climate. In general, the best answer is the "layer" system whereby a camper puts on or peels off clothing to keep comfortable. Even when summer days are scorchers, it's still wise to bring along a change of warm clothing, especially for children.

Now, with all the equipment gathered, a campground must be selected. First-timers should pick one close to home. A family can contact their state's office of tourism or check with recreational services for a listing of public and private campgrounds in the vicinity.

Summer months are usually the peak season for camping. However, national parks and forests, within reach of most major metropolitan areas, offer a year-round spectrum of outdoor recreation. Families in Brunswick, Maine, and Jacksonville, Fla., as examples, are offered mountain tops and seaside escapades, respectively.

Within half a tank of gas from Brunswick lies White Mountain National Forest and Acadia National Park.

White Mountain, in New Hampshire, encompasses more than 1,500 square miles of rolling, round-shouldered Appalachian mountains and dense hardwood forest, including the 15-mile Presidential Range. Dozens of hiking trails beckon the family into the forest. And Acadia National Park on Mount Desert Island offers surf-splashed cliffs crowned with mountain forests and lakes sheltered by steep slopes. A system of gravel roads constructed in 1915 (for carriages) forms bike trails over the island. Today, the park preserves about 16 miles of the road system free from "Detroit Iron" for cyclists.

Jacksonville families have several Florida state parks bordering the Atlantic with white sand beaches, caverns, springs, and clear streams for a hodgepodge of recreational activities. A unique adventure also waits northwest of Jacksonville just across the state line. There the Okefenokee National Wildlife Refuge sprawls over the southeastern corner of Georgia.

In this vast swamp, where you can get a fascinating glimpse of wildlife, channels form a maze through the moss-covered cypress trees. At the main entrance, you can choose from among self-guided or guided tours, walking trails, canoe trips, swamp exhibits, and picnic facilities. General camping is not permitted but campers can rent a canoe and follow well-marked canoe runs into the swamp. Other more developed campgrounds are located in Waycross State Forest, north of Okefenokee.

With a park or forest selected, the car loaded, the family packed in, an outdoor vacation in America's heritage begins.

Once a campsite is found, park the family car, set up camp, and begin to enjoy the natural beauty on foot or on family bicycles.

When you and your family become confirmed campers, you can turn any three-day weekend into a mini-vacation and find any excuse for a weekend camping jaunt. The only limitation on how often your family camps is your family budget.

Wilderness Camping

As campers gain experience, a new adventure beckons many into one of today's thrill sports—wilderness camping.

There are still a few isolated areas in America where the stillness is disturbed only by the rustle of wildlife or the rambling of a mountain stream. To enjoy this special experience, you'll have to pack what you need on your back and hike into the wilderness on foot.

Millions of Americans find wilderness camping forces them to choose between essentials and desirables. Backpacking equipment is expensive and money should be spent on only essential equipment. Urban life fosters many dependencies but in the wilderness you depend upon yourself and the few worldly goods on your back....

Wilderness buffs in Bremerton, Wash., are at the threshold of the Olympics, one of the nation's wildest mountain ranges, and the North Cascades or the American Alps.

Beautiful as the areas are, they shouldn't be tackled solo. Backpackers should travel in pairs or in groups of four as recommended by backpacking experts.

Both Olympic National Park and North Cascade National Park offer wilderness trails where you can enjoy an old-fashioned family picnic or an extended trek. In addition, part of the National Trail System's Pacific Crest Trail runs along the base of Mount Rainier and through the North Cascades, offering a once in a lifetime wilderness adventure.

The North Cascades embrace alpine scenery, snowcapped peaks, cascading streams and foothills covered with softwood forest crisscrossed with about 350 miles of hiking trails. In the Olympics, more than 600 miles of trails thread through a forest of evergreen giants and alpine meadows.

Meanwhile, the Puget Sound area offers an endless array of seaside campgrounds for family enjoyment. And, in several cases, an ordinary family picnic can be turned into a vacation with short trips to nearby beaches and longer trips by bus or ferry to various other beaches surrounding the Sound.

City Vacations

For those who prefer the sights and sounds of the city to a wilderness experience, most urban areas offer possibilities. While the family car sits in the garage, your family can spend an inexpensive vacation on the city streets by using the local mass transit system or by trying family bicycling. The key to a city vacation is to take shorter, more frequent trips, especially on weekends, and to select destinations and activities that will interest both youngsters and adults.

Freebies

With the annual outbreak of spring fever, many cities plan open-air concerts, special displays, street fairs, art exhibits and other programs aimed at helping city dwellers forget the heat and smog while not ruining their budgets. These summertime freebies can turn an ordinary weekend into a stimulating mini-vacation. To find out about these programs, consult your local newspaper or call your local park authority.

Parks and Zoos

In the San Diego area, families can enjoy extended family picnics at several city and state parks or take a vacation trip into California history, science, culture and recreation.

San Diego parks and its nationally famous zoo offer educational and recreational adventures for a family. First obtain a list of parks in the area from the local chamber of commerce, plan a daily itinerary of parks to visit, and check the bus schedule and routes. To save money, plan a picnic menu or make a list of inexpensive restaurants for lunch. What your family sees and does, is limited only by what's available, your imagination and your budget.

Amid 1,400 wooded acres, San Diego's Balboa Park forms a center of recreational and cultural activities. Housed within are a variety of sporting facilities such as tennis and basketball courts along with the zoo, a space theater and a museum of man.

At the San Diego Zoo, more than 4,000 animals attract visitors to a day's safari. Its botanical garden of exotic plants and flowers is perfect for a nature trip.

After the zoo safari, take a one-day outer space stroll into the $4.5-million Reuben H. Fleet Space Theater and Science Center. The computerized planetarium can project 10,000 stars on the nation's largest hemisphere dome and duplicate, as well, space trips to the moon and other planets. . . .

Families looking for an endless bounty of salty adventures have several parks and miles of beaches to enjoy such as Torrey Pine State Park. Torrey, a reserve for the rare torrey pine trees, overlooks the rugged California shoreline where swimming, skin diving, and sunbathing are favorite pastimes.

Museum Touring

Another city vacation is museum touring. In most large cities and neighboring communities, a wide selection of art galleries and educational and cultural museums are open to the public.

Museum admission fees run the gamut from free to more than $5; however, many museums are free only at specific hours and days. With careful planning, a family could have a free museum touring vacation by taking advantage of these times. Your only cost would be food and bus fares.

To plan your tour, first contact the local chamber of commerce for a listing of museums and art galleries. Plan an itinerary of shows and exhibits and lay out a tour in conjunction with local bus routes and schedules. In between museum visits, a family can also plan a mini-tour of local restaurants to sample different cuisines—or, the family's gourmet can pack an epicurean picnic lunch.

In the Great Lakes area, families can fend off the summertime blues and heat by visiting several museums along the local bus routes. A few museums open for a family's summer touring offer attractions ranging from the more than 500 strange and bizarre oddities assembled by the famous journalist Robert L. Ripley to an antique auto exhibit of more than 100 restored classics along with a 1930s arcade. On the scientific side, a family can push buttons, turn cranks, lift levers and operate computers in hundreds of exhibits demonstrating scientific principles and industrial applications. Or, they can venture into the primordial world of 150 million years ago through exhibits of fossilized prehistoric remains and artifacts of early civilization.

Historical Villages

A vacation planned around history and historical figures offers yet another inexpensive and energy conscious vacation for families. American history encompasses each community and most record their heritage with landmarks and monuments or restored villages.

A vacation starts by contacting the local chamber of commerce or state office of tourism for a listing of historical sites, planning an itinerary of places and checking on bus routes and schedules.

Our nation's capital holds numerous avenues for families living there to retrace American history. Historical monuments and sites are open to the public as are many government buildings such as the Bureau of Engraving and Printing and the FBI that offer public tours Monday through Friday. All are easily reached on the city's mass transit system.

Many cities across the United States are preserving their heritage in the restoration of villages. Several such villages are within easy commuting distance of the D.C. area.

On its outskirts lies Old Town Alexandria, Va., with its colonial flavor and imposing brick houses accented with ultra-modern offices and shops. Several of the historical houses and shops have been restored to their original states.

Visitors stroll the main streets of "Virginia's Gateway to the South" and step back into history through the doors of Ramsey House, the 1724 home of the city's Scottish founder and first postmaster, and the Carlyle House, Alexandria's grandest mansion and the house where English governors proposed taxation without representation, one of the hated laws that helped spark the American Revolution.

Walk along the cobblestone streets of Gentry Row and Captain's Row to view the early American homes (now privately owned) that belonged to sea captains when Alexandria was a thriving seaport. And stop in at the Old Apothecary Shop, now a museum of early medical ware and handblown glass containers.

A short bus ride south to Fredricksburg, Va., once a major port of colonial Virginia and a strategic civil war city, will give you an unusual one-day break.

After its founding in 1727, Fredricksburg emerged as a major port and crossroad town on the main road from the North to the South. It was for this reason during the Civil War that both sides fought for control of the principal land route between Richmond, Va., and Washington, D.C..

Visitors can wander across the battlefields of Fredricksburg, Chancellorsville, the Wilderness, and Spotsylvania Court House or visit the Jackson Shrine, the spot where Confederate General "Stonewall" Jackson died, and the Richard Kirkland Monument, a sculpture of Confederate Richard Kirkland giving water to Union soldiers wounded during the Fredricksburg campaign.

But not all the sights are of war memorials in "America's Most Historic City." Fredricksburg is the home of the James Monroe Law Office-Museum and Memorial Library, High Mercer Apothecary Shop, and the Rising Sun Tavern. These buildings and many more were preserved so that today's Americans could sample southern living and hospitality.

With the above cost-conscious ideas in mind, plus their own imaginative additions, family members can enjoy successful, inexpensive vacations. They can take the time to learn about their own parts of America.

Record your finishing time. Then answer the comprehension questions.

Comprehension Exercise for Unit 7

1 This passage is mainly about
   a Going on vacation without spending a lot of money
   b Spending your vacation at home
   c Going to Europe
   d Going to museums

2 If children are going along on the camping trips it's a good idea to bring along
   a Suntan lotion
   b A first-aid kit
   c Candy bars
   d Games, books, and playing cards

3 Although most camps have plenty available, it is always a good idea to bring an emergency
   a Water jug
   b First-aid kit
   c Wood supply
   d Food supply

4 In heavily used campgrounds there is often a shortage of _____, which is very seldom supplied.
   a Fresh water

b Food
c Pots and pans
d Wood

5 The bike trails on Mount Desert Island were originally
a Horse trails
b Bike paths
c Carriage roads
d Hiking paths

6 The key to a city vacation is
a Preselection of destinations and activities
b Shorter trips
c Less frequent trips
d All of the above

7 When planning trips to parks and zoos, money can be saved by
a Taking the bus
b Planning your trip with another family
c Bringing a picnic lunch
d None of the above

8 The author of this passage thinks that vacations should be
a Very educational
b Uncomfortable
c At least a month long
d Inexpensive

9 In Washington, D.C., many government buildings offer tours Monday through Friday; among them are tours of
a The White House
b The Pentagon
c The Bureau of Engraving and Printing
d The Smithsonian Institution

10 Just a short drive from Washington, D.C., families can enjoy "Virginia's Gateway to the South" by strolling the streets of
a Old Town Alexandria
b Richmond
c Fredricksburg
d Kirkland

Check your answers using the key on page 314.
Refer to the chart on the next page to get your reading rate. Then plot your rate and comprehension on the progress chart on page 320.

Time-Rate Table for Unit 7

"COST-CONSCIOUS VACATIONS" (2445 words)

Time in seconds converted to rate in words per minute

Time	Rate	Time	Rate	Time	Rate
3:00	815	11:00	222	19:00	129
:10	772	:10	219	:10	128
:20	734	:20	216	:20	126
:30	699	:30	212	:30	125
:40	667	:40	210	:40	124
:50	638	:50	207	:50	123
4:00	611	12:00	204	20:00	122
:10	587	:10	201	:10	121
:20	564	:20	198	:20	120
:30	543	:30	196	:30	119
:40	524	:40	193	:40	118
:50	506	:50	191	:50	117
5:00	489	13:00	188	21:00	116
:10	473	:10	186	:10	116
:20	458	:20	183	:20	115
:30	445	:30	181	:30	114
:40	431	:40	179	:40	113
:50	419	:50	177	:50	112
6:00	408	14:00	175	22:00	111
:10	396	:10	173	:10	110
:20	386	:20	171	:20	109
:30	376	:30	169	:30	109
:40	367	:40	167	:40	108
:50	358	:50	165	:50	107
7:00	349	15:00	163	23:00	106
:10	341	:10	161	:10	105
:20	333	:20	159	:20	105
:30	326	:30	158	:30	104
:40	319	:40	156	:40	103
:50	312	:50	154	:50	103
8:00	306	16:00	153	24:00	102
:10	299	:10	151	:10	101
:20	293	:20	150	:20	100
:30	288	:30	148	:30	100
:40	282	:40	147	:40	99
:50	277	:50	145	:50	98
9:00	272	17:00	144	25:00	98
:10	267	:10	142		
:20	262	:20	141		
:30	257	:30	140		
:40	253	:40	138		
:50	249	:50	138		
10:00	245	18:00	136		
:10	240	:10	135		
:20	237	:20	133		
:30	233	:30	132		
:40	229	:40	131		
:50	226	:50	130		

Understanding Reading Comprehension

Everything you read was written by someone. This simple idea is the basis for understanding reading comprehension. If you think of the material you read as a message written to you by an author, the important aspects of the process become clearer. Each time a message is read, both the author and the reader bring something to the process.

The author has a certain set of experiences in his or her life that causes the message to be written. The author also has some language patterns and skills that determine how the message is formed. In addition, the author has some purpose in writing the message, or it would not be written at all.

The reader also has a background of experience, a set of language habits and skills, and a purpose for reading.

When all of these elements are present, the reading-comprehension process takes place. However, there are several ways in which the process can fail to produce the effect desired by the writer and the reader. To take an obvious example, the message must be written in a language that the reader understands. If the reader does not have a vocabulary which contains the most important words in the message, there will be little successful communication.

In addition to the elements we have discussed, the reader also needs to have the ability to concentrate on the material. How often have you discovered that you have just gone over some reading material while thinking about something else? In such cases, comprehension is very low or even nonexistent. Sometimes such "empty reading" takes place because the material is dull or badly written. Other times it is the result of the reader's simply not paying enough attention. If the reading material is interesting, and the reader has a strong purpose for obtaining the information in the material, a high level of comprehension is likely to result.

Experts who study reading often talk about three levels of comprehension. The first level is called "literal comprehension"; the reader simply reads and understands the literal meaning that the author presents. If you recognize and understand all of the words and identify what it is that the author said, you are getting the literal meaning. You might be able to identify and retain details and main ideas, but you would not go beyond the facts and ideas presented by the author.

At the second level of comprehension, called "interpretation," you do more than simply understand the literal meaning. You look for meaning in the details given and recognize relationships among ideas. Some facts and ideas are much more important than others. At this level, you grasp the structure of the material and interpret the ideas given. You draw inferences and conclusions from the ideas presented.

If you have successfully comprehended the material at the lower two levels, you are then ready to move to the highest level of comprehension, the "applied" or "creative" level. You bring in more of your own experiences and values. You understand and interpret the author's ideas, but you also have ideas of your own. You evaluate the author's ideas. You might disagree with the author. You might take some of the author's ideas and apply them to some new situations or problems. Comprehension at this third level is really a mixture of your ideas and the author's ideas.

Since the primary focus of Part 1 is on the development of efficient reading rates, we will not be working on comprehension a great deal yet. We will continue to have comprehension questions in each unit to insure that you are understanding what you read for practice. However, as you may have noticed, the questions are generally factual and require primarily literal comprehension. We will not be asking you to do a lot of interpretation or evaluation of the material.

We are really interested in having you develop higher rates of reading. To do that, you need to practice reading easy material much faster. The best way to do that is to read without a lot of concern for comprehension. If you focus your attention on the comprehension process, your reading rate will not increase as much. In fact, if you find that your comprehension scores on the practice exercises are all very high, you are probably not reading as fast as you should be. If you are really pushing hard to increase rate, you probably will not be able to recall all of the specific details asked for in the questions. The kind of reading necessary to insure that you could answer *all* detailed questions correctly is really study-type reading. It is not what you should be doing for rate practice. You should be able, though, to answer questions about the *important* facts in each exercise.

Now let's get ready for another rate exercise. This time we will add another element to the process. Try to become extremely active as you read. That doesn't mean you should physically move around. It does mean that you should be more actively involved in the process. Reading, like any other activity, will be done more efficiently if you put more energy into it. This time try to do just that. Sit up straight, put your feet flat on the floor, and hold the book in your hands. After recording your starting time, read rapidly and actively. Keep looking ahead for the next thing the author is going to say!

finishing time _____

starting time _____

reading time _____

Sugar
How Sweet It Is — And Isn't

Sugar, "that honey from reeds," as one author described it more than 2,000 years ago, has been a part of mankind's diet for as long as anyone cares to remember.

Cave drawings tell us of prehistoric man's taste for honey, figs, and dates. The beekeeping practices of Egyptians are depicted in the artwork in tombs dating around 2600 B.C.

The Bible tells us that the "promised land" flowed with milk and honey. It turned into a flood once sugarcane was discovered.

In the writings of an obscure officer in Alexander's army during its invasion of India, one finds the first written mention of sugarcane. That was around 325 B.C.

Yet, despite this long history, the use of sugar in the diet has become a controversial issue in recent years that has involved doctors, scientists, nutritionists, private citizens, the Government, and the industry itself.

Why all the fuss?

Because there is a growing body of expert opinion that believes Americans would be healthier if they ate less sugar, not because it's bad for you, but because its only real contribution is taste and Calories.

Because sugar has become the leading ingredient added to foods in the United States today. That is, most of the sugar consumed is added before it gets to the consumer.

Because most people don't know how much sugar they eat, and many want to know. This is a principal reason the Food and Drug Administration wants the total amount of all sugars identified on more foods. The total would include both naturally occurring and added sugar.

Because sugar, though blamed wrongly for many ills, is one of a number of contributors to dental caries. Americans are spending $10 billion a year for dental care.

To most people, sugar is what you find on the kitchen table, put into coffee, or mix in a cake. This, of course, is the sugar refined from cane and beets.

Actually, there are more than a hundred substances that are sweet and which chemists can correctly describe as sugars. Sucrose, or table sugar, is just the most common and abundant of them all.

Industry literature describes sugar as a cheap source of food energy, a major contributor to food processing and general nutrition, and a substance that makes many foods with other nutrients taste better.

"Good nutrition," says a brochure from the Sugar Association, "begins with eating."

Its point, of course, is that if food is sweetened, people will eat the foods with the nutrients they need. However, many nutritionists and others concerned with American eating habits dispute sugar's value.

In a 1976 evaluation of the health aspects of sucrose as a food ingredient, the Federation of American Societies for Experimental Biology (FASEB) stated in a report to FDA: "Unlike most other foods, sucrose furnishes virtually only energy."

Many nutritionists concur and describe sugar as an "empty Calorie." If sugar is to be part of the diet, they say, it is preferable to get it from fruits, vegetables, and other items where it's a natural part of the product.

As it does with most other carbohydrates, the body converts sugar into glucose, the primary fuel of the body. During digestion it is broken down into equal parts of two simple sugars: glucose (dextrose) and fructose (levulose).

These components enter the bloodstream through the walls of the small intestine, and the blood carries the sugars to the tissues and the liver. There it is used or converted into glycogen and stored until the body needs it. The hormone insulin makes it possible for glucose, or blood sugar, to enter nearly all the cells of the body, where it is used as an energy source.

When more energy is needed, the liver converts glycogen into glucose, which is then delivered by the bloodstream to other organs or muscle tissue. Glucose not needed by the cells is metabolized in the liver into fatty substances called triglycerides. The body can call upon this stored energy during dieting and fasting.

Because of these energy reserves, nutritionists discount the argument that sugar is useful for quick energy needs before physical activity.

Americans get about 24 percent of their Calories from sugar—of which 3 percent comes in natural form from fruits and vegetables, 3 percent from dairy products, and the balance from sugar added to foods.

If sugar provides about 20 percent of a person's Calories, he must get the other 80 percent by selecting foods that supply the other nutrients his body needs—which is not easy to do, say some nutritionists, if one is trying to lose weight.

For many Americans, weight is a problem. A study released in 1978 by the National Center for Health Statistics indicated that one-third of the population was overweight.

In a study of 13,600 people whose weights between 1971 and 1974 were compared with adults of equivalent height a decade earlier, the Center found that men and women under 45 were, on the average, 3.8 and 4.7 pounds heavier, respectively. Those over 45 had gained an average of 4.8 pounds.

There is no accurate measurement of how much sugar the average American eats. The best available barometer of sugar use is the per capita consumption figures of the U.S. Department of Agriculture (USDA).

Although the per capita figures do not tell how much a person actually eats, they do show the amount of sugar that "disappears" into the marketplace—that is, the amount shipped by sugar products for industrial, home, and other uses.

Citing USDA figures, sugar industry spokesmen maintain that sugar consumption in the United States has been relatively stable for more than 50 years now, at around 100 pounds a year per person.

However, that figure refers only to the consumption of refined cane and beet sugar. It does not reflect the growing impact of a variety of corn sweeteners now in use. The term "corn sweeteners" includes various corn syrups (high fructose corn syrup, glucose) plus other Caloric sweeteners, such as dextrose, that are derived from corn.

Refined sugar, corn syrup, and corn sugar account for the bulk of the sweeteners consumed in this country. Among the remainder are honey, maple, and other edible syrups.

All of these are Caloric, and when all are taken into account, USDA figures show a rise in per capita consumption from 122 pounds in 1970 to 128 pounds in 1978.

Per capita consumption of just refined sugar hovered around the 100 pounds per year level between 1960 and 1974. Since then, the trend generally has been downward, falling below 93 pounds in 1978, according to USDA. Fred Gray, an agriculture economist for USDA, predicted a further drop of several pounds for 1979.

The decline in refined sugar consumption has been more than offset by the steady rise in corn sweetener usage—from a per capita rate of 19 pounds in 1970 to almost 34 pounds in 1978.

Norris Bollenback, scientific director for the Sugar Association, said the primary impetus for the increase has come from the growing industrial use of high fructose corn syrups, especially by soft drink producers.

The use of high fructose corn syrups was negligible—less than a pound per capita, on the average—in the early 1970's. The industry was in its infancy then, and food and beverage manufacturers relied almost entirely on cane and beet sugar for their products because those sugars were cheap and plentiful, selling for about 11 or 12 cents a pound wholesale.

The rapid escalation of sugar prices in 1974—up to around 33 cents a pound wholesale—compelled the food and beverage industries to turn to other sweeteners, and the most attractive of them all was the high fructose corn syrups.

By the end of 1975, USDA figures show that per capita consumption of those corn syrups had risen to 5 pounds and 3 years later up to 11 pounds. Gray predicted that high fructose corn syrup usage would reach 15 pounds in 1979 and 18 pounds by the end of 1980.

Bollenback cited figures that showed that high fructose corn syrup producers have maintained their product's price consistently below that of refined sugar—roughly from 3 to 10 cents a pound less at the wholesale level. Last year, the wholesale price of high fructose corn syrup was around 13 cents a pound compared to 20 cents for refined sugar.

"If (refined) sugar proponents think things will be back the way they were, they are being unrealistic," Bollenback noted.

Things also aren't the way they used to be in how sugar gets to our stomachs. Fifty years ago, two-thirds of the sugar produced went directly into the home, which meant control was directly in the hands of the housewife or individual who bought it. The balance was used mostly by industry.

Now, the reverse is true. Sixty-five percent of the refined sugar produced today is being consumed by the food and beverage industries and only 24 percent is going for home use.

The beverage industry—comprised of soft drink bottlers and beer and wine producers—is the leading industrial user of refined sugar and of high fructose corn syrups. It used 26 percent of the 9.8 million tons of refined sugar shipped in 1978 and about 40 percent of the high fructose corn syrups.

Although there has been a considerable amount of public controversy over the amount of sugar in cereals, the bakery and cereal industries combined used only 13.4 percent of all the sugar produced for food purposes in 1978. USDA figures did not separate the two.

Producers of confectionery products had the next highest usage at 9.2 percent, followed by 7 percent for the processed food and canning industries, and 5.6 percent for dairy products.

The consumer today is confronted by a wide variety of sugars and other nutritive sweeteners, and there is no significant difference in the amount of Calories each provides.

Below is a brief explanation of the more common sugars and sweeteners:

Sucrose, obtained in crystalline form, from cane and beets, is a double sugar or disaccharide and is composed of two simple sugars, glucose and fructose. It is about 99.9 percent pure and is sold in either granulated or powdered form.

Raw sugar, tan to brown in appearance, is a coarse, granulated solid obtained from evaporation of sugarcane juice. FDA regulations prohibit the sale of raw sugar unless impurities—dirt, insect fragments, etc.—are removed.

Turbinado sugar is sometimes viewed erroneously as a raw sugar. Actually, it has to go through a refining process to remove impurities and most of the molasses. It is produced by separating raw sugar crystals and washing them with steam. It is edible if produced under proper conditions. However, some samples in the past have been found to contain contaminants, the Sugar Association warns.

Brown sugar consists of sugar crystals contained in a molasses syrup with natural flavor and color. However, some refiners make brown sugar by simply adding syrup to refined white sugar in a mixer. It has 91 to 96 percent sucrose.

Total invert sugar, a mixture of glucose and fructose, is formed by splitting sucrose in a process called inversion, which is accomplished by the application of acids or enzymes. It is sold only in liquid form and is sweeter than sucrose. It helps prolong the freshness of baked foods and confections and is useful in preventing food shrinkage.

Honey is an invert sugar formed by an enzyme from nectar gathered by bees. Its composition and flavor depend on the source of the nectar. Fructose, glucose, maltose, and sucrose are among its components.

Corn syrups, produced by the acton of enzymes and/or acids on cornstarch, are the result of hydrolysis of starch. High fructose corn syrup is a derivative of corn. The amounts of fructose vary with the manufacturer. One major producer's syrups contain 42 percent, 55 percent, and 90 percent fructose. Dextrose comprises most of the balance.

Levulose, or fructose, is a commercial sugar, considerably sweeter than sucrose, although its sweetness actually depends on its physical form and how it is used in cooking. Fructose, known as a fruit sugar, occurs naturally in many fruits.

Dextrose, or glucose, is also called corn sugar. It is made commercially from starch by the action of heat and acids, or enzymes. It is often sold blended with regular sugar.

Lactose, or milk sugar, is made from whey and skim milk for commercial purposes. It occurs in the milk of mammals. The pharmaceutical industry is a primary user of prepared lactose.

Sorbitol, mannitol, maltitol, and *xylitol* are sugar alcohols or polyols. They occur naturally in fruits but are commercially produced from such sources as dextrose. Xylitol is a sugar alcohol made from a part of birch trees. Sorbitol, mannitol, and maltitol are about half as sweet as sucrose; xylitol has a sweetness about equal to sucrose.

Although fructose and the other sugar alcohols are promoted as suitable substitute sweeteners, especially for diabetics, many health scientists question their supposed advantages pending more research and long-term studies.

Record your finishing time. Then answer the comprehension questions.

Comprehension Exercise for Unit 8

1 Sugarcane was first mentioned in the writings of an officer under the command of _____.
   a   George Washington
   b   Napoleon
   c   Alexander the Great
   d   Marco Polo

2 This passage is about
   a   Cane sugar
   b   All kinds of sugar
   c   Honey
   d   Sucrose

3 Sucrose (table sugar) furnishes _____ for the body.
   a   Several vitamins
   b   Five nutrients
   c   Vitamin C
   d   No nutrients or vitamins, only energy

4 The hormone _____ makes it possible for glucose to enter all the cells of the body.
   a   Estrogen

    b Testosterone
    c Glycogen
    d Insulin

5 According to the author Americans now eat
    a Less sugar than they used to
    b Much less brown sugar than they should
    c Almost no sugar at all
    d More sugar than they used to

6 In the past fifty years the United States has consumed about _____
pounds for each person per year.
    a 1000
    b 100
    c 50
    d 75

7 Because of the price of sugar the beverage industry has begun using
_____ in place of refined sugar.
    a Corn syrup
    b Brown sugar
    c Honey
    d Lactose

8 _____ is found naturally in many fruits and is considerably sweeter
than table sugar.
    a Levulose
    b Dextrose
    c Raw sugar
    d Sorbitol

9 _____ consists of sugar crystals contained in molasses syrup with
natural flavor and color.
    a Sucrose
    b Turbinado sugar
    c Brown sugar
    d Raw sugar

10 _____ is a sugar alcohol made from a part of birch trees.
    a Brown sugar
    b Honey
    c Xylitol
    d Dextrose

Check your answers using the key on page 314.
Refer to the chart on the next page to get your reading rate. Then plot your
rate and comprehension on the progress chart on page 320.

Time-Rate Table for Unit 8

"SUGAR: HOW SWEET IT IS—AND ISN'T" (2183 words)

Time in seconds converted to rate in words per minute

Time	Rate	Time	Rate	Time	Rate
2:40	819	10:00	218	17:00	128
:50	770	:10	215	:10	127
3:00	728	:20	211	:20	126
:10	689	:30	208	:30	125
:20	655	:40	205	:40	124
:30	624	:50	202	:50	122
:40	595	11:00	198	18:00	121
:50	569	:10	195	:10	120
4:00	546	:20	193	:20	119
:10	524	:30	190	:30	118
:20	504	:40	187	:40	117
:30	485	:50	184	:50	116
:40	468	12:00	182	19:00	115
:50	452	:10	179	:10	114
5:00	437	:20	177	:20	113
:10	423	:30	175	:30	112
:20	409	:40	172	:40	111
:30	397	:50	170	:50	110
:40	385	13:00	168	20:00	109
:50	374	:10	166	:10	108
6:00	364	:20	164	:20	107
:10	354	:30	162	:30	106
:20	347	:40	160	:40	106
:30	336	:50	158	:50	105
:40	327	14:00	156	21:00	104
:50	319	:10	154	:10	103
7:00	312	:20	152	:20	102
:10	305	:30	150	:30	102
:20	298	:40	149	:40	101
:30	291	:50	147	:50	100
:40	285	15:00	146	22:00	99
:50	279	:10	144		
8:00	273	:20	142		
:10	267	:30	141		
:20	262	:40	139		
:30	257	:50	138		
:40	252	16:00	136		
:50	247	:10	135		
9:00	243	:20	134		
:10	238	:30	132		
:20	234	:40	131		
:30	230	:50	130		
:40	226				
:50	222				

Study-Type Reading

Reading for study purposes is somewhat different from the rapid-practice reading you have been doing in this book so far. It is much more intensive and not usually done at very high rates. The main focus is on understanding and retaining the information given by the author.

Good reading skills are required for effective study. In addition, there are some other characteristics of a good study situation.

1 Motivation helps. A highly motivated student will learn a great deal more than one who has little or no interest in learning.

2 Intense or exciting experiences produce more learning and longer retention. Some experiences are really unforgettable.

3 Material for which you have appropriate background will be learned more easily.

4 Good concentration helps. The more you can eliminate distractions, the better you will learn.

5 Self-testing, or "recitation," helps—probably because self-testing creates a learning situation similar to the experience you will have later when you are tested on the same material.

6 Well-organized material will be learned more quickly and retained longer. We will demonstrate this principle by having you learn something right now!

Stop immediately and try to memorize the following number series:

1 2 4 8 1 6 3 2 6 4

Be sure you can repeat the series without error before you go on. We will come back to this series later in the unit. Use any technique you can to memorize it so that you could repeat it from memory in a day or two.

Ways to Improve Study-Type Reading

The learning principles we have listed will suggest some ways to improve your study. They can be applied to your own learning in a variety of ways.

The fact that motivation is important suggests a good review of your own reasons for learning. If you are a student in school or taking a course for some specific purpose, you might want to think about the advantages of learning the course material. The more you can specify your objectives, the more likely you are to stick to the task and the easier it will be to learn. If you are simply in school because you have nothing else to do or because someone else wants you to be a student, it is quite difficult to maintain enough motivation for effective study. Sometimes a careful examination of long-term plans, perhaps with the aid of a counselor, will clarify your goals and objectives.

Making a learning experience unforgettable because it is intense or exciting is a real challenge. Some teachers manage to make even the most routine material very interesting by the way they present it. Unfortunately, however, the burden of learning and remembering really falls on you.

There are some things that can be done to increase involvement in the situation. For example, taking organized notes on a lecture or reading assignment tends to get you more involved. Most important, it requires some physical activity. We learn by various modes; visual and auditory are the most common. However, sometimes other senses are involved; we learn about skunks by smell. Other forms of learning involve taste or touch. Other than the visual and the auditory, one of the most powerful modes is through the use of physical actions. Physical learning and skills are extremely resistant to being forgotten. (You may have heard the old saying that you never forget how to ride a bicycle.) You can take advantage of the increased memory of physical actions by building some activity into your study techniques.

As we have said, taking notes is one such method. Information that is written down is remembered better. In addition, taking notes gives you a more efficient way to review than rereading. In some cases, you may encounter a term, a formula, or other specific thing that is difficult for you to remember. Another technique that is used with learning disabled persons but that can be helpful to most people involves writing and finger tracing.

Let's say, for example, that you have a difficult time remembering how to spell the word "ceiling." (You can apply the "i before e, except after c" rule, but you are never sure whether "ceiling" is an exception.) To lock the word in your memory system, first write it down in very large letters, using a whole sheet of paper. Then you put down your pencil and trace the word with your finger as you say it to yourself (preferably aloud). Do the tracing several times. Then close your eyes and visualize the word as you say it to yourself. Then write the word in large form again without looking at the one you wrote before.

Try the writing and tracing technique on some word, phrase, or formula that you have trouble remembering. You will find that it will not be a problem again.

Another of the learning principles we discussed has to do with background. Material for which you have adequate background is learned most easily. Other material that is new to you will be more difficult. One way to improve your learning in a new area of study is to read a lot of related material. Many teachers recognize the need for a broad background in their subject. They provide for it to some extent by suggesting or requiring supplementary readings. You will be well-advised to spend some time on related readings, especially in an area of learning that is new to you.

Improving your ability to concentrate will also make learning easier. One good way to improve concentration is to pay more attention to the things and ideas that distract you. When you find that your mind is wandering from the task at hand, observe what it is that is demanding your attention. It may be an unfinished task or a personal problem that keeps coming up. One way to deal with such distractions is to stop and finish the task or solve the problem. In most cases, however, you don't have the time or information to do so. The best way to handle such a situation is to make a definite plan to deal with the distracting situation at a later time. "I will write that letter tomorrow after lunch." Or "I will spend some time after lunch tomorrow trying to work out the problem with Mary." Making a definite plan will allow you to put the problem out of your mind for the moment and will help you concentrate.

Some distractions are in the room around you. It may be noisy, poorly ventilated, or otherwise bad for study. If you can't change the conditions in the room, perhaps you can arrange to study in a library or other more appropriate place. You need a place that is quiet, well-lit, not too hot or cold, and not cluttered up with pictures and objects that will remind you of other things. Sometimes simply removing a picture from your desk will solve the problem!

One good way to improve your success in school is to take the tests in advance. It almost always helps to do a lot of self-testing. Look over the material and try to decide what information or skills you will need. Pretend to be the teacher. What would you have on the test? Try to predict test questions. Then test your ability to answer them without looking at books or notes.

In some courses you can use flash cards to do systematic self-testing. Put the question on one side and the answer on the other. Or if you are studying a foreign language, put the English word on one side and the foreign language equivalent on the other side. Flash cards are especially useful in areas of study in which you have a lot of specific, detailed information to memorize. When you practice with flash cards, it is important to shuffle them periodically. This prevents knowing them only in a certain sequence. The teacher is not likely to ask for the information in exactly the sequence in your deck of cards.

Now we come to the last of the principles we discussed—the one having to do with organization. Remember the number series you memorized at the beginning of this unit? Can you write it now without error? If you can, you probably organized it in some say. Perhaps you made it into five 2-digit numbers:

12 48 16 32 64

Perhaps you used some other technique. Would you remember the series in a week? A month?

Let's look at it again, and notice that the numbers have an organization of their own. Each one is twice the last—a simple doubling series:

1 2 4 8 16 32 64

If you had discovered this organization before, you would have had no trouble remembering the series. Now that the organization is clear, notice that it is easy to remember. You would probably be able to come up with it in a week, a month, or even a year. There are also some other benefits. If a number is left out, it is easy to remember what is missing:

1 2 4 __ 16 32 64

Additional, added information also makes more sense. If you needed to remember the next number in a longer series, you would know that it had to be 128 (twice 64).

This little demonstration shows the advantage of trying to create or discover the organization of the material to be learned. It will make learning easier, memory longer, and understanding more intense.

Much of the material you learn is already well-organized. Some attention to that organization will help. Look, for example, at the table of contents in a textbook. It will tell you a lot about the organization of the material, if you think about it a little. Sometimes the author explains the organization of a book in the preface. Other clues to organization are to be found in chapter titles, page headings, section subtitles, and other graphic aids in the book. It is well worth your time to examine a book to discover the way it is organized. The best time to do so is before you begin reading the book.

We will be working on developing study-type reading skills later in this book. For the moment, however, let's get back to our plan to build up high reading rates on easy material. By now you should have raised your rate on these practice exercises a great deal. Let's continue that improvement on the practice exercise which follows. Try to read it at a higher rate than any of the earlier units. Sit up, put a lot of energy into it, and keep looking ahead for the next idea or fact to be presented.

Don't forget to record your starting time and finishing time.

finishing time _____

starting time _____

reading time _____

Life as It Used To Be

In 1933 little had changed in the everyday lives of the vast majority of rural Tennessee Valley people since the turn of the century. Some had left the farms for jobs in town, but even many of those were back now, deprived of their new livelihood by the Great Depression which had swept across the face of the land.

The automobile had beat out the horse and wagon, except in the most remote and poverty stricken hollows.

The spinning wheel, a familiar sight in the living room corner for 100 years, was all but gone, replaced by "store-bought calico," purchased along with shoes, farm implements, coffee, sugar, and gasoline at the general store down the road a few miles. But the skills required to card, spin, and weave the fiber into fabric were still fresh on the minds of most women.

Electricity was known on only three farms in a hundred. Light came from a kerosene lamp, refrigeration from a cool spring or cellar, and heat from a fireplace or wood-burning stove.

Home-grown vegetables, fruits, and livestock provided the food, which was cooked in dark kitchens with wood stoves. A reservoir on the side of the stove or a kettle on top was the only source of hot water.

The simple act of getting water required back-breaking labor. The family with a good spring near the back door was fortunate indeed. Hand-dug wells provided water for many families. Buckets or tubes had to be lowered to the bottom of the well, 30, 40, or 50 feet down, and the water pulled to the surface by rope. Ingenious combinations of winches, pullies, and cranks were contrived to make this job easier.

Monday was washday, and a busy day it was. Gallons of water had to be carried from the closest source, often a nearby stream. Fire was kindled under a cast-iron pot to boil the clothes, which were then scrubbed and rinsed by hand before being hung out to dry. The warm, soapy water left over was used to scrub the spring house, outdoor toilet, animal quarters, or anything else needing a good cleaning. The rinse water was used on the flowers. Nothing so hard obtained was wasted. The clothes were ironed with heavy flatirons heated on the kitchen stove.

Repairs to automobile, plow, cooking utensil, clothing, or shoes were made at home. The period between supper and bedtime provided an ideal time for such chores, particularly if they could be brought inside by the fire in winter. Food for the next day's meals also was made ready for cooking at this time.

Every member of the family, young and old, had work to do. Women were responsible for most of the chores around the house. During peak planting and harvesting seasons, they also joined their husbands and sons in the fields. The well-off and the poor shared in common many of the same chores.

Hard as it was in the 1930s, life in the Tennessee Valley Region had a rhythm and from this rhythm the people derived security and peace and happiness. It was a style familiar in many respects to the pioneers who first settled the region 200 years before. But it was a style soon to be caught up in the web of change and progress which was even then beginning.

Norris and Wheeler Dams, the first major projects of TVA, transformed the landscape and helped bring the marvel of electricity to the rural people. The building of these projects provided thousands of jobs at a time when no other work was available.

Factories followed the power lines and the developed river into the Valley Region, bringing a new industrial revolution.

New TVA-developed fertilizers and modern farming practices sparked another kind of revolution, this one in Valley agriculture.

These and other economic and social forces nudged the Valley Region closer to the mainstream of modern American life and further from its nostalgic past.

Today, only small, scattered fragments of the old life styles remain in isolated pockets deep in mountain coves. Artifacts preserved in simulated museums designed for tourists provide modern-day Valley residents with their only visible link to a culture which even many of them experienced in childhood and which was the only way of life known to their parents and grandparents.

Record your finishing time. Then answer the comprehension questions.

Comprehension Exercise for Unit 9

1   The everyday lives of the people in the rural _____ _____ had not changed from the turn of the century through the 1930s.
  a   Appalachian mountains
  b   Tennessee Valley
  c   Southern states
  d   Imperial Valley

2   This passage is mainly about changes brought about by
  a   The automobile
  b   The spinning wheel
  c   Fertilizer
  d   Electricity

3   Only three farms in 100 had _____.
  a   Running water
  b   Refrigerators
  c   Electricity
  d   Bathrooms

4   Getting water for many families was
  a   Helped by government aid
  b   A back-breaking job
  c   Easy because water was always close by
  d   Helped by the building of a new water system

5   The rinse water from the washing of clothes was used on the _____.
  a   Flowers
  b   Outdoor toilet

c   Floors
d   Automobile

6   According to the author life today for people in the Tennessee Valley
a   Is much worse than it used to be
b   Is not much different than it was
c   Is only slightly different than it was
d   Is very different than it was

7   The lifestyle in the Tennessee Valley in the 1930s was similar to that of
the _____ .
a   Pilgrims
b   Plantation owners
c   Early city dwellers
d   Pioneers

8   Norris and Wheeler Dams were the first major projects of the

_____ .
a   TWA
b   TVA
c   NRA
d   WPA

9   Once power lines began to appear _____ came into the picture.
a   Railroads
b   Highways
c   Automobiles
d   Factories

10   Today most of the people of the Tennessee Valley _____ .
a   Still cling to the old ways
b   Are closer to the mainstream of modern American life
c   Are still rebelling against the changes brought about by the introduction of
electricity
d   Feel they have been taken advantage of

Check your answers using the key on page 314.
Refer to the chart on the next page to get your reading rate. Then plot your
rate and comprehension on the progress chart on page 320.

Time-Rate Table for Unit 9

"LIFE AS IT USED TO BE" (724 words)

Time in seconds converted to rate in words per minute.

Time	Rate		Time	Rate
:50	869		5:00	141
1:00	724		:10	140
:10	620		:20	136
:20	543		:30	132
:30	483		:40	128
:40	434		:50	124
:50	395		6:00	121
2:00	362		:10	117
:10	334		:20	114
:20	310		:30	111
:30	290		:40	109
:40	272		:50	106
:50	256		7:00	103
3:00	241		:10	101
:10	229		:20	99
:20	217		:30	97
:30	207		:40	94
:40	197		:50	92
:50	189		8:00	91
4:00	181		:10	89
:10	174		:20	87
:20	167			
:30	161			
:40	155			
:50	150			

Reading to Discover Organization

In Unit 9 we discussed briefly the fact that material that was well organized could be learned more easily and remembered better. (At that time you also learned a series of numbers beginning with 1 2 4 8 1 6 __ __ __ __. Can you complete the series now?)

There are two major ways that you can use the organization of reading material to improve your understanding and retention. The first and most important is to be alert to the ways in which authors organize ideas. They sometimes tell you what they are doing by giving a summary at the beginning. On the other hand, they sometimes wait until the very end to give the most important information. In a short story by O'Henry, for example, you usually find some surprise twist to the story at the end that gives the whole thing meaning.

Newspaper reports follow a definite pattern in which the most important information is given very early in the story. Reporters are trained to put the who, why, where, what, and when of the story into the first paragraph or two. Details follow in descending order of importance in later paragraphs. There are at least two good reasons why reporters follow this pattern. One is that newspaper readers do not always read all of the paper. If the reader only gets to the first or second paragraph of the story, at least the most important facts are there. The other reason for the way news reports are written has to do with the way editors put the paper together. Sometimes a reporter will turn in a story that is longer than the editor can use. The space available in the paper determines how much the editor will use. If the least important information is at the end of the story, it can be cut and no great harm is done.

Other patterns of organization can be discovered if you look for them. Some authors use a straight narrative style in which everything is described as it happens in a time sequence. Other authors use the same technique but periodically put in flashbacks, with events out of chronological order. If you are not aware that the author is presenting a flashback, you can become extremely confused about what is going on in the story.

Some writing is designed to present an organized argument. Facts, interpretations, and conclusions are presented in sequence to convince you of the logic of the author's position.

Descriptive material is sometimes presented as though you were observing it—right to left, top to bottom, or near to far. The author is trying to produce a mental picture in your mind that matches the one being described.

Another way of organizing material is to present some extremely interesting, humorous, or controversial statement at the beginning. Then the statement is supported, elaborated, explained, or somehow expanded in the rest of the passage.

If you give some attention to the way the author has organized the material it will pay off in better comprehension of the material and in longer and stronger retention.

The second major way you can use the organization of the material to increase understanding and retention is to use the various graphic aids provided. You may not have noticed it much, but this book has a definite organization, much of which can be seen in the way it is printed. Consider the following points:

1   There is a table of contents at the beginning.

2   Each unit starts on a new page.

3   Each question is numbered.

4   Each article has a definite place to record reading time.

We could go on with this list, but you already understand the point. Notice, also, that numbering the points above sets them apart and makes it easier to memorize them if you had to.

> Notice that material in a box
> stands apart and is noticed more.

If the author wants to emphasize a point, one way to do it is to put it in italics.

Material that is surrounded by an
unusual amount of blank space tends
to be seen and remembered.

Figures, pictures, drawings, and graphs can also help. The old saying, A picture is worth a thousand words, applies equally well to figures and graphs. Some readers tend to ignore figures, graphs, and pictures and as a result, get less information than the good reader.

We are now going to go on to the practice exercise for this unit. It is an example which uses subheadings to show the organization of the material. Notice how the subheadings lead you from one topic to the next.

The selection is taken from a booklet published in 1955 to explain the social security program. The program had been in effect for twenty years at that time but had been changed somewhat, and many people were covered who had not been involved earlier. This is one of two selections relating to social security. The next unit, "Critical Reading," contains a selection that is closely related to this one. Try to remember as much as you can from this selection so you can compare it with the next one. Remember to record your starting time.

finishing time _____

starting time _____

reading time _____

Your Social Security

Social Security has been a part of American life since 1935. The 1954 amendments to the social security law extended and improved the Old-Age and Survivors Insurance program that has become familiar to almost a generation of Americans.

With these amendments, Federal Old-Age and Survivors Insurance has become a more effective weapon against family insecurity caused by old age or death. The 1954 changes extended its protection to 9 out of 10 working Americans and their families, increased benefit payments, and improved the law in a number of other important ways.

Federal Old-Age and Survivors Insurance

What It Is

Old-Age and Survivors Insurance is protection for you and your family based on your earnings in work covered by the Federal social security law.

If you work in employment or self-employment covered by the law, you will make social security tax contributions during your working years to provide an income for yourself and your family in case your earnings are cut off by old age, and for your family in case of your death. If you are employed, you and your employer share the tax; if you are self-employed, the rate of your tax is three-fourths as much as the total tax of employer and employee on the same amount of earnings.

The amount of your benefit payment depends on the amount of your average earnings.

Other members of your family may be entitled to payments based on your social security account while you are receiving benefits and after your death. Payments to them—to your wife, or to children under 18, for example—are figured from the amount of your old-age insurance benefit.

The amount of monthly payments to your family, therefore, depends on three things: your earnings, the number of your dependents, and the age of each member of your family.

Becoming Insured

To qualify for monthly payments when you reach 65 and retire, or to make payments possible for your survivors in case of your death, you must have been in work covered by the social security law for a certain length of time. The amount of work required is measured in "quarters of coverage."

A quarter of coverage, in a general way, corresponds with a calendar quarter of work. A calendar quarter is a 3-month period beginning January 1, April 1, July 1, or October 1. The exact meaning of a quarter of coverage is different, however, for certain different kinds of work.

You get 4 quarters of coverage for a year in which you have $400 or more in net earnings from self-employment.

After 1954, you get 1 quarter of coverage for each $100 of cash wages paid to you in a year as a farm employee (but no more than 4 in a year).

For all other kinds of employment you get 1 quarter of coverage for each calendar quarter in which you are paid $50 or more in wages.

You can also earn quarters of coverage through railroad employment and active military service.

You may have earned quarters of coverage by working as an employee at any time after 1936 and by self-employment after 1950.

The number of quarters of coverage you have is used only in figuring whether or not a payment can be made. The amount *of the payment is figured from your average monthly earnings.*

If at the time you reach 65 you have enough quarters of coverage to be "fully insured," you are eligible for retirement payments. You may also earn needed quarters of coverage after you are 65. "Fully insured" means only that *some* amount of benefits can be paid, not necessarily that the maximum amount will be paid.

If at the time of death you are either "fully insured" or "currently insured," your survivors may be eligible for benefit payments.

Amount of Your Old-Age Insurance Benefit

The amount of your old-age insurance benefit is determined from your average monthly earnings over a certain period of time. Payments to your dependents and to your survivors are figured from the amount of your benefit.

The exact amount of your payments can be determined only after an application has been made, but you can get an idea of the amount by using the tables and the simplified methods given here.

The period of time over which your average earnings are figured can start with January 1, 1937, or with January 1, 1951.

Most people will receive higher benefits under the formula given in the 1954 amendments, using average monthly earnings after 1950. *It is not necessary for you to select which method will be used to figure your payments. When you make your application for payments, the Social Security Administration will figure the benefit in all ways and will pay the highest possible benefit.*

Who Pays for It?

Federal Old-Age and Survivors Insurance is paid for by a contribution (or tax) on the employee's wages and the self-employed person's earnings from his trade or business.

If you are employed, you and your employer will share equally in the tax. If you are self-employed, you pay only three-fourths as much as an employee and his employer would pay on the same amount of earnings.

Manner in Which Taxes Are Paid

If you are employed, your tax is deducted from your wages each payday. The employer sends it, with an equal amount as his own tax, to the District Director of Internal Revenue with a report on Form 941. Employers of house-hold workers may use a special envelope report, Form 942. Special reporting procedures for farm workers are provided by the Internal Revenue Service.

If you are self-employed, you must report your earnings and pay your tax each year when you file your individual income tax return.

A special method of reporting is provided for self-employed farmers.

As long as you have earnings that are covered by the law, you continue to pay the social security tax regardless of your age.

The following table shows the present tax percentages and scheduled increases:

Calendar year	Employer	Employee	Self-employed
1955–59	2	2	3
1960–64	$2^1/_2$	$2^1/_2$	$3^3/_4$
1965–69	3	3	$4^1/_2$
1970–74	$3^1/_2$	$3^1/_2$	$5^1/_4$
1975 and after	4	4	6

Those who have earnings from both employment and self-employment pay the tax on their wages from employment; if these wages amount to less than $4,200, they also pay the tax on that part of their net earnings from self-employment necessary to bring the total up to $4,200 for a year.

From the social security tax report your wages and self-employment income are entered on your individual record by the Social Security Administration. This record of your earnings will be used to determine your eligibility for benefits and the amount you will receive.

If a worker has been employed so little under social security that he has not become insured, there is no provision under the law which permits refund of the social security taxes paid.

The Trust Fund

The social security taxes collected by the Internal Revenue Service are deposited in the Federal Old-Age and Survivors Insurance Trust Fund and are used to pay all the benefits and administrative expenses of the program. They may be used for no other purpose. The reserve portion of the trust fund—that is, the part not required for current disbursement—is invested in interest-bearing United States Government securities.

The schedule of tax rates given above is designed to meet the future obligations of the program and keep it on a self-supporting basis.

Account Number Cards

If you are employed or self-employed in any kind of work covered by the Social Security Act, you must have a social security account number. Your social security card shows your account number, which is used to keep a record of your earnings. You should use the same account number all your life.

There are 130 million names in the social security records, but your account number as shown on your social security card distinguishes your account from the social security accounts of other people who have names similar to or exactly like yours. Both your name and account number are needed to make sure you get full credit for your earnings. If you are employed, show your card to each employer so that when reporting your wages he may use your name and account number exactly as they appear on the card. If you are self-employed, copy your name and account number on the schedule you use to report your net earnings for social security credit.

Your nearest social security office will issue you a social security card or a duplicate card to replace one that has been lost. If there is no social security office in your town, ask at the post office for an application blank.

If your name has been changed, ask your social security office for a new card showing the same account number and your new name.

The account number on your card is the key to your social security account. The benefits payable to you or to your family are figured from the earnings recorded in your social security account.

Checking Your Account

Each employer is required by law to give you receipts for the social security taxes he has deducted from your pay. He must do this at the end of each year and also when you stop working for him. These receipts will help you check on your social security account because they show not only the amount deducted from your pay but also the wages paid you. You should keep a record of the amount of self-employment income you have reported.

You may check your official social security record as often as once a year by writing to the Social Security Administration, Baltimore, Md., and asking for a statement of your account. You can get an addressed post card form at your social security office for use in requesting wage information.

If an error has been made in your account, the social security office will help you get it corrected. You should check on your account at least once each 3 years, since there is a limit to the period within which certain corrections can be made.

Social Security Offices

The Social Security Administration has district offices (formerly called "field offices") conveniently located throughout the country. These local offices have representatives who go regularly to other communities to serve the public.

If you have any questions about old-age and survivors insurance, call at one of these district offices, or get in touch with it by telephone or mail. The people who work there will be glad to answer questions and to explain your rights.

When you need a social security card—either a new one or a copy of a card that has been lost—your nearest district office is the place to go. This office will also help you get a statement of the wages credited to your social security account, and will assist you in correcting errors in your account.

Record your finishing time. Then answer the comprehension questions.

Comprehension Exercise for Unit 10

1 What did the 1954 amendment to the social security law do?
   a Decrease benefits
   b Legislate that all workers in the United States be covered by social security
   c Extend its protection to nine out of ten working Americans and their families
   d Make the law very hard to interpret

2 Old Age and Survivors Insurance is protection for you and your family based on
   a Where you are employed
   b Your earnings in work covered by the federal social security law
   c How long you live
   d The number of years you worked

3 If you die before you are eligible to collect social security _____.
   a Your children over 18 can collect your social security
   b Your wife and children under 18 can collect your social security
   c No benefits are paid to anyone
   d You can name a friend to get your benefits

4 To qualify for monthly payments when you reach 65 and retire you must have _____.
   a So many quarters of coverage
   b So many years that you have paid into the fund
   c Paid a certain amount of money into the fund
   d Been employed for a certain length of time

5 How can you find out what the exact amount of your benefits will be?
   a By calling the Social Security Administration
   b By writing your Congressman

c   By using tables published by the Social Security Administration
d   By making an application to the Social Security Administration

6   If you are employed, your employer pays
a   All of your social security costs
b   Half of the amount paid into social security
c   Three-fourths as much as you do
d   One-third of the total amount

7   This passage describes social security as a kind of
a   Insurance
b   Tax
c   Charity program
d   Supplemental income

8   A person who has not paid enough into social security to become in-sured can
a   Get a refund of all the money paid in
b   Get a partial refund of the money paid in
c   Not get back any of the money paid in
d   Not get back the portion the employer has paid in

9   The author's purpose in this passage is mainly to
a   Warn
b   Sell
c   Inform
d   Insult

10   Your employer is required by law
a   To give you receipts for the social security tax deducted from your pay
b   To report to you the amount of money in your account
c   To make your share of the payments if you fail to pay
d   To make payments to your dependents if you die

Check your answers using the key on page 314.
Refer to the chart on the next page to get your reading rate. Then plot your rate and comprehension on the progress chart on page 320.

Time-Rate Table for Unit 10

"YOUR SOCIAL SECURITY" (1833 words)

Time in seconds converted to rate in words per minute

Time	Rate	Time	Rate	Time	Rate
2:10	846	9:00	204	15:00	122
:20	786	:10	200	:10	121
:30	733	:20	196	:20	120
:40	687	:30	193	:30	118
:50	657	:40	190	:40	117
3:00	611	:50	186	:50	116
:10	579	10:00	183	16:00	115
:20	550	:10	181	:10	113
:30	524	:20	177	:20	112
:40	500	:30	175	:30	111
:50	478	:40	172	:40	110
4:00	458	:50	169	:50	109
:10	440	11:00	167	17:00	108
:20	423	:10	164	:10	107
:30	407	:20	162	:20	106
:40	393	:30	159	:30	105
:50	379	:40	157	:40	104
5:00	367	:50	155	:50	103
:10	355	12:00	153	18:00	102
:20	344	:10	151	:10	101
:30	333	:20	149	:20	100
:40	323	:30	147	:30	99
:50	314	:40	145	:40	98
6:00	306	:50	143	:50	97
:10	297	13:00	141		
:20	289	:10	139		
:30	282	:20	137		
:40	275	:30	136		
:50	268	:40	134		
7:00	262	:50	133		
:10	256	14:00	131		
:20	250	:10	129		
:30	244	:20	128		
:40	239	:30	126		
:50	234	:40	125		
8:00	229	:50	124		
:10	224				
:20	220				
:30	216				
:40	212				
:50	208				

Critical Reading

Suppose you read the following in the sports section of a school paper:

District Baseball Championship Game:
Elmtown 7, Maple Valley 5

Or this:

Elmtown Wins District Championship in Brilliant Finish

It was a bright summer day and the Elmtown baseball team was having a good day. They were playing Maple Valley for the district championship. Elmtown scored runs in the third, fourth, and fifth innings but were still behind in the ninth inning. A homerun by Sam Jones in the ninth won the game for Elmtown. It was an exciting and rewarding afternoon for the new district champions in Elmtown.

Or this:

Maple Valley Loses to Elmtown
after Leading throughout Game

In the heat and dust of last Saturday afternoon, Maple Valley traveled to Elmtown for the district baseball championship game. It was a long game, with Maple Valley leading throughout the afternoon. Finally in the last inning, Elmtown's star batter hit a homerun, scoring two base runners. It was a frustrating and disappointing end to the season for Maple Valley.

The first notice simply gives the minimum facts, without comment. The second and third reports are written from a definite point of view. Notice that it would not be difficult to guess whether it was an Elmtown paper or a Maple Valley paper in which the last two accounts appeared.

The authors of the last two accounts of the game are probably not trying to distort the story. They are simply writing from different points of view. They are also writing for different readers.

Much of the material you read every day is written in an effort to express a particular point of view. Some of the issues that influence our lives are being debated in the press. It would be difficult, if not impossible, to say very much about a truly controversial subject without saying things that many would disagree with. For example, consider the following questions that are debated in public at times:

Should stricter gun control legislation be enacted?

How much foreign aid should our government provide?

Should there be prayers in the public schools?

Should capital punishment be abolished?

Should divorces be made easier to obtain?

Should a pregnant woman be able to choose to have an abortion?

In writing about controversial issues, facts as well as opinions are presented. However, the facts that are chosen can influence the reader. Good readers are the ones who are alert to the author's purpose. Why was the topic chosen? What facts and opinions are presented? What facts are left out or underemphasized? Why did the author take the particular approach that you see in the material? Is the author a person to be relied upon? Is the author an expert in the field? What does the author want you to do or believe?

Some things you read will be deliberate efforts to get you to do something specific. The writer may want you to buy a product, vote for a candidate, or contribute to a cause. In such cases it is usually quite easy to determine the author's purpose.

The process of reading critically involves three levels of understanding. First, you need to get the literal meaning. This means that you understand the words and sentences and are not missing any of what the author says. Second, you must be able to interpret what you read. This involves grasping the main ideas, recognizing the importance of the facts given, and drawing conclusions and interpretations from combinations of ideas. The third level of comprehension involves a recognition of the relationship between the author and the reader. Not only do you know what the author says and understand it; you also evaluate the ideas and compare them with your own. You consider the author and his or her motives. You may accept what the author says, or reject it, or suspend judgment about it. You may believe it, suspect it, doubt it, question it, or disbelieve it. The choice is yours. Simply because a statement is in print does not mean that it is true, complete, or reliable. As a good reader, you have to make that judgment for yourself.

In this part of the book our primary purpose is to work on reading rates, so we will not go into great detail on the topic of critical reading. However, it is important to be able to shift gears in reading, slowing or stopping sometimes to ponder some of the questions discussed here. Otherwise you can be in danger of rushing through reading material, accepting what the author is saying without question.

Let us continue now with some practice on material which illustrates the need for critical reading. In the previous unit you read a selection from a government booklet about social security, issued in 1955. The selection in this unit was written at about the same time by a national organization. As you read it, think about how different it is from the selection in Unit 10. It illustrates the fact that even widely used textbooks can contain serious errors of fact. In this particular case, the topic of social security has become the subject of public concern, partly because of the misinformation given to people about it when this passage was written over twenty years ago. Some of the information in it has changed.

Remember, your task in this exercise is to read as rapidly as possible while understanding what you read. Try to increase your rate beyond that on the earlier units.

Record your starting time and begin reading.

finishing time _____

starting time _____

reading time _____

What's Your IQ
on Social Security

Social Security—Its Purpose!

In 1935, Congress established a new program. Commonly called Social Security—it is technically known now as "Federal Old-Age, Survivors and Disability Insurance Benefits."

Social Security now pays four major types of monthly benefits to:

Retired workers;

Their dependents;

Family survivors of deceased breadwinners;

Workers at 50 who are totally and permanently disabled.

In each case, benefits are paid because of a presumed "loss" of wages or salary due to old age, disability or premature death. That is, the family breadwinner is no longer able to work—or has died.

Benefits are intended to be sufficient so that most recipients will not have to ask for relief. That is, they are a "floor of protection."

Benefits are paid in cash. Finally, benefits are paid according to provisions and conditions in the law, and without a "means test"—or "pauper's oath"—as is the case in relief programs.

What's in a Number . . . Your Social Security Number?

When you started working, you probably filed an application for a Social Security number. Soon you received a card which said "Social Security Account Number 000-00-0000 has been established for John A. Doe."

What is this "account"? It means that the Social Security Administration has an account with your name and number in which is recorded what you earned (up to a maximum specified in the law) in any job covered by Social Security. IT DOES *NOT* SHOW THE *SOCIAL TAXES* YOU

HAVE PAID—AND THAT YOUR EMPLOYER HAS PAID. In fact, the government doesn't keep a record over the years on that.

This earnings record shows your Social Security coverage—and this is *one* condition of eligibility for Social Security old-age benefits.

What *other* conditions are there?

Another condition is age 65 for a man, and 62 for a woman. Congress says that at these ages, a man or woman may not be able to keep on working—because of age—and may file a claim for benefits.

And *another* condition of eligibility for old-age benefits—! When Congress established the age requirement, it added a companion condition of eligibility known as the "work test" or "retirement test." This was because benefits were intended only when a person presumably could no longer support himself by working. Thus, today, if a person (under 72) earns more than $1200 a year in a job, he is presumably able to support himself by working and is not eligible for all of his monthly Social Security benefits. And for most people, their Social Security account will show if they're still able at 62 or 65 to support themselves by working—or not.

Finally, the earnings recorded in your "account" are used to determine the amount of benefits for you, your dependents, or your survivors.

About Social Security

What They're Teaching Johnny...
...Isn't So!

The Scene—

A high school, a civics class, almost anywhere in the United States. The teacher calls on Johnny to discuss Social Security, and he recites:

The Social Security program is a vast government insurance program. Almost all Americans who work are under its protection. A person entering the system is given a card, which bears a number. This number is not just a tag to identify him; it is the number of a special account (like that of a savings account in a bank).

Each payday part of the earner's wages is taken from him and placed to his credit in the Federal Treasury. And another sum is taken from his employer and placed in the Treasury. When the employee becomes 65, he can retire from work and receive income from the savings taken from him and his employer during his working years. In this way the law requires an individual to save so that he has an income when he is no longer employed. In case the worker dies before he reaches the age of 65, all the money he paid in, plus interest, is given back. The benefits belong to the worker as a matter of right. They are bought and paid for. They are not a handout.

And so on and on.

That is what Johnny would answer, if he studied Social Security from more than a dozen high school civics textbooks that give as much as a chapter to the subject (samples of which are shown on the following pages). Using these books (from which everything in Johnny's answer was quoted), the teacher would give him a big shining "A" for his recitation.

Yet, every single statement in Johnny's answer is wrong!

The program is not insurance. The Social Security number does not identify anything like a bank account. There is no tax money credited to any earner. The benefits are not automatically payable *at* age 65; there are *other* conditions to be met. And what is paid in is not given back if the worker dies, though his family may—and may not—draw benefits.

It is bad enough that millions of high school youngsters are being given such erroneous information about the biggest welfare program of this government. The real damage grows out of the fact that Johnny and his schoolmates are getting the wrong *concepts*. These authors simply do not grasp the *idea* of Social Security, its nature, its purpose or the way it works.

Social Security is not run on insurance principles at all. All insurance companies are careful to collect premiums from their policy holders, that will cover what they must pay out. But no one—not even the Government's actuaries—knows whether Social Security *under the present law* will go broke in the next 40 years, or pile up hundreds of millions of dollars in surplus funds. There may not be enough money to provide the benefits that are promised. Or, there may be a huge, contingency fund such as staggers the imagination. *Nobody* knows which.

From the beginning Congress has declared the aim of the system is to give working people—on certain conditions—a floor of economic protection—basic protection for their families, in some cases, if they die; and a basic income in old age. But this is not done on the basis of each one paying for what he gets, and getting what he pays for. Nor is it done on the basis of need. There are records kept in the names of the holders of more than 110 million Social Security numbers, but these records do not show what taxes these people paid, or what was paid by their employers. All the record shows is the total covered earnings, and the names of the employers.

From the day they start to work, Social Security will be a big factor in the lives of these children now in high school. Under existing law, it will take amounts up to $8^{1}/_{2}$ per cent of their covered earnings in social taxes and it will promise them much, but not everything!

To make the best of the system, people need to know the facts about it, and to understand what they know. For this understanding they depend on our schools, and the textbooks from which they learn.

As Robert J. Myers, the Social Security chief actuary, has wryly said, "The situation would seem to indicate that those preparing textbooks should do more adequate research."

It would indeed!

Typical Textbook Errors

Do your children study these books?

> In case the worker dies before he reaches the age of 65, all the money he has paid in plus interest is paid to him.

The fact is: There is no such refund.

> The employed person and his employer must pay equal sums into the person's Social Security account.

> Every three months your employer banks this money for you with the Government. . . . *The money belongs to you.*

> On each payday, a part of the earner's wage is taken from him and placed to his account in the Federal treasury.

> Every payday . . . the Administration makes a record of the amount received, credits it to Joe's account, and then deposits the money in the United States Treasury.

The fact is: Social Security does not credit any tax money to the account of any individual.

> This latter group [Social Security beneficiaries] is not taking funds from the public coffers as charity gifts . . . They are paying their own way.

> . . . the benefits belong to you as of right. . . . The benefits are yours— bought and paid for. They are not a handout.

The fact is: No person now drawing benefits has paid in social taxes anything near the value of what he probably will receive. Few who become eligible in this century will have "paid in full" for the value of the benefits promised them. And the so-called "right" can be wiped out by the Congress at any time.

> The amount of the pension depends upon how much has been credited to the worker's account during the years of his employment.

> The size of the annuity will vary with the number of years of employment.

The fact is: The Social Security benefit will not be fixed by the worker's total "credits" nor by how long he worked, but by his "average" covered monthly wage.

These [old-age] payments go to an insured worker at the age of 65 or over . . .

Each qualified individual shall be entitled to a monthly payment from the time he attains the age of 65 until the date of his death.

The fact is: The payments begin at age 65 if the worker complies with the conditions now in force, or new ones that may be adopted in years to come. Whether the payments will go on for the rest of his life depends on whether the conditions are changed, as they were in 1950 when many thousands of persons lost their "rights" to benefits, not because of anything different they did but because Congress changed the rules. Whether he gets old-age benefits the rest of his life will also depend on how much he earns after retirement age—on whether or not he is presumed to be self-supporting in a job.

Record your finishing time. Then answer the comprehension questions.

Comprehension Exercise for Unit 11

1 Social security was intended to be sufficient for most recipients
   a To live comfortably in old age
   b To have a "floor of protection" to avoid the need for relief
   c To retire early
   d To remove the need for other retirement benefits.

2 According to this article, social security is technically known as
   a Federal Social Security and Disability Insurance Benefits
   b United States Social Security Insurance Benefits
   c Federal Old Age Survivors and Disability Insurance Benefits
   d Federal Retirement and Disability Insurance Benefits

3 The author of this article feels that social security
   a Has been misrepresented
   b Is harmful to the economy
   c Should be scrapped
   d Is too generous to retired persons

4 The Social Security Administration keeps a record of
   a All the social security taxes you have paid
   b All the social security taxes your employer has paid

c   What you earned up to the maximum specified in the law
d   All the money you and your employer have paid

5   When this article was written in 1956, the law stated that if you were under 72 and earned more than $1200 a year in a job you would
a   Get your full social security benefits
b   Get no social security benefits
c   Have to pay more into social security
d   Not be eligible for full social security benefits

6   According to this article social security benefits go mainly to
a   People who are working full-time
b   Persons over 65 who have retired
c   Small children
d   Veterans

7   The social security program is
a   Like an insurance company, where they collect enough premiums from their policy holders to cover what they must pay out
b   Unlike an insurance program, in that the government actuaries do not know whether under the present law there is enough money coming in to pay out all the future benefits
c   Funded by putting the money into individual trust accounts
d   Designed so that each person's contributions pay for his or her benefits

8   The purpose of this booklet was
a   To stop the social security program
b   To encourage more people to work under the social security program
c   To make people aware of the incorrect ideas about social security
d   To make sure no changes were made in the social security program

9   This booklet states that few people receiving social security benefits in this century will have
a   Paid into social security as much as they will receive
b   Paid more into social security than they will receive
c   Paid for all the benefits they will receive
d   Paid for twice as many benefits as they will receive

10   Workers cannot be sure of their benefits under social security because
a   Congress could change the rules
b   The income of people who continue to work beyond age 65 may be too high for them to receive full benefits
c   The system could run out of money
d   All of the above

Check your answers using the key on page 314.
Refer to the chart on the next page to get your reading rate. Then plot your rate and comprehension on the progress chart on page 320.

Time-Rate Table on Unit 11

"WHAT'S YOUR I.Q. ON SOCIAL SECURITY" (1687 words)

Time in seconds converted to rate in words per minute

Time	Rate	Time	Rate	Time	Rate
2:00	844	8:00	211	14:00	121
:10	779	:10	207	:10	119
:20	723	:20	202	:20	118
:30	675	:30	198	:30	116
:40	633	:40	195	:40	115
:50	595	:50	191	:50	114
3:00	562	9:00	187	15:00	112
:10	533	:10	184	:10	111
:20	506	:20	181	:20	110
:30	482	:30	178	:30	109
:40	460	:40	175	:40	108
:50	440	:50	172	:50	107
4:00	422	10:00	169	16:00	105
:10	405	:10	166	:10	104
:20	389	:20	163	:20	103
:30	375	:30	161	:30	102
:40	362	:40	158	:40	101
:50	349	:50	156	:50	100
5:00	337	11:00	153	17:00	99
:10	327	:10	151	:10	98
:20	316	:20	149	:20	97
:30	307	:30	147	:30	96
:40	298	:40	145		
:50	289	:50	143		
6:00	281	12:00	141		
:10	274	:10	139		
:20	266	:20	137		
:30	260	:30	135		
:40	253	:40	133		
:50	247	:50	131		
7:00	241	13:00	130		
:10	235	:10	128		
:20	230	:20	127		
:30	225	:30	125		
:40	220	:40	123		
:50	215	:50	122		

SKIMMING AND SCANNING

Introduction

Skimming and scanning are two forms of selective reading. In normal reading, all the words are seen and read; in selective reading, only some of the material is read. Your eyes skip around and skim over some of the words.

In Unit 7 we talked about what your eyes are doing in reading. We noted that you only have clear vision of a small part of the page on each eye fixation. If you move smoothly along the lines, making eye fixations every word or two, you will see all of the words clearly and will be doing normal reading. If you move your eyes along the line or over the page too rapidly to be able to see all the words, you will be skimming or scanning. You will not be able to get complete comprehension of the material by skimming or scanning. However, you will be able to get a great deal of information if you do an efficient job of selective reading.

There are times when selective reading is the only efficient thing to do. To take an obvious example, you would not read a telephone book from the beginning to end to find someone's telephone number. The process you use, in which you skip large sections and read only an occasional word, is called scanning.

Scanning

"Scanning" is the term used to describe a selective reading process in which you are searching for certain facts or information. There are several levels of scanning, depending on what information you are seeking and why you are looking for it.

1 *Scanning to find a single word.* At this level your purpose is to locate a single word (or number) such as a name, date, phone number, price, place, or other single item that can be easily identified.

2 *Scanning for a particular fact.* This level of scanning requires slightly more attention and a somewhat higher level of comprehension. You are looking for a fact that is probably expressed in a phrase or sentence.

3 *Scanning for a section to be read.* This level of scanning makes more use of the general organization of a book or other source. Once the section or sections you are seeking are identified by a scanning process, they will probably be read quite carefully. An example of this level of scanning is the situation in which you have a test coming up and know that you need to study a certain topic. You scan to find the topic, then read carefully.

4 *Seeking all the information on a topic.* This level of scanning is often used by students who have a paper or report to write. If you have to write about a certain topic, you might go to the library and scan the card catalog for books on the subject. Then you would scan the books to find the information.

Skimming

Skimming is the other major type of selective reading. It differs from normal reading in that not all of the material is read. Chunks of material of various sizes are skipped over. It differs from scanning in that it is an effort to get general information rather than specific facts.

Skimming is a way of covering material quickly, with comprehension that may be complete enough for many purposes. You may not have the time, the interest, or the need to read many items carefully. On the other hand, it may be very useful to skim over something quickly to get the main idea, to build up your general background on the topic, or to satisfy your curiosity about the topic without spending a lot of time on it.

Skimming is particularly useful to students who have a great deal of supplementary reading in addition to required textbook reading. It is usually much better to skim a variety of materials on a topic than it is to cover one or two readings in depth. You tend to build up a better background on the topic that way.

Most readers already use skimming some of the time without any formal training or organized practice. It happens naturally when they read material that has only a small amount of relevant content. They begin to skip over the parts that are not interesting or useful. Some readers become quite good at skimming. Unfortunately, most readers need to have the kind of guided practice that is provided in this book.

When you begin to practice skimming you may find that it is not much faster than normal reading. However, with a little practice you should be able to cover material at two to four times the rate of normal reading, with comprehension that will be adequate for many purposes.

Our goal is to enable you to skim *when it is appropriate to the material and your purpose.* Skimming will never be a complete substitute for reading and should not ever be confused with reading.

Levels of Skimming

You may remember that we talked earlier about levels of comprehension in reading. There are also levels of skimming. Sometimes you are only interested in finding out what an article or book is about, so you are skimming simply to identify the topic. At other times you may want to know much more. The following will give you some idea of the various levels of skimming.

1 *Skimming to identify the topic.* This is the easiest and most rapid level. All you want to know is what the book or article is about. Sometimes you can find out by simply reading the title and perhaps taking a quick look at the material.

2 *Skimming to identify point of view.* You may know what the topic is but want to know where the author stands on some issue. In an editorial, for example, you probably do not need to read much to know whether the author is for or against an issue. Probably the first or last paragraph will tell you.

3 *Skimming to find out what kind of information is given.* You want to know what facts the author presents. You will probably have to glance over most of the material to get a good idea, but you should not have to read it all.

4 *Skimming to identify the author's style.* The author may present the material in a humorous or serious way. It may be in descriptive or narrative form. It may be a dialogue. Only a reading of selected parts of the material will tell you.

5 *Skimming to discover the organization.* At this level, you want to know how the author has organized the ideas being presented. They might be in a time sequence, a formal argument, a comparison or contrast, or in some other form. This level of skimming is extremely useful for material that must be studied and remembered. It will take a little more time than the other simpler levels but will pay off in better understanding and retention. Preview skimming to observe organization is an excellent way to start studying a chapter in a textbook, for example.

6 *Skimming to understand the content.* This level is the closest to normal reading. Perhaps you will actually read as much as half of the material. (The problem is to decide how much *not* to read!) On most reading material, a high level of comprehension can be obtained by skimming at this level. You are covering the material fairly carefully but skipping over those parts that are clearly unimportant or not useful to you.

For convenience, we can divide skimming purposes into three major categories: previewing, overviewing and reviewing. Each has its own special uses and techniques.

Preview Skimming

As the name implies, preview skimming involves dealing with the material before it is read. You are assuming that you will be reading the material later. The purpose is to find out what the material is about, what kind of facts are presented, how it is organized, and what approach will be most effective if it is to be studied later.

Preview skimming is like looking at a road map before starting to drive somewhere. It gives direction to your reading. You have a better idea of what is coming up and tend to see the article, chapter, or book as more of an organized whole.

Here is a good plan for getting acquainted with a book.

1 Spend *one minute* looking over the material that precedes Chapter 1. (Publishers call this the "front matter." It consists of the title page, copyright information, preface or other introduction, table of contents, and other locator information such as lists of tables or illustrations.)

2 Spend *one minute* studying the table of contents. This will give you a good idea of the organization of the book.

3 Spend *one minute* turning the pages, glancing at headlines, subheadings, charts, graphs, and illustrations. Notice whether chapters have summaries at the beginning or end.

4 Spend *one minute* starting to read one chapter or section. Probably the first part is the best. However, your examination of the book may have led you to some other part as a way to best get an idea of the author's style or method of presentation.

After you have done this four-minute survey of the book, stop and think about what you have learned. You will probably be quite surprised at how much you know, even after such a brief exposure to the book. The author has taught this technique many times in reading improvement classes. Students are always very impressed with how much they can find out in a hurry.

A few years ago a commercial speed-reading company went around the country putting on sales demonstrations. They had students "read" books that were supplied by the audience. The students would look over the book while the speaker explained that they were going to read forty or fifty pages in five minutes. The students would then give a summary of what they had read. Watching this procedure was interesting to the author, because students appeared to be using the same preview-skim techniques described above. They gave excellent summaries of the books they "read," and the audience was extremely impressed.

At the rates the students were covering the material it was clear that they were skimming, not reading, but the level of comprehension demonstrated was very impressive. It showed that preview skimming can be extremely effective as a way of gaining information rapidly.

Overview Skimming

In this form of skimming, you are trying to get as much information as you can in one exposure. You probably do not intend to read the material again. In overview skimming you do a bit more reading than in previewing. You are interested in doing more than discovering the organization and the style. You really want to get as much of the author's message as you can.

Pay special attention to the main ideas presented. If there are summaries of chapters or other units, read them carefully. Keep thinking about how you would summarize what the author is saying.

Overview skimming is the type to be used when you have a lot of material to read and don't have time to read it all. As we indicated earlier in this section, it is usually better to overview-skim a lot of supplementary material than to read one or two items very carefully. (On the other hand there are times when reading carefully is better. For example, if the teacher wants a written or a verbal report on one supplementary reading, you would want to read it carefully.)

Some research studies indicate that a very good reader will get more information from an efficient skimming than a poor reader will get from a careful reading. In addition, there is evidence that any reader will get more out of reading if the material has been skimmed beforehand.

Review Skimming

As the name implies, review skimming is done on material that has already been read. The purpose is usually to refresh your memory. Often the reason is to prepare for a test. Review skimming has been shown to improve retention of study material. The best times to review are (1) right after the material is learned and (2) just before a test. Since it takes very little time to review-skim, many good students use this technique to keep their memory fresh all through a course. A good time to do this review skimming is while you are waiting for things to get started at the beginning of a class period. It gets you in the mood for the topic and refreshes your memory of the background material.

In some cases, you may be able to review-skim material with the assistance of study aids you have developed earlier. If you have underlined important ideas, made marginal notes, or taken separate notes on the material, you will be better able to review efficiently, since you will not have to search for the most important content.

All of the above skimming methods—preview, overview, and review—are excellent ways to increase the effectiveness of your study time. They all have the advantage that they save study time and increase your learning.

Eye-Movement Patterns in Skimming and Scanning

In reading, the best eye-movement pattern is a smooth, regular one; left to right on each line with as few fixations and backward looks as possible. In skimming and scanning there really is no pattern that will always be best. However, there are some things we know that will help you develop an efficient attack on particular materials. It depends on your purpose and the nature of the material.

If your purpose is to overview, for example, you want to get as much of the content as possible in one exposure. Your eye-movement patterns are likely to be very similar to normal reading, except that you will skip some things. A good pattern to try on most material is one in which you start reading each paragraph and stop when you have the main idea. The eye-movement pattern might look something like the one shown on page 113.

The majority of eye fixations occur in the first few lines because in most writing that is where the main ideas will be found.

Another eye-movement pattern that has been observed is one in which the reader moves more or less randomly down a column of print. Eye fixations occur when something on the page seems to stick out and is noticed. Some experts have described this process as "floating" down a page. The idea is to be very relaxed about where you are looking while still maintaining a high level of attention on the material. We suggest that you try various techniques in an effort to discover the one that works best for you. The major concern is that you cover the material rapidly without reading all of it, getting the most information possible.

Eye movements in scanning are not greatly different from skimming. The main difference is that regular reading patterns along a line do not occur

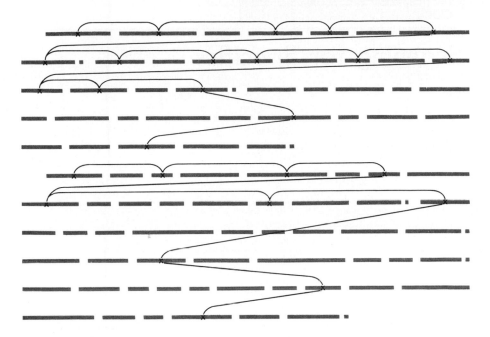

as often. In scanning, you are looking for a particular thing, and that will determine to some extent where your eye fixations occur. If you are looking for a number, for example, you are pretty sure to make eye fixations on any number that appears in a paragraph. On the other hand, if you are looking for a name, you might tend to overlook numbers and focus on any names that appear.

Locating specific information is usually aided by headings and subheadings, so you should pay particular attention to them while scanning.

Energy Levels in Skimming and Scanning

Before we begin a series of practice exercises in skimming and scanning, we want to point out that an efficient job of selective reading takes more than a casual, relaxed approach. You need to be unusually alert, with a high level of energy, to do a good job. Some people tend to think that because you are not doing a total reading of the material, that you can loaf along, noticing whatever comes to mind. Actually, the job of selecting the material to read and putting it together into a meaningful whole is more difficult and demanding than just reading.

As you do the exercises that follow in Part 2, keep in mind that you will have to work hard at it if you really want to improve your ability to get information rapidly.

Scanning for Specifics

This is the easiest and fastest type of scanning. You are looking for a single word, date, number, place, price, or other highly specific thing. A good example is a word in a dictionary or a telephone number in a directory.

You will be applying this technique to the pages which follow. Unlike the reading selections you have been doing, where the questions were at the end, you will begin with the questions. Remember that scanning is a search for specific information. You should always know what it is you are looking for before you begin to scan.

We will *not* be computing a reading rate on these exercises because it would be quite meaningless. On the other hand, you want to be sure that you are doing the job rapidly and efficiently. You will keep time, much as you did in the earlier exercises, and also check the accuracy of your answers using the key at the back of the book. We will give you some goals to work toward so you can tell whether you are making progress.

On this unit, record your starting time when you begin reading the questions. When you have found and recorded the answers mark down your finishing time. Try to complete the unit in less than five minutes (the average time for a good reader).

finishing time _____

starting time _____

scanning time _____

Scanning Exercise for Unit 13

1   What is the address of the house for sale that advertises a boat dock on a bayou?

_____

2   What is the highest price listed on the page of houses for sale?

_____

3   How many houses are listed as "open"?

_____

4   At what address would you find a waterfall?

_____

5   At what address would you find a sauna?

_____

6   What two kitchen appliances are listed at the house at 1020 Village Green?

_____

7   How many houses would you have to choose from if you needed three bedrooms?

_____

8   At what address is a down payment mentioned?

_____

9   Two houses list formal dining rooms. One is at 1939 Holmes Street. Where is the other one?

_____

10   You would like a house with an antique brick front. Which one has it?

_____

Record your finishing time, and check the answer key.

TWO ACRE RANCHETTE

3 Br., 2 bath, split level home, 20 minutes from downtown. $32,000 419-6672

OPEN HOUSE
SUNDAY, APRIL 15
2-4 P.M.
1939 HOLMES STREET

Beautiful brick 2 story Tudor home in Chelsea Heights. 3 bed $2\frac{1}{2}$ baths formal dining room, large lot $54,000 779-4311

FAMILY HOME

One-year-old 3 bedroom, 2 bath home on large lot. Beautiful kitchen, spacious living room, City water & sewer $37,900, 646-1008

OPEN HOUSE 1-5

1020 Village Green Dr. 3 Br., 2 B., family room, dishwasher, disposal, other extras. By owner. $37,500, terms, 331-4112.

COUNTRY CLUB SHORES

3 Br., 2 B., pool, boat dock. A buy at $71,500. Call 377-5216 for appointment. Owner.

OPEN HOUSE—SAT & SUN., 2-5.

3 Br., 2 B., elec. kit., wall to wall carpet, sauna. Landscaped. Maintenance free. $57,900, $6,000 down. 781 Tartan Drive, 383-1634.

TOWNHOUSE

3 Br., $2\frac{1}{2}$ bath condominium. Tennis, pool, and much more. Great family complex. Assume Mortgage of $20,500 636-3980.

COLONIAL TERRACE

New 3 bedroom, 2 bath home in prime residential area. Large family room, 2 car garage, many trees. Priced at $52,000 347-9880

OPEN 11-5
721 CANTERBURY DRIVE

New two bedroom, two bath home with family room, double car garage, central heat & air, wall to wall carpeting, antique brick front on 100×150' lot. 721-7666.

ST. JOSEPH'S PARISH

4 bedroom, 2 bath, wall to wall carpeting, nice yard, walking distance to stores. Owner, 331-7999.

OPEN HOUSE 2-5
744 BILTMORE DRIVE

3 bedrooms, 2 bath home. Large rooms including paneled family room, large living room, formal dining room, two car garage. Good financing. 417-1121.

SAILBOAT WATERS

2791 Bayside Shores, 3 Br., beautifully decorated, new shag carpet, lush tropical landscaping, complete with waterfall and Garden pools. $72,500 221-7863.

OPEN 2-5
1410 RIVER DRIVE

Unusual contemporary home near Oyster Bay. 2 bedrooms, 2 baths with spacious lanai, caged pool, boat dock on bayou open to bay. $62,500, terms, 646-1798.

GOLF, SWIM & TENNIS. A

beautiful home well maintained, 2 Br., 2 bath, family room, 2 car garage. $61,600. 467-2232.

Scanning for Specifics II

This exercise is the same type as Unit 13, except for the type of material being scanned. In this exercise, you are looking for specific information in an index from a book for nursing aides.

Follow the same procedure as you did on the last unit. Record your starting time before you begin to read the questions. When you have located and recorded the answers, mark down your finishing time. Then check the answer key at the back of the book.

Try to complete this unit in less than four minutes.

finishing time _____

starting time _____

scanning time _____

Scanning Exercise for Unit 14

1   On what page would you find a discussion of adjustment to the environment?

2   How many different subheadings are listed under "Elderly"?

_____

3   Where would you find out how to meet emergencies?

_____

4   Where would you read about how to care for dying patients?

_____

5   On what page are drainage tubes discussed?

_____

6   Where would you turn to find out about epithelial tissue?

_____

7   Where would you look to find out how to take care of the personal needs of the elderly?

_____

8   Where would you look to find out about postoperative care of dressings?

_____

9   You heard the doctor use the term "epidermis." Where could you find out what it means?

_____

10 You want to know about using an endotracheal tube. Where would you look?

_____

Record your finishing time, and check the answer key.

Scanning for a Single Fact

This level of scanning is very similar to the ones you have just finished. The difference is that in this unit you are seeking a fact that may be expressed in a short phrase or sentence.

Follow the same procedure as you did on the last unit. Record your starting time before you begin to read the questions. When you have located and recorded the answers mark down your finishing time. Then check the answer key at the back of the book.

Try to complete this unit in less than five minutes.

finishing time _____

starting time _____

scanning time _____

Scanning Exercise for Unit 15

1   How many miles a year does the average American drive?

2   How do you avoid using your auto air conditioner, according to the article?

3   How do you save gas when you approach a hill?

4   When your engine is cold, how much should you pump the accelerator?

5   What does the article suggest about meal stops?

6   What kind of "foot work" saves gas?

7   How much of the typical American's driving is for social and recreational purposes?

8   How many gallons a day does the average American use?

9   What does the article suggest about long engine warm-ups?

10 What kind of route should you choose to save gas?

_____

Record your finishing time, and check the answer key.

Stretching Your Gas

The typical American drives more than 11,000 miles a year and uses a little more than two gallons of gasoline a day—that's on an average. Of that, about 33 percent is used for social and recreational driving, including vacation trips and pleasure rides.

Whether it's a weekend trip or a long vacation, drivers can really cut gasoline consumption if they're careful. The following tips can help you stretch that gallon of gasoline on your next vacation trip.

Choose a vacation where you won't need to use your car.

Plan motoring vacations with friends and share costs.

Pack carefully. Unnecessary weight in your trunk will cut fuel economy; packing baggage on a roof rack creates fuel-robbing air resistance.

Plan driving routes which allow you to travel at a steady speed.

Avoid driving during rush hours and other peak traffic times.

Start early in the day so you'll minimize the need to use your air conditioner.

Plan your meal stops to coincide with peak traffic periods.

Travel at moderate speeds.

Use smooth "foot work" for good gasoline mileage.

Avoid extended warmups.

When the engine is cold, depress the accelerator once to set the automatic choke—added pumping only wastes gas.

When you approach a hill, build up speed early. With manual transmissions, shift as soon as possible before the engine begins to "lug."

The most fuel-efficient time to use air conditioning is during open road driving. The least efficient time is in stop-and-go traffic.

Be sure spark plugs are clean and firing properly.

Check points.

Replace clogged or dirty air filters.

Make sure automatic choke functions properly.

Adjust carburetor air-fuel mixture.

Make an oil change a part of every tuneup and use the weight oil recommended in the owner's manual.

Make sure tire pressure is correct and wheels are properly balanced and aligned.

When you fill up with fuel, use the correct octane for your car.

Taken alone, each measure only effects a nominal saving; together they can have a significant impact on dollars saved at the pumps and better gas mileage.

UNIT 16

Scanning for Material to Be Read Carefully

At this level, scanning is a search for material that is of some special interest. It may be for some study purpose, or it may be that you need to find some information for your own practical use. A good example of this level of scanning is a search for a recipe in a cookbook. If you are trying to decide what to cook, you look through the cookbook, guided by the headings and subheadings and perhaps the index. You are looking for recipes for cooking the food you have on hand or want to buy. Once you find the recipe you want, you will read it very carefully, following the directions in it.

Another example of scanning for material to be read carefully is a study situation when you know you will be tested on a certain topic. You want to be sure you are familiar with the particular topic.

Our practice exercise for this unit is one that might be applicable in a psychology course. Imagine that the teacher has talked some about a test that is coming up soon and has said something that leads you to believe that there will be important questions on the effects of anxiety on the human body.

On the next few pages you will find a section of a book in which the author covers the topic of anxiety.

Your task is to search through the material to find the parts that deal with anxiety and its effects on the human body. Then read those parts carefully and answer the questions which follow.

We will not time the reading and scanning part separately, but you should keep a record of how long the whole process takes. Try to do the scanning and question answering in less than twelve minutes.

Before you begin, record your starting time. Then when you have answered the questions, record your finishing time, and check the answer key at the back of the book.

finishing time _____

starting time _____

scanning time _____

Anxiety

We define *anxiety* as an emotion characterized by feelings of anticipated danger, tension, and distress and by sympathetic nervous system arousal. You may recall that R. M. characterized the affect as a negative, "tight" one. Anxiety and fear are sometimes distinguished from one another on two dimensions. (1) The object of a fear is easy to specify, while the object of an anxiety is often unclear. (2) The intensity of a fear is proportional to the magnitude of the danger. The intensity of an anxiety is likely to be greater than the objective danger (if it is known). In real life, anxiety and fear are not easy to differentiate, so we will use the two terms interchangeably, as many psychologists do. In this section we examine several questions. What triggers anxiety? What shapes its intensity? How does anxiety influence learning? How does it contribute to health?

Triggers of Anxiety
A number of triggers of anxiety have been described. Freud listed two: (1) real-world dangers and (2) anticipation of punishment for expressing sexual, aggressive, or other forbidden impulses or engaging in immoral behavior. In the first case, anxiety is caused by actual situations which lead to physical pain; in the second case, by cognitions. Behavioral scientists tend to emphasize one or the other source. Cognitive psychologists stress conflicts between expectations, beliefs, attitudes, perceptions, information, conceptions, and the like, which lead to *cognitive dissonance* (described in Chapter 10). Humanistic psychologists focus on mental conflicts too, especially on those that arise while choosing a fulfilling and meaningful life-style. Behavioristic psychologists believe that most anxieties are established by *conditioning,* as an "object" of some type is accidentally associated with an anxiety-arousing experience, often one that may be dangerous. (Chapter 5 treats the conditioning of fear in more detail.) Both cognitive conflicts and

potentially perilous situations, then, appear to be able to excite anxiety. Recent research suggests that the two types of anxiety have their own distinct physiological patterns [29].

Influences on the Intensity of Anxiety

Physical responses to the same threat may be mild or intense. Twin studies and investigations of infant differences, mentioned earlier, suggest that genes influence human reactions to stress. Experiences mold an individual's anxiety level, as well. In rats, too few or too many fear-arousing experiences in infancy are associated with a higher-than-average level of anxiety later in life [30]. Too many stresses during infancy and throughout the life cycle are definitely harmful to human beings. After continuous exposure to danger during combat in World War II, for instance, soldiers reached a point of no return. Responses to stress became exaggerated. When the soldiers returned to civilian life, they reacted to minor pressures (such as loud noises, bright lights, or exercise) as though they were confronting a major emergency. Their bodies recovered slowly. The mechanisms that ordinarily restore equilibrium conditions seemed to have broken down [31].

Although people show characteristic levels of anxiety, responses to any specific event depend to some extent on thoughts and perceptions. There is evidence that both laboratory animals and people experience less tension when they feel in control—when stresses are predictable and coping is possible. Rats, for example, that are shocked immediately after a tone are less likely to develop ulcers, a severe reaction to anxiety, than those that are shocked randomly without warning (but with the same number of shocks). Similarly, rats that can make a response that will terminate a shock develop fewer stomach lesions than animals that are exposed to identical shocks without being able to control them in any way [32].

A sense of control helps people handle stress, too. In one investigation, psychologists David Glass and Jerome Singer and their coworkers studied the effects of noise on forty-eight undergraduate women. Some research participants listened to a tape recording of superimposed sounds: voices of a Spaniard and an Armenian, a typewriter, a desk calculator, and a mimeograph machine. Subjects in one group heard the discordant noise at high volume; those in another group, at low volume. For some individuals in each group, the clatter appeared at regular (predictable) intervals; for others, at random (unpredictable) intervals. After listening to the tape, the research participants were asked to work paper-and-pencil tasks (some of which were insoluble). Another group of women, who had been spared the noisy experience altogether, tackled the same problems. Students who had been exposed to any noise at all were less persistent on the insoluble tasks than the others. Randomly spaced noise, even at low volume, decreased persistence more than regularly spaced noise. Similar results were obtained on male college students and on city-dwelling residents of both sexes. Later laboratory experiments have shown that when people feel that they can control the presence of noise, its aversive effects are reduced [33]. Unpredictable noise which cannot be regulated may lead to a sense of helplessness that increases anxiety and decreases ability to tolerate frustration and think clearly. In real life, unpredictable, uncontrollable noise adversely affects academic achievement and possibly mental health [34].

Research by James Geer and his colleagues and many other psychologists suggests that it is the *perception of control,* not the actual control, that is of critical importance [35]. He and his coworkers gave student subjects ten painful six-second electric shocks. After each one, the research participants had to press a switch immediately "to provide an index of their reaction time." To assess anxiety, Geer measured the students' sweat-gland activity. After the first series of shocks, half the subjects were told that they could cut the duration of the next ten shocks in half if they reacted quickly enough. These people perceived themselves in control. The remaining research participants were informed merely that the next ten shocks would be shorter. Though all students received the same three-second shocks, those who believed that they were in control showed significantly less sweat-gland activity (and presumably less anxiety) than the others.

Helping people feel that they have control over frightening circumstances is likely to reduce the anxiety level in a great many settings. When patients are prepared for surgery beforehand, for example, they adjust more easily to the tensions of the postoperative period than unprepared patients do. They complain less, require less sedation, and seem to recover more quickly [36].

Anxiety's Effects on Learning

Anxious students sometimes report blocking or choking up on tests and being unable to retrieve information that they know. Anxiety can affect learning at different stages. In terms of our memory model (Chapter 8), anxiety may influence encoding, storage, and/or retrieval. Effects on the various memory processes are not easily separated from one another. In the past, psychologists simply administered different types of learning tasks in the laboratory to people who identified themselves (on tests) as feeling either much or very little anxiety in academic situations. The overall performances of the two groups were subsequently compared. The relationship between anxiety and overall performance under these circumstances appears to be complicated. In general, anxiety seems to facilitate success on simple tasks and to hinder complex achievements [37]. People with high anxiety levels are especially likely to perform poorly on difficult or ambiguous test items (which are apt to be misread or misinterpreted). They do particularly badly in pressured, stressful situations such as important exams [38]. When materials are loosely organized and when rote learning, or memorizing, is required, highly anxious individuals tend to perform worse than less anxious ones, as well [39]. Recent studies suggest that highly anxious people may experience encoding problems that interfere with putting information into memory in the first place. Psychologist John Mueller has found that research participants with high anxiety appear to encode fewer dimensions of the material to be learned than less anxious ones. They use less complicated organizing strategies as they process information. When adaptability is required, they tend to be less flexible than less anxious people in switching from tactic to tactic [40].

In view of these findings, we would expect highly anxious people to perform rather poorly in school. To investigate this issue, psychologist Charles Spielberger examined the grades and scholastic aptitude test scores of male college students. Anxiety level appeared to have relatively little influence on the academic performance of students with either very high or very low aptitudes. Regardless of reported anxiety level, men who scored low on aptitude tests made relatively poor grades generally. High scorers tended to make relatively good marks. Excessive anxiety did appear to adversely affect the great majority of students, those who scored in the middle range on the aptitude test. Among these middle-aptitude people, high anxiety was associated with low academic performance [41].

A number of techniques can help anxious students cope with their tension. Charles Spielberger and his associates counseled highly anxious university students in groups to increase their sense of control in the classroom. The psychologists focused on practical topics, including studying and preparing for exams, figuring out what the instructor wanted, handling individual academic difficulties, managing dormitory life, and selecting a vocation. This program raised the anxious students' grade points by one-half point on the average [42]. Systematic desensitization, a relaxation technique described in Chapter 16, is frequently successful in helping students lower their anxiety. Jogging and thinking about calm, happy, comfortable experiences appear to be effective tension reducers for anxious students, too [43].

Anxiety's Effects on Health
Early in his career, the endocrinologist Hans Selye (b. 1907) . . . discovered that animals responded similarly to many different types of stresses, including intense cold, conflict, injury, bacterial agents, and surgery. The victim, Selye came to believe, experienced a *general adaptation syndrome* (GAS) in three stages:

> *Stage 1: Alarm reaction.* During this stage, the sympathetic nervous system and the adrenal glands mobilize the body's defensive forces. In

this way energy production is maximized to handle the emergency—to resist the stressor. If the tension is prolonged, the body enters a second stage.

Stage 2: Resistance. As an animal fights off a specific stressor, its body remains highly aroused. But a price is paid for this emergency preparedness. Systems responsible for growth, repair, and warding off infection do not operate well under these conditions. Consequently, the organism is in a weakened state and very susceptible to other stresses, including disease. If the old stressor continues or new ones arise, the animal enters a third stage.

Stage 3: Exhaustion. The body cannot maintain its resistance indefinitely and gradually shows the signs of exhaustion. After the sympathetic nervous system has depleted its energy supply, the parasympathetic system takes charge. Body activities slow down and may stop altogether. If the stressor continues, the worn-out victim will have great difficulty coping. At this time, continued tension leads to psychological problems, including depression and psychotic behavior, and/or to physical illness or even death [44].

Before looking at some of the health-related implications of Selye's general adaptation syndrome, it is important to know that the model has been amended by subsequent research. The GAS is more apt to occur after a stress of long duration, and not after brief, abrupt strains [45]. Not all prolonged pressures produce the syndrome. Exercise, fasting, and heat, for instance, do not [46]. It is currently unclear whether intense joys activate the response [47]. Moreover, as indicated earlier, physiological reactions during emotion depend on the situation and the organism involved. Diverse stresses produce different reactions. A given stressor—say, electric shock—does not influence all bodily systems that participate in the stress response in the same way. Some systems may be severely taxed, while others are hardly affected or even benefited [48]. Experience and genetics influence the precise responses. In sum, animals undergoing crises probably react somewhat similarly with the core responses Selye described. But a great many individual differences are observed.

The general adaptation syndrome is a mixed blessing. On the one hand, it offers people and other animals the necessary energy for fighting or fleeing. If action is required, organisms are apt to perform and feel better as the adrenalin level rises [49]. But modern strains, such as crowded highways, tight budgets, social conflicts, and competition, more frequently demand clear thinking over a long period rather than quick action. For this reason, some scientists believe that our autonomic and hormonal stress-related responses have outlived their usefulness. They are, in fact, often harmful. The sugar summoned from the liver to provide energy, for example, is converted to fat if it isn't used, creating conditions that lead to artery disease. Excessive adrenalin and noradrenalin damage organs and contribute to headaches, sinus attacks, high blood pressure, ulcers, allergic reactions, and many other illnesses. These disorders are often labeled *psychosomatic*. (They are the result of an animal's bodily, or *somatic,* responses to tension, a psychological condition.) Many diseases that were once thought to be caused entirely by physical mechanisms are now believed to be influenced by stress [50]. We examine evidence for this hypothesis.

Disease and Stress

In the late 1960s, Thomas Holmes, Richard Rahe, Minoru Masuda, and others began a massive research program to explore the connections between personal experiences and health. Initially, these behavioral scientists developed a questionnaire to measure the stressfulness of forty-three common *life changes*. Nearly 400 people were asked to indicate how much readjustment was required by these experiences. Each event had to be compared with marriage (arbitrarily assigned the value 500) and rated accordingly. The ratings of diverse groups were very similar.... This research has enabled psychologists to explore the question: Is the number of life change units in a specific time period, say one year, associated with later health problems? In one of many studies of this topic, Richard Rahe and his coworkers had 2,500 naval officers and enlisted men fill out a questionnaire reporting significant experiences throughout the preceding six months. As the navy men went about their sea duties, the investigators gathered health information. During the first month of the cruise, the men who had been recently subjected to a great many readjustments came down with 90 percent more first illnesses than those who had made few such adjustments. For each subsequent month of the voyage, men who had experienced many previous stresses reported more new illnesses than the others [51]. Similar studies find small but significant associations between life changes and heart attacks, cancer, leukemia, asthma, tuberculosis, pregnancy complications, hernias, warts, colds, skin disorders, menstrual difficulties, depression, suicide attempts, anxiety, and schizophrenia [52].

Daily stresses and strains may be just as injurious to health as major life changes are, or even more so. All over the world, poor people exhibit greater health-related problems than more fortunate people[53]. The tension associated with poverty may be an important contributor to ill health. Recent research on black Americans living in urban and rural areas supports this idea. People who had been exposed to a great many daily strains experienced a significantly greater incidence of high blood pressure and related disorders (such as strokes and hypertensive heart conditions) than those leading more stable lives [54]. Though this body of correlational research is far from being airtight proof that stresses of varied types cause illnesses, it has called attention to the consistent relationship between the two phenomena. We look more closely now at peptic ulcers, heart attacks, and sudden deaths and the evidence suggesting that stress contributes to each condition.

Peptic Ulcers

Peptic ulcers will probably afflict one in every ten Americans now living at some time during the life cycle. A peptic ulcer is essentially a sore in the lining of the stomach or duodenum (the first section of the small bowel). During digestion, hydrochloric acid and enzymes produced by the body break food down into usable components. In the case of the peptic ulcer victim, excessive amounts of hydrochloric acid erode the mucous layer that protects the inner wall of the stomach or duodenum. Then the acid begins to digest the wall itself.

Stress appears to play a major role in the production of excessive secretions of hydrochloric acid. Numerous experimental studies link the ulcers of animals to severe stresses [55]. When people undergo intense, prolonged strains, during migrations, floods, earthquakes, and wars, for example, a relatively high number develop peptic ulcers or other gastrointestinal disorders [56]. Air traffic controllers, burdened every day by life-and-death decision making, have an unusually high rate of ulcers and other stress-related problems [57].

Observations on Tom (the man with the partially exposed stomach described earlier) suggest that there is a direct connection between tension and ulcers. When Tom became angry, increased acid secretions took place just as though his stomach were full of food that needed to be digested. During two weeks of intense agitation, he secreted excessive quantities of gastric juices and developed bleeding sores in his stomach.

Stresses do not produce ulcers in all laboratory animals or all people. Apparently, ulcer victims are predisposed to respond to tension by increasing gastric secretions. This tendency is associated with a *high pepsinogen level,* a characteristic which appears to be influenced by heredity. (Pepsinogen is a substance secreted by the gastric glands in the stomach and later converted into pepsin, a major ingredient in the gastric juices. Pepsinogen level may be thought of, then, as an index of gastric activity.) Research shows that a high pepsinogen level often precedes the formation of ulcers. In one study supporting this notion, psychologist Herbert Weiner and his colleagues measured the level of pepsinogen in more than 2,000 newly inducted male military draftees. The investigators then selected the men with the highest and lowest pepsinogen levels for further observation. No soldier showed signs of ulcers at the time. When the subjects were reexamined during the eighth and sixteenth weeks of basic training, nine of them were developing ulcers. All nine came from the high-pepsinogen group. A similar association between high pepsinogen level and ulcer formation has been found in children and civilian adults [58]. Presumably, a genetic propensity to secrete gastric juices under stress and prolonged tension combine to produce ulcers. Other factors are undoubtedly involved. Since the mid-1950s, there has been an absolute decline in ulcer cases in the United States. Right now, no one knows the causes of this trend [59].

Heart Attacks

Heart disorders kill approximately 700,000 Americans every year [60]. The causes of coronary diseases are known to be multiple, but are not well understood. Many studies suggest that the stresses and strains of life are a contributing factor.

The pioneering research of cardiologists Meyer Friedman and Ray Rosenman has related heart attacks to a particular personality pattern, called *type A*. Type A people struggle continually to accomplish too many things in too little time or against too many obstacles. They appear aggressive (sometimes hostile), ambitious for achievement and power, competitive, and compulsive. They are habitually racing against the clock, and they rarely "waste time" by relaxing. Type A college students frequently ignore fatigue as they push themselves in the laboratory. Type A individuals talk loudly, quickly, and explosively. Even when no time constraints exist, they like to act with speed. People with this personality pattern show exaggerated sympathetic nervous system responses to laboratory stresses. Resting measures of the autonomic activity of the type A person are not distinctive[61].

A number of well-controlled, long-term studies suggest that individuals with type A personalities (especially men) are more likely than others to develop cardiac conditions. In a typical investigation, scientists classify the personalities of large numbers of middle-aged males who have no history of coronary problems. The research participants are checked periodically thereafter for signs of cardiac disease. Type A people are more apt to develop heart conditions than others. In one study, for example, 70 percent of the coronary cases had initially been categorized type A [62]. Smoking and other known risk factors cannot account for the findings.

While researchers do not know which aspects of the type A personality pattern are associated with heart trouble or precisely how [63], they speculate along these lines: Type A individuals maximize their daily pressures. The resulting anxiety leads to biochemical changes that precipitate the coronary problems. Genetics might predispose people both to heart attacks and type A personalities. This hypothesis is currently being investigated.

Sudden Deaths

Every year approximately 400,000 *sudden deaths* are reported throughout the United States [64]. Walter Cannon was one of the first scientists to show an interest in the abrupt deaths which occur without clear medical cause. He examined reports of *voodoo deaths* from all over the world and then visited Africa to investigate firsthand. By asking questions such as "Did the death occur rapidly?" and "Were poisons available?" Cannon tried to rule out alternative causes of death. He concluded that voodoo deaths were legitimate and followed a predictable pattern. The victim, usually a male, was cursed and a "spell" was cast. People surrounding the "target" withdrew their support. Consequently, the individual was alone, isolated, and in many cases, treated as already deceased. The individual expected imminent death and experienced intense anxiety. Death often occurred within twenty-four hours of being "targeted" [65].

In modern civilizations, sudden deaths take place under a wide range of circumstances. Occasionally, chronically ill people in hospitals are thought to "lose the will to live" and to die of no specifiable cause [66]. Individuals in prisoner-of-war camps sometimes "turn their faces to the wall" and give up on life [67]. A substantial number of unexpected deaths follow the loss of a close human relationship, the confrontation of danger, reduced status, lost property, failure, and even triumph [68]. Lesser animals die abruptly under varied conditions too—after fights without injuries or when transferred to unfamiliar locations, immobilized, stimulated excessively, or deprived by death of a mate or master [69].

How can animals, including people, die of psychological causes? Many sudden deaths are thought to result from deadly cardiac irregularities which are more easily triggered after the prolonged sympathetic nervous system arousal that accompanies stresses. Investigations by Bernard Lown and his coworkers support this hypothesis. In one experiment, the scientists allowed some of their dog subjects to rest in their cages while they stressed others. Then, they paced the dogs' hearts artificially in the *ventricular fibrillation pattern,* a lethal irregular rhythm, using progressively stronger currents. The anxious animals were more sensitive to the irregular pattern at lower current intensities [70]. The precise link between sympathetic nervous system activity and irregular heart rhythms is not well understood.

Scanning Exercise for Unit 16

1   Who studied the effects of *perception of control* on sweat-gland activity?
   a   James Geer
   b   Sigmund Freud
   c   David Glass
   d   Charles Spielberger

2   Who studied the General Adaptation Syndrome (GAS)?
   a   Walter Cannon
   b   H. Wiener

    c   Hans Selye
    d   Sigmund Freud

3 When humans are subjected to stress, one result is:
    a   Muscle weakness in the arms
    b   Secretion of acid in the stomach
    c   Sharp pains in the head
    d   Increase in appetite

4 Which are the characteristics of the "Type A" people described by Friedman and Rosenman?
    a   Always in a hurry
    b   Cooperative
    c   Relaxed
    d   Wealthy

5 Who was the scientist who studied voodoo deaths?
    a   James Greer
    b   Hans Selye
    c   H. Weiner
    d   Walter Cannon

Record your finishing time and check the answer key on page 315.

Scanning for All the Information on a Topic

This level of scanning is frequently used by students or others who are writing a paper or report on a particular topic.

The practice exercise in this unit provides you with locator material for just one book, *The Nurse Assistant,* by Donovan, Belsjoe, and Dillon. It is for students preparing to be nurse aides. In actually preparing a paper you would use several books; however, the process is the same for each one. You will find a title page, table of contents, preface, and index from one book. Imagine that you are preparing a report on the topic of food service in hospitals.

Your task is to go through the material provided, looking for information about food and food service. As you scan the material, write down all the page numbers of the places where you would expect to find such information. Then check your list of page numbers against the list at the back of the book. *Do not look at the list* until you have finished writing your list of page numbers.

Record your starting time before you search for page locations. When you have completed your list, record your finishing time. Do not count the time you will spend later checking your list against the key. Try to find all references to food and food service in less than ten minutes.

finishing time _____

starting time _____

scanning time _____

THE NURSE ASSISTANT

SECOND EDITION

Joan E. Donovan R.N., B.S.N.

Formerly Assistant Director, Nursing Service
St. Vincent's Hospital and Medical Center of New York

Edith H. Belsjoe B.A., M.A., LL.B.

Director of Personnel
St. Vincent's Hospital and Medical Center of New York

Daniel C. Dillon B.A., M.A.

McGRAW-HILL BOOK COMPANY

A Blakiston Publication

New York St. Louis San Francisco Auckland Bogota Düsseldorf
Johannesburg London Madrid Mexico Montreal New Delhi
Panama Paris São Paulo Singapore Sydney Tokyo Toronto

Contents

v

Preface

The need for nurse aides or nurse assistants has continued to grow. In our original edition, we noted that there were 400,000 nurse aides in the United States. That was in 1968. We find that number has now tripled. There are approximately 1,500,000 nurse aides currently employed in the United States, and it is expected that this number will continue to rise.

Because the nurse aide has learned more and become a more integral part of the nursing team, we have changed the title of our book to *The Nurse Assistant.* We believe in doing so that we have more fully recognized the value and contribution of the nurse aide to total patient care.

In revising *The Nurse Aide,* we carefully considered critiques from reviewers supplied to us by our publisher. We revised the order of chapters to better service instructors' needs, and added two new chapters, "Care of the Geriatric Patient" and "Care of the Emergency Room Patient," and in general did a major overhaul of all material that had become obsolete. We added functions that

the nurse assistant now performs such as taking blood pressures and CPR.

We hope *The Nurse Assistant* may be an introduction to the nursing field for the LPN, LVN, and RN student. We also hope our book will inspire students to progress from one nursing level to another. Our second chapter, "Orientation," has been expanded to show how vast the nursing field has become and how great the opportunities are.

We wish to thank all those who have made this revision possible. We are grateful in particular to the reviewers who spent considerable time pointing out to us which chapters could be expanded or updated and where new material should be added.

We especially thank Mary Ann Linder and Orville Haberman at McGraw-Hill for their guidance and encouragement, and Irene Gunther at Allen Wayne Technical Corporation, whose staff did a superb job of copy editing.

Joan E. Donovan
Edith H. Belsjoe
Daniel C. Dillon

vii

Index

Skimming to Identify the Topic

In this exercise your task is to skim each brief selection to identify the topic being discussed. Try to identify the topic *without reading all of the passage*.

Notice that we are now working on *skimming,* not scanning. You are not looking for a specific number or name. You are trying to identify the main topic of the selection.

Begin by recording your starting time. Then answer the questions, identifying the topic. When you have finished answering the questions, record your finishing time, and check the answer key at the back of the book.

finishing time _____

starting time _____

skimming time _____

Skimming Exercise for Unit 18

Credit can cost you pennies or dollars. It depends on your character, your capital and your capability to repay, the money market, and other economic factors.

Two choices you frequently have are closed-end and revolving transactions. Under the closed-end plans you ordinarily sign a promissory note, if you are borrowing cash, or a retail installment contract, if

153

you are using sales credit. You agree in advance on the specific amount to borrow, the number and size of weekly or monthly payments, and a due date.

On the other hand, the revolving charge plan is open-ended. A top limit is agreed upon, but purchases are added as they are made and finance charges are figured on the unpaid balance each month.

1 The topic is
a Money market funds
b Cost of credit
c Shopping suggestions
d Economic conditions

Note: There is a 25% discount for 100 or more copies of a single publication mailed to one address.

Cost increases may make it necessary for the Superintendent of Documents to increase the selling price of publications. Therefore, the prices listed in the Catalog may differ from those in the publications.

Operating rules require that receipts must be deposited in the U.S. Treasury within 48 hours. Therefore, your cancelled check may be returned before your order arrives. If this happens, be assured that your order is being processed as rapidly as possible.

2 The topic is
a The U.S. Treasury
b Government services
c Document ordering information
d How to write a check

On January 1, 1972 a Food and Drug Administration ruling of extraordinary significance became effective in all 50 states. This commendable rule—which requires eyeglass and sunglass lenses for use by the general public to be *impact-resistant*—was issued under FDA's authority to regulate medical devices, as spectacles are characterized.

The FDA ruling specifies that *impact-resistant* eyeglass and sunglass lenses must be capable of resisting an impact from a 5/8″ diameter steel ball dropped from a height of 50 inches. Industrial strength safety lenses are verified by being struck with an even larger, heavier, steel ball. Most lenses previously available to the general public could not pass such tests.

Safeguarding eyesight cannot be accomplished with *impact-resistant* lenses alone! All such lenses function best when supported by frames that hold them securely, and which are made of flame-retardant materials.

3   The topic is
   a   Food regulations
   b   Making glass
   c   Steel ball bearings
   d   Impact-resistant lenses

The ground around the outside of a house should be graded in such a manner as to prevent dampness. Your lot should slope away from the house on all sides to allow proper drainage and to prevent water that is draining off other lots from standing on your lot. Water should not be allowed to stand next to a house because it will eventually seep through the foundation walls. When disturbing established lot drainage patterns by installing such items as new lawns, landscaping, patios or planters, extreme care should be taken to maintain proper grades. To assure positive drainage at all times, periodic removal of silt and other obstructions from drainage swales and facilities is required, and areas subject to settlement, wash and erosion may require patching and replanting periodically.

4   The topic is
   a   Patio construction
   b   Drainage
   c   Foundations
   d   Plantings

As the Nation's principal conservation agency, the Department of the Interior has responsibility for most of our nationally owned public lands and natural resources. This includes fostering the wisest use of our land and water resources, protecting our fish and wildlife, preserving the environmental and cultural values of our national parks and historical places, and providing for the enjoyment of life through outdoor recreation. The Department assesses our energy and mineral resources and works to assure that their development is in the best interests of all our people. The Department also has a major responsibility for American Indian reservation communities and for people who live in Island Territories under U.S. administration.

5   The topic is
   a   The Department of Interior
   b   Recreation
   c   Minerals
   d   Indian territories

The general plan of attack in building Hoover Dam was to drive tunnels through the canyon walls around the site, divert the Colorado through the tunnels, build cofferdams to block off the river from the damsite, excavate the site, and build the dam and powerplant.

The narrowness of the canyon, the spread of activity up and down the river, and the possible large fluctuation of the river's flow made the job of diverting the Colorado a ticklish one.

It had been decided to drive four diversion tunnels (two on each side of the river) around the damsite through the solid rock of the canyon walls. Two temporary cofferdams would then be built—one would be upstream, above the site but just below the tunnel inlets; the other would be downstream, below the site but upstream from the tunnel outlets. These cofferdams would block off the river so that the site could be pumped dry and excavated to foundation bedrock.

The four tunnels would serve other purposes when their use as diversion tunnels was completed. The two outer tunnels would become outlets for the huge spillways. The inner tunnels would be utilized for installation of penstocks to convey water from the intake towers in the reservoir to the powerplant or to the outlet valves below the dam.

6   The topic is
   a   The Colorado River
   b   Building the Hoover Dam
   c   Tunnel building
   d   Power-plant building

What are the prospects for acquiring Government land? Is there a lot of free land around? How difficult is it to buy public land? How much land is available for sale each year?

These are only a few of the questions Government agencies receive every day. Many people apparently have read advertisements giving the impression that Uncle Sam is still distributing "free" public land for homesteading or selling it for next to nothing the way the Federal Government did in the days of the Old West.

Bluntly, there is no truth to such claims. There is no free public land available to private individuals, and such parcels as the Government occasionally does sell cost as much as, or perhaps more than, comparable nearby privately owned land. Homesteading on public lands in the Western lower 48 States is a thing of the past.

7   The topic is
   a   Advertising
   b   The old west
   c   Private land costs
   d   Obtaining government land

The National Archives has custody of millions of records relating to persons who have had dealings with the Federal Government. ... These records may contain full information about the person or give little information beyond a name. Searches in the records may be very time consuming as many records lack name indexes. The National Archives is unable to make extensive searches but, given enough identifying information, will try to find a record about a specific person.

8 The topic is
   a   Employment at the National Archives
   b   Personal records in the National Archives
   c   Location of the National Archives
   d   Cost of the National Archives

It is in situations where visual references such as the ground and horizon are obscured that trouble develops, especially for pilots who lack experience and proficiency in instrument flight. The vestibular sense in particular tends to confuse the pilot. Because of inertia, the sensory areas of the inner ear cannot detect slight changes in the attitude of the aircraft nor can they accurately sense attitude changes which occur at a uniform rate over a period of time. On the other hand false sensations are often generated which lead the pilot to believe the attitude of the plane has changed when in fact it has not. This not only compounds the confusion of the pilot but also makes him more susceptible to motion sickness which often accompanies disorientation.

If a disoriented pilot actually does make a recovery from a turn, bank, or spin, he has a very strong tendency to feel that he has entered a turn, bank or spin in the opposite direction. These false sensations may lead to the well-known "graveyard spiral."

Every pilot should be aware of these illusions and their consequences. Flight instructors should provide each pilot with an opportunity to experience these sensations under controlled conditions.

9 The topic is
   a   Pilot disorientation
   b   Flight rules
   c   Aircraft design
   d   Navigation

A *watch,* according to the National Weather Service, means conditions are appropriate for severe weather. It does not mean that there is immediate danger. A *warning,* on the other hand, means that a storm exists and is nearby, and you should seek a safe place immediately.

10 The topic is
  a Meaning of terms *watch* and *warning*
  b History of the U.S. Weather Bureau
  c Safe building construction
  d Weather broadcast frequencies

Record your finishing time, and check the answer key.

Skimming to Identify the Author's Point of View

In this exercise we will look at *why* and *how* authors write what they do. Your task is to skim the passages presented and to answer the questions that follow. Try to discover the author's point of view without reading all of the selection.

First record your starting time. Then skim and answer the questions. When you have answered the questions, record your finishing time, and check the answer key at the back of the book. The unit should take you less then five minutes to complete.

finishing time _____

starting time _____

skimming time _____

Skimming Exercises for Unit 19

You shop for credit the way you shop for anything else. It's best to shop at more than one place. And it's best to know what to look for. A typical household with a good credit rating can save enough for an annual vacation by shopping for the money it "rents" in order to buy now and pay later.

Here are some pointers to help you shop for money for installment buying through contracts and through credit cards and other kinds of revolving charge plans. This chapter will not deal with financing a home or other real property.

1 The author
   a Wants to save you money
   b Doesn't approve of credit buying
   c Is personally in debt
   d Wants to loan money

2 The author thinks that
   a You should not buy on credit
   b You should shop for credit
   c All people should have the same credit rating
   d Credit ratings are not accurate

One of the most striking transformations brought about by the storage of water in the reservoir, officially named Lake Mead, is the change in color and consistency of the Colorado River. Where once it flowed through Black Canyon a brown turbid stream, carrying an average silt load of 300 tons a minute—"too thin to plow and too thick to drink"—the lake is now a dark emerald green in the canyons and a deep blue in more open country, while the river below the dam has regained the sparkling clearness it possessed when it left the mountains.

An unusually scenic and interesting country has been made accessible by the filling of the canyons where the river long held sway. The fiord-like vistas of Boulder, Black, and Iceberg Canyons and the lower reaches of Grand Canyon, the many islands inhabited by desert dwellers secluded there by the rising waters, the deep colors and mirror-like reflections of unusual rock formations, and the ferns, springs, falls and prehistoric dwellings in remote side canyons, are among the sights viewed on exploratory boat trips. Shorter excursions are made at frequent intervals and there are regular schedules from the boat landing to the upstream face of the dam and nearby places.

The lake is being stocked with millions of bass, crappie and bream. Trout also have been placed in the river downstream from the dam, as the temperature of the water will be cool both summer and winter, being drawn from a reservoir depth of 150 to 300 feet.

3 The author
   a Thinks the project was a mistake
   b Approves of what has been done
   c Does not want to talk about it
   d Thinks you should stay away

4 The author thinks the area is improved because
  a Boats can travel past the new dam
  b The area is more primitive now
  c The water is now "sparkling clear"
  d The country is being kept as a wilderness

5 The author apparently thinks that fishing will be
  a Ruined
  b Improved
  c Illegal
  d Difficult

Dear Editor,

   Our city council has lost its sense of what is good for the community. The latest insanity is the proposal to buy the Smith farm to add to the park system. We already have much more park land than we can afford. Parks do not pay taxes. They cost tax money to buy and maintain. A look at the parks we have now will show that we are not taking care of them. In addition, they are becoming impossible to enjoy. They are filled with loud, rude, inconsiderate young people who don't care who they bother with their loud music and their flying saucers.

   The city council should be spending its time doing something about improving conditions in the city for its residents instead of constantly spending tax money on foolishness.

Sincerely,

An Irate Citizen

6 The writer
  a Is a member of the city council
  b Is probably a new resident
  c Likes loud music
  d Doesn't want the city to buy more park land

7 The writer
  a Wants taxes increased
  b Want taxes spent on more parks
  c Wants taxes reduced
  d Enjoys the local parks

8 This letter would probably be found in
  a A magazine
  b A daily newspaper
  c A book
  d A government report

Do you want enduring elegance and timeless style in a residence? The need for quality and taste is as great now as it was in Victorian times. You can still find elegance and style in a Rolls Royce, a Château Lafite Rothschild wine, or a new house built by Prestige Homes. None of these classics ever lose their appeal to the discriminating person.

Prestige Homes has now started a new neighborhood of outstanding residences in the exclusive Westmore Woods section. The area will be secured by discretely placed fences, and an entry gateman will be on hand at all times to screen visitors. The natural appearance of the Westmore Woods will be conserved by keeping the stately oaks intact. Roads will curve gracefully through the woods, and of course all utilities will be underground.

If you want to find your place in this gracious elegance, call for an appointment to visit the neighborhood. Be prepared for a most exciting adventure in prestigious living.

9 The selection above would most likely be found in
   a An advertisement
   b An editorial
   c A book
   d A scientific journal

10 The author wants to appeal to
   a Poor people
   b Wine drinkers
   c Status-conscious people
   d Auto owners

Record your finishing time, and check the answer key.

Skimming to Identify Facts

In this level of skimming you are trying to get as much factual information as possible without reading all of the material. You glance over the material, looking for particular facts. You need to have some idea of the general ideas presented, but your primary focus is on specific facts.

Skim over the selection that follows, paying particular attention to those parts in which facts are being presented. They try to answer as many of the questions as possible.

Be sure you do not study-read the selection. Remember that the purpose here is to *skim* for facts.

First record your starting time. After you have answered the questions, record your finishing time, and check the answer key at the back of the book.

finishing time _____

starting time _____

skimming time _____

How to Buy Meat for Your Freezer

"Can I save money by buying a side of beef?"

This, and similar questions, are often asked by owners of home freezers. There is no easy "yes" or "no" answer. The answer can be found only by making a careful comparison of costs among the alternatives available to you.

Basically, you have three alternatives in buying meat for your freezer: buying a whole carcass, side, or quarter; buying wholesale cuts (loin, round, chuck, etc.); or buying retail cuts.

It is the purpose of this bulletin to help you compare the costs under these alternatives, and also to point out a number of other factors that you should consider. The information provided is intended primarily to answer the questions most frequently asked by consumer-buyers—those relating to costs, grades, kinds of cuts, and yields of usable meat.

Points to Consider

Wholesomeness . . . quality . . . how much to buy . . . cost . . . convenience . . . service . . . and getting good value for your money . . . these are all factors you should take into account in buying meat for your freezer.

You should also consider the amount of meat you can store in your freezer, the amount your family can use within a reasonable time, and the kinds of cuts and quality your family prefers. And you should be aware of the kinds and quantity of the various cuts that you get from a carcass or wholesale cut.

As in any buying situation, success in buying meat for your freezer depends upon your knowledge of what you are purchasing.

Carcass, Side, or Quarter

When you buy a whole carcass or side (half a carcass, including both fore and hind quarters), you will get a wide variety—the entire range of cuts, both high- and low-priced. These will include some you might not normally buy, such as the brisket, short ribs, and shank. But most locker and freezer provisioners, who specialize in preparing meat for the freezer, will convert cuts that you do not want to use "as is" into ground meat or stew meat. In addition, they will usually age meat to the extent desired and will cut it to your order.

A carcass, side or quarter is normally sold by its "hanging" or gross weight. This means the weight before cutting and trimming. The amount of usable meat you take home will, of course, be considerably less—how much less can vary substantially.

For a beef carcass, cutting loss (bone, fat trim, shrink, etc.) could vary from 20 to 30 percent or more. A 25-percent cutting loss, which is not unusual, means that a 300-pound side of beef would yield 225 pounds of usable meat cuts.

A rule of thumb for carcass beef is: 25 percent waste, 25 percent ground beef and stew meat, 25 percent steaks, and 25 percent roasts. Not all of the steaks and roasts, however, are from the loin and rib, the most tender portions.

Buying a quarter involves many of the considerations already mentioned. In addition, you should be aware of the difference in the kinds of cuts you get from a hindquarter as compared with a forequarter.

A hindquarter of beef will yield more steaks and roasts, but will cost more per pound than a forequarter. In 1975, this difference in price averaged about 25 cents a pound. A forequarter of beef, while containing the delectable rib roast, has more of the less-tender cuts than the hindquarter. The chuck, or shoulder, makes up about one-half of the forequarter's weight. The yield of usable lean meat, however, is greater in the forequarter than in the hindquarter.

Buying Beef

In determining whether or not you can save money by buying meat in quantity, over and above what it would cost to buy it at the retail store, remember you will have to take into account the yield of meat you will get from the carcass, the quality of the meat, and the costs of cutting, wrapping, and quick-freezing. You should find out, when buying carcass meat, whether these costs are included in the price per pound, or if you'll have to pay additional for them. The usual charge is 12 to 18 cents per pound for cutting, wrapping, and quick-freezing, whether it is charged separately or added onto the price per pound. . . .

Quality Grades

Beef varies in quality more than any other meat. Making sure of the quality you get when you buy in quantity, then, is even more important for beef than for other meats.

USDA quality grades offer a consistent, reliable guide to the tenderness, juiciness, and flavor of beef. That is, for any given cut—for example, a sirloin steak—the higher the grade, the greater the degree of tenderness, juiciness, and flavor .

You should be aware that some cuts of beef are naturally more tender than others. The most tender are those from the less used muscles along the back of the animal, the rib and loin sections. The less tender cuts, such as the chuck (shoulder), flank, and round, come from the active muscles. . . .

Each USDA quality grade is a measure of a distinct level of quality—and it takes eight grades to span the range. They are: USDA Prime, Choice, Good, Standard, Commercial, Utility, Cutter, and Canner. The three lower grades, USDA Utility, Cutter, and Canner, are seldom if ever sold at retail but are used instead to make ground beef and manufactured meat items such as frankfurters.

The highest grade, USDA Prime, is used mostly by hotels and restaurants, but a small amount is sold at retail and by dealers supplying freezer meat. The grade most widely sold at retail is USDA Choice. It is produced in the greatest volume and most consumers find this level of quality to their liking. In buying for your freezer, you would be well advised to select beef from the higher quality grades. . . .

Yield Grades

As mentioned earlier in this booklet, the yield of usable meat from a beef carcass can vary greatly—regardless of quality grade. This variation is caused, primarily, by differences in the amount of fat on the outside of the carcass. Beef carcasses must be graded for yield at the same time they are graded for quality. Yield Grade 1 denotes the highest yield, and Yield Grade 5 the lowest.

Little grading of pork carcasses is presently being done, but it may be possible to order by grade through a wholesale meat dealer. A U.S. No. 1 pork carcass will yield more than 53 percent of its weight in the four major lean cuts, the ham, loin, Boston butt, and picnic shoulder. A U.S. No. 2 will yield 50–53 percent in those cuts; U.S. No. 3, 47–50 percent, and U.S. No. 4, less than 47 percent.

If you're thinking of buying a pork carcass or side, you'll want to get it from a place that is equipped to render the lard and cure the bacon, hams, and other cuts that you may not want to use fresh. If you cannot obtain this service, you would probably find it better to buy wholesale cuts of fresh pork, such as shoulders, loins, and hams.

In buying pork, look for cuts with a relatively small amount of fat over the outside and with meat that is firm and a grayish pink color. For best eating, the meat should have a small amount of marbling.

How Much Should I Buy?

How much meat you should buy at any one time depends, of course, on how much you want to spend at one time, the amount of freezer storage space you have available, and how much your family consumes. You will need to do some figuring.

Properly wrapped meat cuts, stored at 0 degrees F., or lower, will maintain their quality for a long time. This varies, however, with the kind of meat. In the table below, the times indicated represent a range within which you can store the meat with reasonable expectation that it will maintain its quality. Meats can be kept safely frozen for longer periods than indicated, but they are apt to lose quality.

**SUGGESTED STORAGE TIMES FOR
MEAT AT 0° F.**

Beef	8–12 months
Lamb	8–12 months
Pork, fresh	4–8 months
Ground beef and lamb	3–4 months
Pork sausage	1–3 months

On the average, one cubic foot of freezer space will accommodate 35 to 40 pounds of cut and wrapped meat, though it will be slightly less if the meat is packaged in odd shapes.

Meat should be initially frozen at −10° F. or lower, and as quickly as possible. If you are freezing it yourself, allow some space for air to circulate between the packages.

The amount of food frozen at one time should be limited in order to get as quick and efficient freezing as possible. Only the amount of unfrozen food that will freeze within 24 hours should be put into the freezer. Usually that will be about 2 or 3 pounds to each cubic foot of freezer capacity. The speed of freezing will be slower if the freezer is overloaded with unfrozen food.

For large meat purchases, it is usually best to get the freezing done by a commercial establishment properly equipped to do the job. Quick freezing causes less damage to the meat fibers. Slower freezing causes more of the cells to rupture, due to formation of large ice crystals, so that more meat juices are lost when the meat is thawed.

Proper wrapping of meat for the freezer is as important as proper storage. Use a moisture-vapor-proof wrap, such as heavy aluminum foil, heavily waxed freezer paper, or specially laminated papers. Wrap the meat closely, eliminating all air if possible. Double thicknesses of waxed paper should be placed between chops and steaks to prevent their sticking together. Seal the packages well and mark them with the date. The rule in using frozen meat should be: First in, first out.

Improperly wrapped packages will allow air to enter and draw moisture from the meat, resulting in "freezer burn" or meat which is dry and less flavorful.

It is perfectly safe to refreeze meat that has been kept refrigerated after thawing. However, refreezing of defrosted meat is not usually recommended because there is some loss of meat quality.

Skimming Exercise for Unit 20

1   You buy a carcass or side of beef by its
   a   Original weight
   b   Finished unfrozen weight
   c   Boneless weight
   d   "Hanging" weight

2   A typical cutting loss would be
   a   10 percent
   b   25 percent
   c   40 percent
   d   50 percent

3   Compared with forequarters, hindquarters
   a   Are more tender
   b   Are less expensive per pound of meat
   c   Are more expensive per pound of meat
   d   Have more usable lean meat

4   Processing charges include
   a   Cutting
   b   Wrapping
   c   Freezing
   d   All of the above

5   Quality grades are a measure of
   a   Cost
   b   Size

c Quality
d Age

6 The top quality grade is

a Commercial
b Standard
c Good
d Prime

7 In the four major lean cuts a U.S. No. 1 pork carcass will yield more than

a 25 percent
b 33 percent
c 53 percent
d 61 percent

8 In buying pork, look for meat that is

a Brownish in color
b Sand-colored
c Tinged with green
d Grayish pink in color

9 Meat should be frozen at temperatures below

a 40°F
b 32°F
c 0°C
d 0°F

10 One cubic foot of freezer space will hold about

a 10–12 pounds
b 20–22 pounds
c 35–40 pounds
d 70–90 pounds

Record your finishing time, and check the answer key.

Skimming to Identify the Author's Style

In this level of skimming you are trying to determine the general approach being taken by the author. It may be descriptive, humorous, narrative; it may be a dialogue, an argument, or some other form.

Skim over the selections which follow and then answer the questions. The questions all deal with the author's style and general approach.

Before you begin, record your starting time. Then when you have answered all of the questions, record your finishing time, and check your answers with the answer key in the back of the book.

finishing time _____

starting time _____

skimming time _____

Skimming Exercise for Unit 21

The National Archives has records of births, marriages, and deaths at U.S. Army facilities, 1884–1912, with some records dated as late as 1928. It will search these records if provided with the following: *birth records*—name of child, names of his parents, place of birth, and month and year of birth; *marriage records*—names of contracting parties; *death records*—name, date, place, and rank of deceased.

1 The material is
  a Humorous
  b Descriptive
  c Dialogue
  d Poetic

"Mother," he said. "I just can't go to school today. The kids don't like me, the bus drivers pick on me, and the principal doesn't want me around at all."

"Son," the mother replied. "You have to go. Everybody expects you to be there. You have a lot of good qualities. You're a bright person, and a leader. Besides, you are 41 years old and a teacher."

2 The author's style is
  a Poetic
  b Descriptive
  c Artistic
  d Humorous

3 The form of the selection is
  a Dialogue
  b Descriptive
  c Poetic
  d Historical

The Colorado River for centuries, in its wild 1,400-mile descent from the lofty Rocky Mountains to the Pacific Ocean, has gouged great chasms such as Grand Canyon. Fed by melted snows in the spring and summer, the river yearly flooded low-lying farmlands along its route. Then in late summer and fall, the river dried to a trickle. Early settlers diverted water from the river with little success. There was either too much or too little. Floods destroyed crops, lives, and property, and often crops and livestock withered and died when the river ran too low to be diverted.

The disastrous floods in 1905-07 which swept through Imperial Valley in southern California provided added incentive for action. The Colorado River had to be controlled and regulated, but it was a long, drawn-out job.

Representatives of the seven Colorado River Basin States met in Santa Fe, N. Mex., in 1922 and drafted the Colorado River Compact. This agreement divided use of the river's water between the upper and lower basins and paved the way for construction of works to control, regulate, and utilize the stream's natural resources. The Congress in 1928 passed the Boulder Canyon Project Act, authorizing construction of Hoover Dam and the All-American Canal System.

4   The approach taken in the above selection is
a   Humorous
b   Historical
c   Persuasive
d   Dialogue

5   The author's description is
a   Matter of fact and impersonal
b   Colorful and interesting
c   Biased
d   General and lacking in fact

Sell Your House Yourself and Save Thousands

Join the many home-owners who are saving large sums of money by selling their houses themselves!

This complete guide, written by two experts who have sold many houses, covers the following topics:

Deciding whether to sell yourself

How to use an appraiser to guide pricing

Where and how to advertise effectively

How to prepare and show the house

Improving appearance inexpensively

Deciding what improvements will pay off

What to tell prospective buyers when they call

How to make up an information sheet on the house

How to get the prospect to make an offer

Sources and types of financing—FHA, VA, etc.

Writing a sales agreement

How to use a lawyer to best advantage

Many other topics are also covered. In addition, the book contains two special features: a GLOSSARY OF COMMON REAL ESTATE TERMS, AND A SPECIAL SECTION ON TAX SAVINGS.

6   The material above is designed to
a   Sell a book to you
b   Entertain you
c   Moralize at you
d   Improve you

7 The general style is to
  a Describe in detail
  b Sample from passages
  c Give testimonials
  d Summarize the contents

8 The authors of the book are
  a Using other people's ideas
  b Probably new at real estate
  c Probably experienced in real estate
  d Not eager to sell the book

Carry Your Own Good Luck—Guaranteed!

If you want to know the real secret of true good luck, ask someone who carries one of our Lucky Shamrocks. It is a true shamrock encased in transparent long-wearing plastic. The Lucky Shamrock is furnished with a ring that allows it to be worn as a pendant or attached to a key chain. The Lucky Shamrock is guaranteed to be genuine. Have good luck, happiness, health, and wealth for only $9.95. Send check or money order.

9 What word in the heading is misleading?
  a Luck
  b Guaranteed
  c Carry
  d Good

10 Which word best describes the text?
  a Poetry
  b Narrative
  c Humor
  d Advertising

Record your finishing time, and check the answer key.

Skimming to Discover Organization

At this level of skimming, you are trying to find out how the author has put the material together. Presumably the author had some kind of outline. If you could see the author's outline, you would know more about how the ideas relate to each other.

Skimming to discover organization has the same effect as seeing the author's outline if it is well done. Often the organization of a book can be seen very clearly from the material furnished at the beginning. You can learn a great deal from a table of contents if it is reasonably complete. In this unit you will examine the table of contents from a sociology book. The practice exercise includes questions about how the book is put together.

Look over the table of contents on the next page, skimming to discover how the author has organized it. Then answer the questions that follow. First, record your starting time. When you have answered the questions, record your finishing time, and check the answer key at the back of the book.

finishing time _____

starting time _____

skimming time _____

C·O·N·T·E·N·T·S

viii

CONTENTS

PART TWO CULTURE AND PERSONALITY

ix

CONTENTS

PART THREE SOCIAL ORGANIZATION

Skimming Exercise for Unit 22

1 How many major parts does the book have?
a Three
b Four
c Five
d Six

2 How is the index organized?
a There is no index
b There is an index of topics
c There is an index of names
d There are two indexes, for names and topics

3 Where is the author's discussion of sociology as a science?
a At the end of the last chapter
b At the beginning of the book
c In the last chapter
d In the preface

4 The author has several chapters on social organization in
a Section 1
b Section 2
c Section 3
d Section 4

5 The chapter called "Social class" is in the part entitled
a "Social organization"
b "Social interaction"
c "Human ecology"
d "Social change and social policy"

6 To help you understand terms used in the book, the author
a Defines all new terms
b Furnishes a glossary
c Lists new terms at the start of each chapter
d Lists new terms at the end of each chapter

7 If you wanted to read more on a topic, you could look at the
a Suggested readings
b Footnotes
c Chapter summaries
d Other sociology books in your library

8 Under which heading does the author include the chapter on population?
a "Human ecology"
b "Social change and social policy"
c "Social organization"
d "Social interaction"

9 Which of the following chapters does the major heading, "Social interaction," contain

    a "Social groups"

    b "Role and status"

    c "Race and ethnic relations"

    d "Social movements"

10 The chapter on the family is found in the section entitled

    a "Social interaction"

    b "Social organization"

    c "Social change and social policy"

    d "Human ecology"

Record your finishing time, and check the answer key.

Skimming to Understand the Content

At this level of skimming you really want to know as much as possible about what the author is saying. However, you do not read all of the material. You should be able to get good comprehension from most material by reading less than half of it.

The process is one in which you are constantly looking for the important ideas and trying to skip over the material that doesn't add much to the message.

In the exercise which follows, try to get the author's meaning without reading everything. The questions will be quite typical of those we asked in Part 1 when you were reading all of the material. Do the best you can to get all of the message, but don't read more than about half of the words.

Begin by writing down your starting time. When you have finished answering the questions, record your finishing time and check the answer key at the back of the book. You should be able to do this exercise in less than seven minutes.

finishing time _____

starting time _____

skimming time _____

The Last of the Copper Kettle Makers

Marian Clover

Robert Picking at age 100 is the last old-style copper kettle manufacturer in the country. He joined the family business in 1899, at the age of 20, working on a dirt floor until they laid the present brick flooring. Open windows, now as then, serve as air-conditioning, and his office is heated by a seventy-five-year-old gas stove he claims works better than one you could buy today. "Everything is pretty much the way Grandfather had it when he diversified from the hardware business into making copper ware in 1874," Picking says.

He deals with the grandsons of the men he originally started doing business with. Picking doesn't advertise. "We have too much business now. Can't take on any new accounts. We've never had as large a backlog of orders."

When Picking joined his father and grandfather eighty years ago, he worked a ten-hour day, six-day week. He still comes in every day and expects to continue. He has no secretary, no bookkeeper, no typewriter, not even an adding machine. His safe with the stenciled flowers has served the company for over a century. So has the old rolltop desk. "The Pickings have done their own office work since 1845. If I don't get to it during the day, I take it home at night."

D. Picking & Co. of Bucyrus, Ohio, restores copper boilers, coal scuttles, chafing dishes, and decorative ornaments. He points out two stacks of kettles. One is dented, blackened, bottoms burnt-out. The second pile is smooth-sided and whole, with the rosy sheen only copper can give. His firm also makes new copper candy kettles and tympani. "Copper kettles produce a better tasting candy than stainless steel," Picking says. "They tell me it stirs better in copper. It's a fine conductor of heat. We still make eight hundred to nine hundred candy kettles a year. During the Depression we made nearly two hundred a year for people in business for themselves making caramel corn. It kept many a family alive."

D. Picking & Co. turns out 75 tympani—the kettledrums—a year. They have a good reputation with symphony orchestras.

He leads the way to an enormous copper kettle, six feet in diameter.

"We made Swiss cheese kettles like this one, up until eighteen years ago. A cheese maker could turn 2,800 pounds of milk into a 200–250-pound wheel of cheese, and you had something. We cleaned up one of these kettles and rolled it right out the door and up to Greenfield Village in Dearborn, Michigan, to preserve it for posterity. It was riveted tight as the day it was made."

Picking shuns stamping or welding. Every kettle is cut individually from copper sheeting, formed into a circular shape, the bottom attached using the tongue-and-groove method, then bonded and sealed with a mixture of brass, borax, and water. Stacks of finished kettles illuminate every corner, and the steady *thoup, thoup, thoup* of the planishing hammer resounds through the two-story gray frame building. "The only way to harden copper is with a planishing hammer," he says. The special tool makes a bright spot when it contacts the copper, producing the multi-faceted gleam of the metal. Blemishes and irregularities are also pounded out. Much of the planishing to get the shine is done with hand labor—light, steady blows of uniform pressure. One planisher straddles a bench that is an old tree trunk. Another coppersmith works at an iron bench, indented after more than a hundred years of pounding. Another works on a tree stump used as a table. "We hauled those benches up by rope through the window. They've been here as long as I have," Picking says. One of the few concessions to modernity was bringing in electricity some years ago. Some of the hammers that used to be hand-powered are now belt-driven and give 1800-2000 licks per minute.

But mostly, "Everything is creaking old. People see more antiques here than at a museum. I like things that are selfmade, that have some age to them, and are useful. I admire ingenuity." Like the 135-year-old wooden lock and key. Or the gasoline fan lit with a match that whirs as competently as any electric fan. "It was made before the Civil War," Picking says. "In England, John Ericsson, the inventor of the ironclad warship, the *Monitor,* developed a fan 118″ in diameter. It worked on the same principle."

Picking demonstrates a long wooden instrument. "This is a horse fiddle. Put it against the wall at a shivaree for newlyweds and it would rattle the pictures off the wall. I have three, all with a different tone."

He pats an eighty-year-old wooden hurdy-gurdy. "A man had it on a cart and cranked it on the street when I was a boy. It plays 'Never On Sunday,' and they think that's a new song."

Elephants—teak, ebony, marble, jeweled, enameled, and painted—parade across the windowsills and fill every spare niche in his office. They are part of his collection of over 500; Picking has loved elephants since he was five years old.

"The first time I saw a circus I went home and practiced being an elephant with a washtub and a stick. The Mills Brothers Circus people were friends, and they used to say, 'Make yourself at home,' and I did." Picking rode in the circus parade every year and when people would say, "Where's your dignity?" he told them that word wasn't in his dictionary.

Of the 13,000 centenarians in the country, few are as active as Picking, with his amazing memory. He runs his shop with a firm touch. Dapper, his straw boater perched at a jaunty angle, Picking greets his frequent visitors and then goes back to the job.

"Edison said there is no substitute for hard work, and I love to work," he says. "My business interests me as much if not more than when I started out. Somebody's got to work. Half the people who come in are retired." One more word not in Robert Picking's dictionary.

Skimming Exercise for Unit 23

1 Robert Picking started working in the copper kettle business in
  a 1874
  b 1889
  c 1899
  d 1845

2 Picking began by working
  a An eight-hour, five-day week
  b An eight-hour, six-day week
  c A ten-hour, five-day week
  d A ten-hour, six-day week

3 Picking believes in few modern conveniences for an office; he has
  a A secretary
  b A bookkeeper
  c A typewriter
  d None of the things listed here

4 Copper kettles are better for making
  a Soup
  b Candy
  c Popcorn
  d Perfume

5 Some of the largest kettles, six feet in diameter, were made up to eight-een years ago for Swiss cheese makers. These kettles could turn out a wheel of cheese, that was
  a 200–250 pounds
  b 2800 pounds
  c 18 pounds
  d 280 pounds

6 The only way to harden copper is with
  a Brass
  b Borax
  c Brass, borax, and water
  d A planishing hammer

7 One of the few changes that has been made is the use of
  a Electricity
  b A computer
  c A refrigerator
  d Typewriters

8 In the factory he has a collection of
  a Electric trains
  b Antiques
  c Windmills
  d Electric clocks

9 Picking has a collection of over 500
  a Clocks
  b Kettles
  c Horse fiddles
  d Elephants

10 Robert Picking has two words he claims are not in his dictionary:
  _____ and _____.
  a Old and retired
  b Easy and retired
  c Dignity and retired
  d Lazy and dignity

Record your finishing time, and check the answer key.

PART THREE

READING-RATE FLEXIBILITY

Introduction

You have now completed the first two sections of this book. As you know, our main purpose is to improve your reading at all rates. After all the practice in Part One you should have the ability to read much faster than when we started. In Part Two you were able to practice skills in skimming and scanning. Now we are ready to work on the skills involved in matching your reading rates to the material.

Most people tend to read at pretty much the same rate, regardless of the material or their purpose in reading it. This results in extremely inefficient reading. They should be reading or skimming some material several times as fast as other material. Highly skilled readers often read at rates that vary by over 200 words per minute.

The reasons for inflexibility in reading vary from person to person. In a few cases, visual limitations might set a limit on reading speed. However, most cases of inflexibility result from other causes. Some people do not read a wide enough variety of materials. They may read only the difficult, technical material that is required for their job. Others almost never read at all and never get enough practice to become efficient readers. Some people have never learned to read more efficiently simply because no one ever tried to teach them. In some school systems, reading training is almost entirely restricted to the lower grades. It takes more instruction than is usually offered in elementary schools to produce an efficient, flexible reader.

There are two primary elements in reading that should determine reading rate. One is the difficulty of the material. The other is the purpose for reading. Both elements are very important, and we will be spending some time on each.

Imagine reading a very difficult, detailed legal contract that you are about to sign. It would be very foolish to skim over it briefly without being sure that you understood what you were signing. It should be read and studied very carefully.

On the other hand, imagine that you are going to read a book of short stories. You are not studying them but are simply reading for entertainment. You would not read them as carefully and slowly as you would the legal contract. You want to get enough out of the stories to enjoy them. In most cases that means simply following the story without being confused about what is happening.

Under other conditions you might want to read the short stories very carefully and slowly. For example, if you are taking a writing course and are studying the style of the author, you will need to study the sentences and the author's technique quite carefully. To repeat what we said earlier, your rate should depend on the difficulty of the material and on your purpose for reading. Both are very important.

Factors in Readability

Reading experts have been interested for a long time in discovering what makes reading material difficult. A great deal of research has been done on the topic, and now most experts agree that there are two major factors in reading difficulty. One is the difficulty of the words found in the selection. If they are long, unknown, or technical words, the material is more difficult. The other major factor is the complexity of the sentences. Short, simple sentences are easier to understand. Long, involved sentences with many dependent clauses and other subparts are more difficult.

Some experts have developed ways of measuring the readability or difficulty of material. They usually use measures of the two factors mentioned, word difficulty and sentence complexity. Word difficulty is usually measured by word length or word frequency. (Some words are used in our language many more times than other words.) Sentence complexity or syntactical difficulty is usually measured using the average number of words in the sentences.

The usual purpose of measuring difficulty or readability is to be able to provide reading material to children at a level that matches their reading ability. As a result, readability is usually expressed as a grade level. It is supposed to identify the grade level of the person who can successfully read and understand it. For example, material that is at seventh grade on a readability measure would be much too difficult for most children in the third grade.

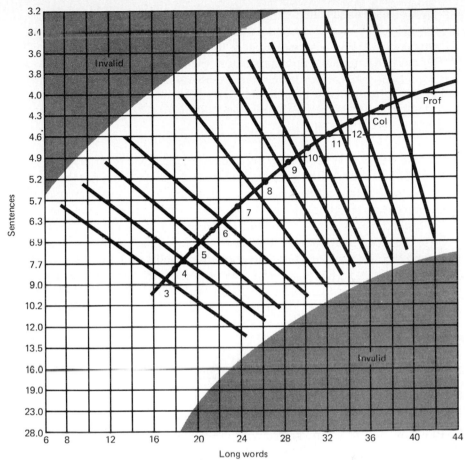

Figure 24-1. The Raygor Readability Estimate.

Measuring Readability

To give you an idea of how readability varies and how to measure it, we are going to do a couple of brief demonstrations. Figure 24-1 shows one of the most widely used readability graphs. Your task is to measure the readability of two 100-word passages. That will show you how to use the graph, but more important, it will give you an idea of how to estimate the difficulty of material by looking it over before you read.

Passage 1

Even the best home buyers sometimes fail to pay on time. Often there is a very good reason. If you can't make a payment on time, you probably have a good reason. It may mean that there is an illness or that you have lost your job. The best thing to do is to tell the bank or other lender right away and try to make up a satisfactory plan to make up the payments as soon as possible. Your lender may be able to suggest ways to help you. Bankers can be very helpful when you have a serious problem.

Passage 2

These behavioral sequences depend to a large extent on heredity. At the time of conception, genetics sets certain potentialities for the organism's structural and functional development, which are only partially complete at the time of birth. The infant's body and nervous system will continue to grow throughout its lifetime. Psychologists frequently use the term "maturation" to refer to the emergence of behavioral patterns that depend on the development of body and nervous system structures. In recent years it has become clear that environmental factors also play a large role in maturation. Before birth the intrauterine environment influences the developing fetus.

Directions

1   Count sentences in each passage, estimating to the nearest tenth.

2   Count words with six or more letters. Count proper nouns, but not numerals.

3   Plot the average on the graph.

Begin with Passage 1. You have probably already noticed that it is the easier one.

1   Count the number of sentences in the passage.
Write the number here. _____

2   Count the number of words with six or more letters.
Write the number here. _____

3   Now look on the graph to find the grade level. Look up the number of sentences on the left side of the graph. Then look up the number of words over six letters on the bottom of the graph. Look across from the number of sentences to where you meet the number of words over six letters. On the graph you will see the grade level of the material. Write it here. _____

Now look at Passage 2 and repeat the process.

1   Count the number of sentences.
Write the number here. _____

2   Count the number of words with six or more letters. Write the number here. _____

3   Look on the graph to find the difficulty level of the material. Write it here. _____

Using this method you should have found that:

1   Passage 1 has seven sentences and seventeen words over six letters. It is at the fourth-grade readability level.

2   Passage 2 has six sentences and forty-two words over six letters. It is at the professional readability level.

Using Readability as a Guide in Reading

Now that you are familiar with at least one measure of readability, you could go through everything before you read it, computing the difficulty. Then you could adjust your reading rate to match. That would be possible but not worth the time. A better plan is to look over material to get a general idea of the difficulty by simply observing the words and the context. You will soon get quite good at it.

Sometimes it is worthwhile to actually do a word count and refer to the graph to find the difficulty. Teachers do it when they select a textbook. You might want to do a quick estimate when you start reading a new textbook that you will be using throughout a course.

You should know that readability estimates have some shortcomings. Material is often variable in difficulty, especially when different parts are written by different people. Also there are some things that the readability estimate will not measure. Reader interest, author style, or special language problems that relate to dialects or ethnic backgrounds are not taken into account. In addition, a few authors use styles of writing that "fool" the formula and seem easier or more difficult than they really are.

Now that you have learned some things about readability, we suggest that you spend some time using that knowledge. Look over the books, magazines, newspapers, and other reading material around you. Try to guess where it would come out on the graph. You might calculate a few difficulty levels using the graph to see how well you can guess.

You are going to be doing some exercises in this book that involve reading materials of varying difficulty—from quite simple levels to very difficult, professional levels. In each case we will give you an estimate of the difficulty before you begin. That way you can start to develop a feel for difficulty as it shows up in the readings.

Purpose

We have discussed the purpose for reading several times already. You know that for some purposes skimming or scanning is the most efficient way to get information. In other situations, with other material, you might want to read very slowly and carefully.

Some of the work you will do in Part 3 of this book will depend on the purpose for reading. We will not be doing as much with varied purposes as we will with difficulty because you have already done a lot in Part 2 that related to purpose. However, we do want to stress the importance of considering *why* you are reading as well as *what* you are reading.

Now let's move on to some exercises that will help you learn to adapt your reading rate to both difficulty and purpose.

Reading Difficult Material

The material you will be reading in this unit will have to be read very carefully. Why? Because we are going to give you written directions, and you are going to use them to make an airplane! On the next page you will find detailed instructions, with drawings, for making a paper airplane. If you have ever made something using written instructions, you will known that the reading has to be done slowly and carefully.

We will not be asking any questions to test your comprehension on this unit. The test will be whether you have read the directions carefully enough to actually make an airplane. The airplane itself will be your evidence that you have read and understood the material.

This exercise will take some people quite a bit longer than others. (Some may already know how to make the airplane.) We are not going to time the unit. Simply do your best to read and follow the directions.

Start now by obtaining an 8 1/2 × 11 inch piece of paper. Then turn the page and begin.

How To Fold A Paper Airplane

1   Take a standard 8 1/2 × 11 inch sheet of paper and fold it, putting point A to point B, making a folded square with an extra strip on one side.

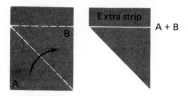

2   Fold the extra strip over the square to weaken it, then cut or tear it off.

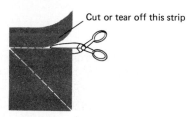

3   Label the corners A, B, C, and D. Open square of paper and fold point C up to point D.

4   Open square of paper, turn it over, and fold it in half, with point A up to point D, and point C up to point B.

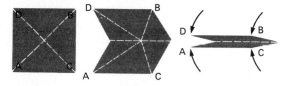

5   Open square, then fold into a triangle, bringing point E inside to meet point F. You should now have a triangle with double "wings".

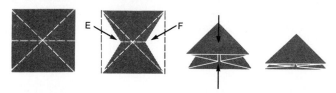

6 Lay the triangle flat with points A and D together on the left. Fold the top down to meet the bottom center. You should now have a "wing" with double tips on each side.

A and D   B and C

7 Fold the top wing tip on the left up until the tip (point D) meets the bottom center. Now fold the same tip up over the center line. Tuck the last fold you made into the slot under it. Repeat, using right wing tip.

Fold top wing only

8 Open the last three folds, until you have the triangle as shown in Step 6. Place the extra strip taken off in Step 2 into the center of the triangle, inside the bottom fold.

Fold Fold Fold

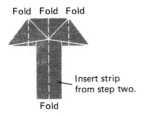

Insert strip from step two.

Fold

9 Refold from Step 6 on, to hold tail in place. Fold the plane up, from tip to tail

10 If you wish, cut or tear the tail to make it look more realistic. You can adjust the glide of your airplane by bending the tips of the tail up or down.

Reading Easy Material

Since it has been a while since we have done an exercise like the ones in Part 2, we will give you a chance to get back to the high rate you developed there.

Read the selection which follows as rapidly as you can while still understanding what you read. Your purpose is to get the author's ideas as quickly as possible.

The material is about ninth grade level.

Remember some of the ideas in Part 2. Sit up straight, with your feet flat on the floor. Put a lot of energy into the process, and read as actively as possible, constantly looking forward to the next idea.

Begin by recording your starting time. When you have finished reading, record your finishing time, then answer the questions. Compute your reading rate from the chart. Then check the answer key at the back of the book and record your reading rate and comprehension scores on the progress chart.

finishing time _____

starting time _____

reading time _____

Women in the Fight for Independence

Lt. Col. Gordon Taylor Bratz

The contributions of women to the American Revolution are not well known or well documented. In fact, historians find it difficult to separate historical fact from traditional legend concerning women's role in the fight for independence. Still, the "Spirit of '76" did capture the hearts of many women.

When the cry of "Revolt" echoed through the colonies in 1775, most women stayed behind to care for children and plow the fields as the men went off to battle.

However, some went to the battlefield to nurse the wounded and cook meals. Others actually went into combat.

Mary "Molly Pitcher" Hays

Mary went with her husband when he joined Procter's Artillery Regiment (Pennsylvania).

Legend has it that she fought at the Battle of Monmouth. Although in the last months of pregnancy, Mary carried water jugs or pitchers to men parched by the heat of the sun and the battle. She became known as "Molly Pitcher." During the battle, she saw that her husband's gun was not firing, so she went to the cannon. She found her husband unconscious from a serious wound. Other men lay about the position wounded or dead.

It's said that the cannon was ordered off the field and would have been had not Molly bravely sprung to action against the enemy. She stayed with the cannon and fired round after round. Legend credits Mary's firing as the turning point of the battle.

Deborah "Robert" Sampson

News of the battles at Lexington and of the shooting at Bunker Hill stirred Deborah's imagination. An orphan who lived in poverty with a kind farmer, she began saving money to buy cloth from which she made a suit of men's clothing.

Dressed as a young man—she was 18 or 19 at the time—and having developed considerable strength by working the farm, she adopted her brother Robert's name and enlisted in 1782.

She bound her breasts tightly to her body. It wasn't necessary to explain the unbearded face when so many soldiers were teenagers.

Legend has it that she volunteered for several hazardous missions. Once, when wounded, she was taken to a hospital. Fearing discovery of her true identity, she left the hospital at night and hid in a nearby cave. There she dug a ball shot out of her leg. After a short time, she limped back to her post.

Later, she and many of her compatriots were seized by "brain fever" and sent to a hospital.

While being examined, the doctor took her pulse by placing his hand on her heart and felt a tightly wrapped bandage. He said nothing but had her moved to his house to give her better care.

While it can't be proven to the satisfaction of historians, legend recounts "Robert" being ordered to carry a letter to Gen. George Washington. After presenting the letter to him, he excused her so he could read in private. Then he called her back in. Without saying a word about her true identity, Washington handed her a discharge from service, gave her some tactful advice and thanked her by giving her enough money to return home.

Margaret "Peggy" Shippen Arnold

Peggy was the beautiful daughter of Pennsylvania's Chief Justice. On April 8, 1779, at the age of 18, she married a 38-year-old widower named Benedict Arnold. Within weeks, the couple began the first negotiations that finally led to an act of treason by her husband.

In June 1780 Arnold learned that he was to become the commandant at West Point, one of the key American defenses of the war. In July, he proposed to British General Sir Henry Clinton to betray this vital American fort to the British.

In September, three patriots captured the courier who passed messages between Arnold and Clinton. In the boots of the man dressed in civilian clothes, who really was Major John Andre, Clinton's adjutant general, was a pass signed by Arnold to permit Andre entrance into West Point.

Andre was hanged as a spy by the Americans; Arnold escaped.

Peggy was fully involved with her husband as a key point of contact between him and Clinton. She coded and decoded messages, and when her husband's treason was discovered, she staged an elaborate hysterical outburst to cover his escape to the British warship, *Vulture*.

After the American victory at Yorktown in October 1781, Peggy and Benedict sailed for England, never to return to the country they betrayed.

"Captain Molly" Corbin

In late fall 1776, the war was not going well for the Americans who occupied Fort Washington on the northern end of Manhattan, where they tried to blockade the Hudson River.

Under attack, the 2,800 soldiers of the garrison found they were no match for the British, Scottish and German regulars who outnumbered them by almost three to one.

During the battle, Molly's husband was killed at the artillery gun which they serviced together. Unafraid, Molly took over the cannon and continued to fire.

But the British pressed the battle and the Americans fell to overwhelming odds. Molly was wounded in her right arm and left side. She survived a bumpy wagon journey to Philadelphia with other wounded soldiers, who were taken prisoner by the British, but she never fully recovered.

Later, after being released, Molly "attached" herself to the Army's Invalid Corps as a camp follower at West Point.

There she received a $30 grant from her home state of Pennsylvania and one half private's pay—$6.33—per month from Congress.

At West Point she called herself "Captain Molly," wore an artillery coat and insisted on being saluted as any other officer. It's reported that the Commandant of West Point denied Molly her portion of rum from her ration because she was a woman, so Molly wrote a complaint to Congress. Not long after she got her rum.

Sybil Ludington

On the evening of April 27, 1777, two years and eight days after the shot heard 'round the world was fired, Sybil volunteered to warn the residents of what is now Putnam County New York of the advance of an estimated 2,000 British Regulars.

Sybil, 16-year-old daughter of a militia captain, mounted one of the family farm horses and rode throughout the night and early morning hours.

Her warnings alerted farmers and militia.

Unlike Paul Revere's ride, which covered some 14 miles and led to his brief arrest by the British, Sybil's similar mission covered nearly 40 miles.

Record your finishing time. Then answer the comprehension questions.

Comprehension Exercise for Unit 26

1 Molly Pitcher's real name was
   a Deborah Sampson
   b Mary Pitcher
   c Molly Corbin
   d Mary Hays

2 Deborah Sampson adopted the name of her
   a Brother
   b Father
   c Husband
   d Boy friend

3 "Robert's" true identity was learned when she was
   a Taken to the hospital after being shot in the leg
   b Captured by the British
   c Taken to the hospital with "brain fever"
   d Shot in the right arm and left side

4 "Robert" was discharged from the army by
   a General Clinton
   b General Washington
   c A doctor
   d Colonel Proctor

5 Margaret Shippen was the wife of
   a Pennsylvania's chief justice
   b General Clinton
   c General Arnold
   d Major Andre

6 Molly Corbin was wounded and captured by the British while trying to keep control of
   a Fort Hudson
   b Fort Manhattan
   c West Point
   d Fort Washington

7 After the war Molly Corbin became a camp follower at
    a Fort Hudson
    b Fort Manhattan
    c West Point
    d Fort Washington

8 Molly wrote a letter to Congress complaining about
    a Her uniform
    b Her pay
    c Her title
    d Her ration of rum

9 Sybil Ludington was the female counterpart of
    a Benedict Arnold
    b George Washington
    c Paul Revere
    d Major Clinton

10 Sybil covered about
    a 50 miles
    b 40 miles
    c 16 miles
    d 14 miles

Check your answers using the key on page 316.
Refer to the chart on the next page to get your reading rate. Then plot your rate and comprehension on the progress chart on page 320.

Time-Rate Table for Unit 26

"WOMEN IN THE FIGHT FOR INDEPENDENCE" (1072 words)

Time in seconds converted to rate in words per minute

Time	Rate		Time	Rate
:20	803		7:00	153
:30	714		:10	149
:40	643		:20	146
:50	584		:30	143
2:00	536		:40	140
:10	494		:50	137
:20	459		8:00	134
:30	428		:10	131
:40	402		:20	129
:50	378		:30	126
3:00	357		:40	124
:10	338		:50	121
:20	321		9:00	119
:30	306		:10	117
:40	292		:20	115
:50	279		:30	113
4:00	268		:40	111
:10	257		:50	109
:20	247		10:00	107
:30	238		:10	105
:40	230		:20	104
:50	222		:30	102
5:00	214		:40	100
:10	207		:50	99
:20	200		11:00	97
:30	195			
:40	189			
:50	184			
6:00	179			
:10	174			
:20	169			
:30	165			
:40	161			
:50	157			

Reading Difficult Textbook Material for Study Purposes

In this unit we get to the type of reading that is typical of the study-type reading. The readability level of the article is at college level. You should read it as though you were studying for a test. The comprehension questions will be like those made up by a college teacher.

Imagine that you are in a science course and are assigned the following reading. It is a brief history of measurement systems.

Before you begin, record your starting time. When you finish reading the selection, record your finishing time, then answer the questions. Check your answers in the answer key at the back of the book.

Remember, this is much more difficult material than in Part 1. Don't try to speed-read or skim it.

finishing time _____

starting time _____

reading time _____

Brief History of Measurement Systems

Weights and measures were among the earliest tools invented by man. Primitive societies needed rudimentary measures for many tasks: constructing dwellings of an appropriate size and shape, fashioning clothing, or bartering food or raw materials.

Man understandably turned first to parts of his body and his natural surroundings for measuring instruments. Early Babylonian and Egyptian records and the Bible indicate that length was first measured with the forearm, hand, or finger and that time was measured by the periods of the sun, moon, and other heavenly bodies. When it was necessary to compare the capacities of containers such as gourds or clay or metal vessels, they were filled with plant seeds which were then counted to measure the volumes. When means for weighing were invented, seeds and stones served as standards. For instance, the "carat," still used as a unit for gems, was derived from the carob seed.

As societies evolved, weights and measures became more complex. The invention of numbering systems and the science of mathematics made it possible to create whole systems of weights and measures suited to trade and commerce, land division, taxation, or scientific research. For these more sophisticated uses it was necessary not only to weigh and measure more complex things—it was also necessary to do it accurately time after time and in different places. However, with limited international exchange of goods and communication of ideas, it is not surprising that different systems for the same purpose developed and became established in different parts of the world—even in different parts of a single continent.

The English System

The measurement system commonly used in the United States today is nearly the same as that brought by the colonists from England. These measures had their origins in a variety of cultures—Babylonian, Egyptian, Roman, Anglo-Saxon, and Norman French. The ancient "digit," "palm," "span," and "cubit" units evolved into the "inch," "foot," and "yard" through a complicated transformation not yet fully understood.

Roman contributions include the use of the number 12 as a base (our foot is divided into 12 inches) and words from which we derive many of our present weights and measures names. For example, the 12 divisions of the Roman "pes," or foot, were called *unciae*. Our words "inch" and "ounce" are both derived from that Latin word.

The "yard" as a measure of length can be traced back to the early Saxon kings. They wore a sash or girdle around the waist—that could be removed and used as a convenient measuring device. Thus the word "yard" comes from the Saxon word "gird" meaning the circumference of a person's waist.

Standardization of the various units and their combinations into a loosely related system of weights and measures sometimes occurred in fascinating ways. Tradition holds that King Henry I decreed that the yard should be the distance from the tip of his nose to the end of his thumb. The length of a furlong (or furrow-long) was established by early Tudor rulers as 220 yards. This led Queen Elizabeth I to declare, in the 16th century, that henceforth the traditional Roman mile of 5,000 feet would be replaced by one of 5,280 feet, making the mile exactly 8 furlongs and providing a convenient relationship between two previously ill-related measures.

Thus, through royal edicts, England by the 18th century had achieved a greater degree of standardization than the continental countries. The English units were well suited to commerce and trade because they had been developed and refined to meet commercial needs. Through colonization and dominance of world commerce during the 17th, 18th, and 19th centuries, the English system of weights and measures was spread to and established in many parts of the world, including the American colonies.

However, standards still differed to an extent undesirable for commerce among the 12 colonies. The need for greater uniformity led to clauses in the Articles of Confederation (ratified by the original colonies in 1781) and the Constitution of the United States (ratified in 1790) giving power to the Congress to fix uniform standards for weights and measures. Today, standards supplied to all the States by the National Bureau of Standards assure uniformity throughout the country.

The Metric System

The need for a single worldwide coordinated measurement system was recognized over 300 years ago. Gabriel Mouton, Vicar of St. Paul in Lyons, proposed in 1670 a comprehensive decimal measurement system based on the length of one minute of arc of a great circle of the earth. In 1671 Jean Picard, a French astronomer, proposed the length of a pendulum beating seconds as the unit of length. (Such a pendulum would have been fairly easily reproducible, thus facilitating the widespread distribution of uniform standards.) Other proposals were made, but over a century elapsed before any action was taken.

In 1790, in the midst of the French Revolution, the National Assembly of France requested the French Academy of Sciences to "deduce an invariable standard for all measures and all the weights." The Commission appointed by the Academy created a system that was, at once, simple and scientific. The unit of length was to be a portion of the earth's circumference. Measures for capacity (volume) and mass (weight) were to be derived from the unit of length, thus relating the basic units of the system to each other and to nature. Furthermore, the larger and smaller versions of each unit were to be created by multiplying or dividing the basic units by 10 and its multiples. This feature provided a great convenience to users of the system, by eliminating the need for such calculations as dividing by 16 (to convert ounces to pounds) or by 12 (to convert inches to feet). Similar calculations in the metric system could be performed simply by shifting the decimal point. Thus the metric system is a "base-10" or "decimal" system.

The Commission assigned the name *metre* (which we now spell meter) to the unit of length. This name was derived from the Greek word *metron,* meaning "a measure." The physical standard representing the meter was to be constructed so that it would equal one ten-millionth of the distance from the north pole to the equator along the meridian of the earth running near Dunkirk in France and Barcelona in Spain.

The metric unit of mass, called the "gram," was defined as the mass of one cubic centimeter (a cube that is 1/100 of a meter on each side) of water at its temperature of maximum density. The cubic decimeter (a cube 1/10 of a meter on each side) was chosen as the unit of fluid capacity. This measure was given the name "liter."

Although the metric system was not accepted with enthusiasm at first, adoption by other nations occurred steadily after France made its use compulsory in 1840. The standardized character and decimal features of the metric system made it well suited to scientific and engineering work. Consequently, it is not surprising that the rapid spread of the system coincided with an age of rapid technological development. In the United States, by Act of Congress in 1866, it was made "lawful throughout the United States of America to employ the weights and measures of the metric system in all contracts, dealings or court proceedings."

By the late 1860's even better metric standards were needed to keep pace with scientific advances. In 1875, an international treaty, the "Treaty of the Meter," set up well-defined metric standards for length and mass, and established permanent machinery to recommend and adopt further refinements in the metric system. This treaty, known as the Metric Convention, was signed by 17 countries, including the United States.

As a result of the Treaty, metric standards were constructed and distributed to each nation that ratified the Convention. Since 1893, the internationally agreed-to metric standards have served as the fundamental weights and measures standards of the United States.

By 1900 a total of 35 nations—including the major nations of continental Europe and most of South America—had officially accepted the metric system. Today, with the exception of the United States and a few small countries, the entire world is using predominantly the metric system or is committed to such use. In 1971 the Secretary of Commerce, in transmitting to Congress the results of a 3-year study authorized by the Metric Study Act of 1968, recommended that the U.S. change to predominant use of the metric system through a coordinated national program. The Congress is now considering this recommendation.

The International Bureau of Weights and Measures located at Sevres, France, serves as a permanent secretariat for the Metric Convention, coordinating the exchange of information about the use and refinement of the metric system. As measurement science develops more precise and easily reproducible ways of defining the measurement units, the General Conference of Weights and Measures—the diplomatic organization made up of adherents to the Convention—meets periodically to ratify improvements in the system and the standards.

In 1960, the General Conference adopted an extensive revision and simplification of the system. The name *Le Système International d'Unités* (International System of Units), with the international abbreviation SI, was adopted for this modernized metric system. Further improvements in and additions to SI were made by the General Conference in 1964, 1968, and 1971.

Record your finishing time. Then answer the comprehension questions.

Comprehension Exercise for Unit 27

1 Humanity's first measuring tools were
   a Sticks
   b Pieces of rope or vines
   c Parts of the body
   d Pebbles

2 Our words "inch" and "ounce" are both derived from the Latin word
   a Cubit
   b Pes
   c Unciae
   d Digit

3 The measurement for a yard dates back to Saxon times and was
  a The distance from the tip of the nose to the end of the thumb
  b The length of 8 furlongs
  c The circumference of a person's waist
  d The length of a furlong

4 The metric system developed by the French Academy of Sciences was based on a _____ system.
  a 10-unit
  b 12-unit
  c 16-unit
  d 10-, 12-, and 16-unit

5 The Commission designed the word "metre" or meter as the unit for
  a Volume measurement
  b The measurement of mass
  c The measurement of temperature
  d The measurement of length

6 The length of the meter was designed to be one ten-millionth of the distance from
  a The equator to Dunkirk, France
  b Dunkirk, France, to Barcelona, Spain
  c The equator to Dunkirk, France, and Barcelona, Spain, along the meridian of the earth
  d The north pole to the equator

7 The metric unit of mass, or gram, is defined as the mass of a cube that is
  a 1 meter on each side
  b 1/10 of a meter on each side
  c 1/100 of a meter on each side
  d 1/1000 of a meter on each side

8 The metric unit of fluid capacity is defined as a cube that is
  a 1 meter on each side
  b 1/10 of a meter on each side
  c 1/100 of a meter on each side
  d 1/1000 of a meter on each side

9 France made the metric system compulsory in
  a 1670
  b 1671
  c 1790
  d 1840

10 The use of the metric system in the United States was first recognized in
  a 1960 when the General Conference adopted a revision of the system and the name International System of Units

b   1968 when the Metric Study Act recommended that the United States change to a metric system
c   1866 when the United States made it lawful by Act of Congress to use the metric system in all contracts and court dealings
d   1875 when the United States signed the Treaty of the Meter along with seventeen other countries

Check your answers using the key on page 316.
Refer to the chart on the next page to get your reading rate. Then plot your rate and comprehension on the progress chart on page 320.

Time-Rate Table for Unit 27

"BRIEF HISTORY OF MEASUREMENT SYSTEMS" (1562 words)

Time in seconds converted to rate in words per minute

Time	Rate	Time	Rate
1:40	937	9:00	173
:50	851	:10	170
2:00	781	:20	167
:10	720	:30	164
:20	669	:40	161
:30	624	:50	159
:40	585	10:00	156
:50	551	:10	154
3:00	520	:20	151
:10	493	:30	149
:20	468	:40	146
:30	446	:50	144
:40	426	11:00	142
:50	407	:10	140
4:00	390	:20	138
:10	375	:30	136
:20	360	:40	134
:30	347	:50	132
:40	334	12:00	130
:50	323	:10	128
5:00	312	:20	127
:10	302	:30	125
:20	293	:40	123
:30	284	:50	122
:40	275	13:00	120
:50	268	:10	119
6:00	260	:20	117
:10	253	:30	116
:20	246	:40	114
:30	240	:50	113
:40	234	14:00	112
:50	228	:10	110
7:00	223	:20	109
:10	218	:30	108
:20	213	:40	106
:30	208	:50	105
:40	203	15:00	104
:50	199	:10	103
8:00	195	:20	102
:10	191	:30	101
:20	187	:40	100
:30	184	:50	99
:40	180	16:00	98
:50	177		

Scanning for Facts

In this unit, we get back to very high speed coverage of material. The idea is to scan the article, seeking particular factual information. *Do not read all of the article.*

Begin by reading the questions. Then scan rapidly to find the answers. The material is of moderate difficulty (about eleventh grade). You are not going to read it, however. You are only going to scan it.

Before you begin, record your starting time. Then read the questions before you scan to find the answers. You should be able to complete this unit in less than ten minutes if you work at it rapidly. We will not be calculating a reading rate on this unit, since you are scanning, not reading.

finishing time _____

starting time _____

scanning time _____

Scanning Exercise for Unit 28

1 Whales migrate to _____ to breed and give birth.
   a Baja, California
   b Monterey, California
   c Mexico City
   d Cape Sarichef, Alaska

2 Laguna Ojo de Liebre was first discovered by whaling captain Charles Scammon in
   a   1857
   b   1860
   c   1936
   d   1947

3 During the early 1900s the gray whale population was at a low point with only about _____ whales left.
   a   15,000
   b   4000
   c   1300
   d   16,000

4 Each year 179 gray whales are allowed to be caught for the use of _____.
   a   American fishermen
   b   Soviet fishermen
   c   International Whaling Commission
   d   American and Soviet Eskimos

5 There are two NOAA counting stations in the United States; one of them is located at _____.
   a   Baja, California
   b   Scammon's Lagoon
   c   Cape Sarichef, Alaska
   d   San Ignacio Lagoon

6 It is difficult to mark whales for study because
   a   They are too big to tranquilize so tags can be put on
   b   They are too dangerous to get close to
   c   Dyes and paints that can safely be used on animals wash off after being in water for long periods of time
   d   The water friction and the whales' muscles work to dislodge anything that becomes embedded below the layer of protective fat.

7 Color-coded nylon streamers were attached to the whale by means of a
   a   Harpoon
   b   Dart shot from a gun
   c   Arrow shot from a crossbow
   d   None of the above

8 After marking, one whale was sighted a month later _____ miles from where it had been tagged.
   a   55
   b   18
   c   150
   d   375

9 One whale was nicknamed
- **a** Big Mama
- **b** Hunchback
- **c** Flipper
- **d** Leviathan

10 What kind of whales were being studied?
- **a** Predator whales
- **b** Killer whales
- **c** Great white whales
- **d** Gray whales

Check the key on page 316. Do *not* record your results on the progress chart.

Leviathans in Scammon's Lagoon

David Withrow

The deep, resonating blows of the California gray whale played obligato to coyote barks and bird chatter. When we awakened, it was 6 a.m., time to dress, gulp a coffee, and climb 20 feet up the observation tower for the morning's first whale watch.

Pregnant gray whales were beginning to arrive in the waters of Baja California, Mexico, where they would deliver and tend their calves. It was early January. By mid-March, most of the cows, calves in tow, would have left for their arctic feeding grounds.

Our research centered around Scammon's Lagoon (Laguna Ojo de Liebre), the largest of the California gray whale's three major breeding and calving areas. The five-year study, now entering its third year, is sponsored by NOAA (National Marine Fisheries Service, National Marine Mammal

Laboratory, Seattle) and PESCA, the Mexican Department of Fisheries. Our research team at last January's field season consisted of five U.S. biologists from NOAA-NML, three Mexican biologists from PESCA, and one Mexican graduate student from the University of Washington.

We are collecting baseline information on habitat usage by gray whales in an area where there is still only minimal human disturbance. We are monitoring whale numbers, movement, and behavior and looking for harassment and other factors that could affect the ecology of the species. Ultimately, we will make recommendations to protect this endangered leviathan.

Each year, gray whales migrate nearly 10,000 miles, from the cold arctic feeding grounds where they spend the summer to the warm quiet waters of Baja California. Here, they breed, give birth, and nurse their young, undisturbed by predators. However, it wasn't always this way. In 1857-58, whaling captain Charles Scammon discovered the entrance to Laguna Ojo de Liebre. Hundreds of whales, including calves, became easy prey for whalers' harpoons and bomblances in this and other secluded bays of Baja California. So many whales were killed so quickly that by 1860-61, less than 4 years after it had begun, whaling in Scammon's Lagoon was considered unprofitable.

Gray whales are thought to have once numbered about 15,000, before Scammon's find. During the early 1900's, the low point, there were probably only 4,000 whales. Today, Scammon's Lagoon is a unique environment, with a denser whale concentration than anywhere else in the world; in just one day's boat survey, we counted over 1,300 of them.

The gray whales were first protected under a 1936 convention, and in 1947, the International Whaling Commission (IWC) prohibited commercial taking of them. Today the gray whale population may have returned to its pre-exploitation level. Gray whales are classified as a sustained management stock by the IWC, and the annual catch limit of 179 is reserved solely for the subsistence use of American and Soviet Eskimos.

Two NOAA-NMML gray whale counting stations—one at Monterey, Calif., which has made 13 annual counts, and the other at Cape Sarichef, Alaska, which has made 2 counts—working independently, in 1979 estimated the gray whale population at 16,000, give or take 3,000 animals.

Though apparently doing well, gray whales may be highly vulnerable to many environmental changes brought about by population growth and industrialization. Two major concerns are the possible impact of oil leases along the migration route and increasing harassment by tourists.

Scammon's Lagoon, the largest and most heavily populated of the three major calving areas, was declared a Mexican National Wildlife Refuge in 1972, protecting the gray whale and limiting tourist vessel traffic. The other two, San Ignacio Lagoon and Magdalena Bay, are located 150 miles and 375 miles south, respectively. Scammon's Lagoon contains many shallow, twisting channels separated by broad tidal flats. These channels, extending over

30 miles into the arid Vizcaino Desert offer protection from the region's heavy winds. The 225-square-mile surface area of Scammon's Lagoon is almost halved at low tide. We had to plan all activities with the 4- to 6-foot tidal difference in mind. By finding ourselves high and dry, we learned to anchor out near the edge of the sand bar when we wanted to use a boat at low tide.

Our camp was situated near the north central portion of the lagoon, 25 miles from the small company town of Guerrero Negro. The town is the home of Exportadora de Sal, the world's largest salt company, evaporating and processing nearly 7 million metric tons of salt a year. We made weekly trips to town to shower, purchase gas and water, and check the post and telegraph offices for news and mail from the northland. Our hour-and-a-quarter trip over a pot-hole riddled trail was rewarded with a shower at the public bath and a meal of fish tacos from our favorite street vendors.

Our work schedule ran in 6-day cycles. Each week, 2 consecutive days were allotted to counting whales from the tower, 2 days to boat surveys throughout the lagoon, and 2 days for miscellaneous experiments and a bad weather allowance. Among the miscellaneous projects were charting the lagoon, taking depth recordings, measuring dead or stranded animals, and conducting necropsies on all fresh specimens.

Numerous photographs were taken for an identification catalog of individual whales to spot their movements between and within lagoons. Researchers in other areas are contributing photographs for this catalog.

Fixed-wing aircraft were used to census whales inside the lagoons and alont the coast of Baja between lagoons. Experiments were conducted to compare the relative accuracy of land, boat, and aerial counts.

To find out whether gray whales stay in the same place within the lagoon, move from area to area in recognizable patterns, or move about randomly, we mark animals. Marking is especially difficult in whales. Built to move smoothly and fast through deep water, the whale's muscles and water friction work together to dislodge anything that becomes embedded below layers of protective fat. For this reason, and because whales are extremely sensitive to tranquillizers used to immobilize other mammals for implants, widespread use of telemetry monitors has proven impractical for anything but friendly whales.

Last season we marked 29 adult whales in an exploratory study to develop a technique for implanting external streamer tags and to see how long the tags would remain implanted. Our streamers were made of color-coded nylon 4.5 inches wide by 3 feet long. There were rolled into a hollow shafted arrow and implanted by means of an 80 pound crossbow. The stainless steel leader and anchor tip were sprayed with a disinfectant and penetrated only the blubber layer, about 1.5 to 2 inches deep.

Most animals reacted to tagging with nothing more than a flinch, much like adults receiving an injection, and no difference in their behavior was noticed afterwards. We hoped the tag would stay put for a month. Due to a heavy storm, we managed to resight only four tagged whales from the observation tower. The longest interval between tagging and resighting was 18 days. One marked animal was reported by fishermen a month later in Laguna Manuela, about 55 miles north of the tagging site.

Tagging was not attempted this year, due in part to a scheduling change, weather, and the late arrival of the whales. However, we were able to obtain some valuable information on movement, time of calving, and date of departure from one conspicuously marked whale. This animal, nicknamed "hunchback" of Scammon's Lagoon could easily be distinguished from all other whales by her greatly enlarged first dorsal hump. From seven resightings, we know that she calved between January 26, 1980 and February 6, and that she probably left the lagoon on her migration north on February 25.

This study is invaluable for our understanding of the gray whale. In addition, knowledge of its biology and behavior and improvements in our sampling techniques may find applications in the conservation of other endangered whale species.

Reading Moderately Difficult Material Rapidly

The material in this unit is at about twelfth-grade to college level. However, it is written in an easy-to-read style and has a very interesting content. Try to read it much as you would if it were a lot easier.

If you can read this selection at a rapid rate and with reasonably good comprehension, you will know that your work on reading rate has paid off. This is the last exercise in this book in which you will be getting a reading rate and comprehension score. Try to end up with a good record of improvement.

Begin by recording your starting time. Then when you finish reading, record your finishing time, and answer the questions. Check the answer key at the back of the book, and record your rate and comprehension results on the progress chart.

finishing time _____

starting time _____

reading time _____

Women and the Winning of the West

Stuart Diamond

The popular version of the lone wagon train, forging its way west, in constant danger of losing the faintly marked trail, its occupants trembling in fear of imminent Indian massacre, is just a Hollywood concoction, says historian Sandra Myres, who has been researching the role of women in settling the American west. She has unearthed vivid accounts of the trail west and of homesteading at the journey's end. The journals, diaries and letters she has read help dispel some long-cherished myths about the American frontier.

Forget the image of the lone wagon train silhouetted against the horizon. The fact was that after the California Gold Rush in 1849, isolated travel was not even a possibility. "You couldn't get lost if you wanted to, because you couldn't get out of sight of another wagon train," explains Myres, professor of history at the University of Texas at Arlington.

"The country was so level that we could see the long trains of white-topped wagons for many miles," observed a pioneer woman, Margaret Frink. "It appeared to me that none of the population had been left behind," she wrote in her *Journal of the Adventures of a Party of California Gold Seekers,* published in 1897:

> It seemed to me that I have never seen so many human beings in all my life before. And, when we drew nearer to the vast multitude, and saw them in all manner of vehicles and conveyances, on horseback and on foot... I thought, in my excitement, if one-tenth of these teams and these people get ahead of us, there would be nothing left for us in California worth picking up.

Another favorite Hollywood image—the wagon train forming a circle at dusk—bears little resemblance to reality. The wagons might have made a circle, but if so it was to enclose livestock which might otherwise wander off and become fair game for rustlers. So the protective stockade of wagons was for the benefit of cows, horses and pigs. Men, women and children naturally preferred to sleep in tents well outside the circle.

In the movies, we know the Indians are going to descend on the settlers as soon as the sun goes down. Hollywood was only preserving misconceptions of the American Indian that had long flourished in popular literature and imagination. The 19th-century pioneers themselves were steeped in simplistic views—many of which still persist today. Nineteenth-century fiction depicted either the good Indian—the noble savage of James Fenimore Cooper's *The Leatherstocking Tales*—or the bad Indian. In Robert Bird's *Neck of the Woods,* for instance, Indians are bloodthirsty and treacherous; the heroic settlers ultimately vanquish them.

Settlers on their way west, however, were more likely to meet Indians who descended on the wagons in order to exploit the possibilities for trade the transcontinental travelers offered. Pioneer women found the Indians extremely helpful in identifying and preparing indigenous food and herbs. "You can't find an Indian attack for anything," says Myres ruefully after reading more than 500 women's journals.

Marauding Indians did occasionally harass the rare party of isolated travelers, but whites and Indians generally regarded each other with a curiosity tinged with mutual apprehension. Pioneer women were keen observers of Indian customs and ceremonies, often recording them in minute detail, very much as a modern anthropologist would. Indian women too were watching their counterparts; some of these accounts have also been preserved in English transcriptions made by interpreters, at times via sign language.

"The 19th century tended to be an age of journals, thank God," says Myres. The virtues of keeping a journal were instilled in young women by their teachers and the flood of ladies' magazines that kept them up-to-date on the latest eastern styles. It was one's duty to keep up a journal which could be read by friends and relations back home who might never be seen again.

Journals were a popular literary genre. Many of the diaries and journals Myres has seen are conscious "literary" efforts, written for a family audience and with an eye to eventual publication.

Women responded to the frontier in many ways. Some shrank from the rigors of the migration west and never adjusted to the upheaval in their lives. Once settled, these women were quick to reaffirm traditional female values and roles. But the adventuresome found that the frontier also offered new roles and new opportunities for women.

The Western territories, eager to attract hard working women to their embryonic settlements, granted them economic rights far more extensive than those women had known in the east and south. In the Oregon territory women were allowed to homestead in their own names and the practice spread rapidly across the west. A woman's right to own property was unequivocal. Women generally had equal, and sometimes slightly preferential, access to credit. In many western communities it was not unusual for women property holders to control a significant proportion of the wealth.

Within a few decades of the settling of the territories an entrepreneurial class of women appeared.

In examining the role of women in the economic life of the west, Myres was directed to a major lode of source material at the Baker Library of the Harvard School of Business: the records of R. G. Dunn & Co., forerunners of Dunn & Bradstreet. The company's agents across the country did more than collect financial data for credit reports; they sent back fascinating snippets of gossip as well. A typical item reveals the "well-known fact in the community that the wife wears the unmentionables in the family and runs the business." The Dunn records constitute "a major source of socio-economic information about 19th century America," according to Myres.

Myres believes that the scope of economic opportunity open to women on the western frontier led in turn to demands for social and political power to match. She points out that eastern and southern women who wielded economic power "tended to use that power silently and through intermediaries throughout the 19th century. Was it the frontier that made the difference?" Myres isn't sure yet, but hopes to have some answers at the conclusion of her research.

Record your finishing time. Then answer the comprehension questions.

Comprehension Exercise for Unit 29

1 The author claims that the popular version of the wagon train is
   a A Hollywood myth
   b Quite accurate in most details
   c Quite accurate in regard to the Indians
   d Useful for creating heroes

2 After the California gold rush in 1849, it was impossible to travel
   a By wagon
   b By stagecoach
   c By train
   d Alone

3 One pioneer woman wrote in her journal that she was afraid
   a That by the time they got to California all the good land would be gone
   b That they would be attacked by Indians
   c They would lose the trail leading west
   d They would run out of supplies before they got to California

4 Myres says that some wagons may have formed circles at night to
   a Have a type of barricade against Indians
   b Block some of the prairie winds

    c Keep livestock contained and safe from wild animals and rustlers
    d Help have a sense of community

5 The author claims that after reading more than 500 women's journals, she found
    a Many Indian attacks
    b Only a few Indian problems
    c No Indian attacks
    d Only helpful Indians

6 According to Myres, Indians often went after the wagon trains
    a To steal things
    b To trade with the settlers
    c To swap stories
    d To try to kill the settlers before they took too much land

7 The nineteenth century tended to be an age of
    a Enlightenment
    b Literature
    c Journals
    d Homesteaders

8 Women were often granted more rights in the west than in the south or east. In _____ territory women were allowed to file homesteads in their own names.
    a Nebraska
    b Utah
    c California
    d Oregon

9 Women were often granted access to _____.
    a The polls
    b Credit
    c Bank accounts
    d Saloons

10 Myres feels that these rights led the way to demands for
    a Job opportunities
    b Equal rights
    c Higher education
    d Social and political power

Check your answers using the key on page 316.
Refer to the chart on the next page to get your reading rate. Then plot your rate and comprehension on the progress chart on page 320.

Time-Rate Table for Unit 29

"WOMEN AND THE WINNING OF THE WEST" (1033 words)

Time in seconds converted to rate in words per minute

Time	Rate	Time	Rate
:30	2066	6:00	172
:40	1549	:10	167
:50	1239	:20	163
1:00	1033	:30	159
:10	885	:40	155
:20	775	:50	151
:30	688	7:00	148
:40	620	:10	144
:50	563	:20	141
2:00	517	:30	138
:10	477	:40	135
:20	443	:50	132
:30	413	8:00	129
:40	387	:10	126
:50	365	:20	124
3:00	344	:30	122
:10	326	:40	119
:20	310	:50	117
:30	295	9:00	115
:40	282	:10	113
:50	269	:20	111
4:00	258	:30	109
:10	248	:40	107
:20	238	:50	105
:30	230	10:00	103
:40	221	:10	102
:50	214	:20	100
5:00	207	:30	98
:10	200	:40	97
:20	194	:50	95
:30	188		
:40	182		
:50	177		

READING COMPREHENSION

Introduction

In the first half of this book you focused on the need to cover reading material rapidly and efficiently. You did not work directly on comprehension skills, even though some of the exercises included information about comprehension.

In Part Four all of the units are designed to improve comprehension. You will be doing exercises to improve such skills as reading for the main idea, reading for details, reading to discover organization, using reference materials, critical reading, and special reading skills for various academic content areas.

In Part One we gave some information about various comprehension skills in the introductions to the rate-building exercises. However, we did not provide practice on those skills. In Part Four we will do that.

You may remember than in Unit 8 we gave a brief introduction to the idea of levels of comprehension. We will now go back to that idea and give a bit more information about it before you go into the next section.

Levels of Comprehension

The amount of information gained in reading will vary greatly depending on several factors. One is the reason for reading. If you only want to find a particular fact, such as a date, name, or place, it would be silly to begin at the opening of a book and study the whole thing carefully. On the other hand, if you want to have a very complete understanding of a topic, you will not get it by skimming over the book quickly and superficially.

For most reading purposes your best approach will be somewhere between a quick skimming and a total, all-out effort to completely master the material. That means that you have to decide in each case how slowly and carefully to read. We usually do so without thinking about the process of deciding on an approach. For example, think about how you approach the telephone book. You don't usually spend time deciding whether to skim, scan, read, or study it. You go ahead and scan it, looking for the one number you want. However, if you didn't already know how the telephone book was organized you would have to pay some attention to how to find what you wanted. In many cases when you begin looking at a new book, you do need to spend a moment examining it and deciding how to proceed.

It may help to understand the comprehension process if you look at it the way many experts in reading do. They often talk about three levels of comprehension. Each level involves more of an active role on the part of the reader.

1 *Literal comprehension.* This level of comprehension represents the minimum of involvement on the part of the reader. It is the simple understanding of the words and ideas of the author. The author's message is received but not examined, evaluated, or utilized in any way.

2 *Interpretive comprehension.* At this level the reader not only knows what the author said but goes beyond that simple knowledge. It involves an effort to grasp relationships, compare facts with personal experiences, understand sequences, see cause-and-effect relationships, and generally interpret the message. It requires a more active participation on the part of the reader.

3 *Applied comprehension.* At this level the reader does more than merely receiving and interpreting the message. The reader evaluates the author's ideas, either accepting or rejecting them or applying them to some new situation. In some cases the author's message is designed to produce some application. For example, the author may be giving instructions for some activity, such as the assembly of a toy or use of a tool. The author's message is received, understood, and utilized in some way, mentally or physically.

Generally the emphasis at this level of comprehension is on actively bringing the reader's general understanding to bear on the ideas and concepts contained in the reading passage. This synthesis is necessary for higher comprehension, especially on difficult material.

Reading for Main Ideas

Skilled authors usually try to organize their material around a particular point or "main idea." Many readers—even some very good readers—have difficulty in picking out the main idea of a reading selection. We have all overheard conversations in which two people are arguing and both seem to be missing the point the other is trying to make. Missing the point of a reading passage is very much like this, except that the author is not there to straighten you out.

It is extremely important to be able to recognize main ideas. Every time you read a letter to the editor of your newspaper, receive a notice from a utility company, answer an essay test question, get a letter from the government, or read anything of importance to you, you *must* understand the main idea before you can proceed. In much modern writing, the main idea is not as clear as it might be and it takes skill and practice to recognize it. Consider, as an example, the following note from a utility company:

Metro Electric Company
Box 72
North Branch, Iowa

Dear Customer:

We have been pleased to provide you with service for some time now. It has been our policy to allow a significant grace period for unpaid debts and payments. Owing to inflationary setbacks and shortfalls in our projected real income we have been forced to modify this policy. You fall into the category of customers who are immediately affected by this policy change. This is to notify you that unless the unpaid balance of your bill is remitted to us by June 15 your electric service will be terminated. We regret that we are forced to take these measures and hope you will be able to comply. If you have already mailed your payment please disregard this notice.

Sincerely,

S. A. Adams
Service Manager

Although the main idea of the above letter is somewhat hard to discover, its message is fairly simple: "Pay what you owe by June 15 or have your electricity shut off!" Obviously, if you thought that this letter was about what a good customer you were or the effects of inflation on utility companies, you might be heading for an unpleasant surprise.

We have broken the task of identifying main ideas into four basic subskills: (1) recognizing topic nouns, (2) distinguishing topic sentences, (3) recognizing main idea, and (4) avoiding irrelevant ideas. The following exercises are designed to teach you these subskills and thereby increase your ability to recognize main ideas. When you have completed the exercises, check your answers in the back of the book.

Comprehension Exercises for Unit 31

Exercise 1: Recognizing Topic Nouns

For most passages, the first step in getting the main idea is to determine what single word best describes the person, place, or thing that is central to the author's point. This single word (occasionally it will be a phrase) is called the topic noun. If a paragraph is about horses, for example, the topic noun is "horses." In the following exercise choose the topic noun for each paragraph.

1 Rocks found on the surface of the earth are divided into three classes: igneous, sedimentary, and metamorphic. Molten material becomes igneous rock when it cools. Sedimentary rocks are formed from materials deposited by glaciers, plants, animals, streams, or winds. Metamorphic rocks are rocks that once were igneous or sedimentary but have changed as a result of pressure, heat, or the deposit of material from solution.

Topic noun _____

2   Heiroglyphic writing was extremely difficult to read and write, even during the period when it was in common use. Trained professionals, known as scribes, were employed to do all the writing and reading of heiroglyphics.

Topic noun _____

3   At the beginning of the Expressionist movement, we see the work of Van Gogh. Not at all concerned with producing a copy of what he painted, he used color and form to express his feelings about his subject. He also used broad brushes and palette knives and sometimes squeezed paint directly from the tube in his haste to get his feelings onto the canvas.

Topic noun _____

4   Water is fairly inexpensive and easy to obtain. This makes it a good tool for use in fighting many kinds of fires. Its properties as an extinguishing agent should be studied well.

Topic noun _____

5   The kind of alcohol present in drinks (ethyl alcohol) is a strong depressant drug. Its action is very similar to barbiturates and other depressant drugs. Because it is sold legally as a beverage many people forget that it is a drug. In our society, people are conditioned to fear "hard drugs" such as heroin and opium. At the same time they think of drinking alcohol as a socially acceptable thing to do.

Topic noun _____

6   This jacket has a heavy, water-repellent outer shell with a draw cord at the waist. Attached hood also has a draw cord and can be hidden in the zipper pouch in collar. The heavy-duty front zipper has a protective storm flap. Comes in green, brown, or blue.

Topic noun _____

7   Parole is an arrangement that allows for the early release of a person convicted of a criminal offense. Following this release the person must obey certain rules and regulations and remain under the supervision of a parole agent.

Topic noun _____

8 Car cards are the advertising messages one sees in the overhead tracks in buses, subways, streetcars, and trains. The size of these cards has been standardized at a height of 11 inches and a width of 28 to 56 inches.

Topic noun _____

9 Like lamb, pork usually comes from young animals and is therefore less variable in quality than beef. U.S. Department of Agriculture grades for pork reflect only two levels of quality: acceptable and unacceptable.

Topic noun _____

10 The major support system for the upper body is the spine. The spine is a stack of blocks. Between the blocks are cushions of cartilage known as discs. The spine was never designed to support the weight of an upright human body standing on two feet. The spine is designed for people who walk on all fours. It was meant to be a suspension bridge rather than a supporting column.

Topic noun _____

Exercise 2: Distinguishing Topic Sentences

The topic sentence of a paragraph is the sentence that best expresses the main idea that the author is trying to get across. Often the topic sentence will be the first sentence of the paragraph, although it occasionally comes later and may even be the last sentence of the paragraph.

In the following exercise underline the topic sentence.

1 The vampire is probably the most frightening of the legendary monsters. Vampires are believed to turn into bats at will and suck the blood of living victims, usually causing their deaths. They cast no reflection in mirrors and cannot cross water. They are repelled by holy objects, and it is said that the only way to kill a vampire is by driving a stake through its heart.

2 In the early days of big-city post offices, a great deal of time was spent in getting mail from the main station to the substations and from stations to trains. Then compressed air came into use as a means of speeding up the movement of mail from place to place. Long tubes were built under the ground to connect different mail-handling sites, and hollow containers were made to fit the tubes. Mail was put into the containers, the containers were put into the tubes, and compressed air was used to propel the containers to their destinations. Some cities still have many miles of mail tubes. Smaller tubes are used in many libraries, stores, and factories.

3 The risk of premature death from all causes is much greater among ciga-rette smokers than among nonsmokers. This alone should be a good reason

to quit smoking. The risk of premature death from coronary artery disease is 1.7 times greater among smokers. The risk of death from bronchitis and emphysema is 6 times greater among smokers. The risk of premature death from lung cancer is 10 times greater among smokers. It is clear that smoking affects not only your day-to-day health but your life span as well.

4   Today's marketplace is crowded with sellers competing for your money and your attention by offering different services, prices, specials, bonuses, and quality of goods. There are so many kinds of stores and deals that it is hard to keep them straight. To get the best bargain you need to carefully weigh the advantages and disadvantages of each deal before making your final selection.

5   The class of drugs know as depressants act to slow down the functioning of the central nervous system. They relax the body and are often used to induce sleep or alleviate pain. When too large a dose is taken, depressant drugs induce a state of drunken intoxication and produce slurred speech, blurred vision, slowed reaction time, and loss of coordination. The depressant drugs are highly addictive and include alcohol, opiates, barbiturates, and minor tranquilizers.

6   Poultry, ground meat, and seafood become unsafe to eat when they start to spoil. The bacteria present in these foods multiply rapidly. When these foods have thawed completely, they should not be refrozen. If the food still has ice crystals in it you may refreeze it immediately. Usually this is safe, although it may reduce the quality of the food. If the food is completely thawed and its condition appears poor or questionable, get rid of it. It might be dangerous.

7   If your car is stopped in a blizzard, by all means stay in it. Trying to walk outside in a blizzard can be extremely dangerous. In blowing and drifting snow, disorientation comes very rapidly. Being lost in open country during a blizzard can be fatal. If you stay in your car you are most likely to be found, and the car will provide a great deal of protection from the elements.

8   Poison oak and poison ivy can usually be destroyed with herbicides with little or no danger. Typically, one stands at a distance from the plants and sprays the herbicide, preferably with the wind at one's back. Most herbicides can be sprayed using equipment with nozzles on extensions of 2 feet or more. The primary danger of poisoning comes from careless handling of clothing and equipment after the work is finished.

9   A sensitive and observing parent will find countless opportunities during the day to make such comments as, "Thank you for coming in for dinner without being called"; "I know you're in a hurry and I appreciate how you took time to put your toys away"; "You were really good while I was on the phone"; "I'm glad you shared with your little brother." Taking this approach allows you to "catch" your child being good. Encouraging good behavior is always more rewarding for everyone involved than punishing bad behavior.

10   Most of today's magazines contain advertising for vitamin and mineral supplements. It is hard to get through a day without hearing or participating in a conversation where vitamins and minerals are a major topic. Today's consumers are more aware of the need for vitamins and minerals in the human body than any previous generation. The increasing sales of vitamin-mineral supplements attest to this awareness.

Exercise 3: Recognizing the Main Idea
There are two mistakes that readers commonly make in identifying the main idea of a reading passage. One is to pick out a small part of the topic and assume it is the main idea; a main idea identified in this way is too specific. The other common mistake is to state a main idea that is too general and covers more than the author intended.

In the following exercise read the passages and then decide whether each of the sentences following it is too specific, too general, or the main idea. (There may not be one of each.)

1   Nitrogen is sometimes called a "lazy" gas. There are not any very interesting simple experiments that can be done with it. It is, however, important to us. We are not built to survive in pure oxygen. The nitrogen in the atmosphere weakens or dilutes the oxygen so that the air is right for us. The nitrogen serves the same purpose in the air that water serves in lemonade. Lemonade made of pure lemon juice and sugar would be too strong. To make lemonade right for us, we add water.

   a   Nitrogen is important because it dilutes oxygen so that the air is right for us.

   _____

   b   Lemonade without water would not be very good. _____

   c   Nitrogen is very important to us. _____

2   Handling children's anger can be very distressing to adults. Often the distress is the result of being unable to deal with our own anger. Parents, teachers, counselors, and others who deal with children need to remember that they may not be very good at dealing with their own anger. As children many of us were taught that anger was bad and were made to feel guilty for expressing anger.

   a   Children can be very hard for adults to deal with. _____

   b   Our own anger can make it hard to deal with children's anger.

   _____

   c   Children sometimes make us angry. _____

d Teachers must learn to handle their own anger in order to learn how to deal with children's anger. _____

3 Lead, cadmium, and mercury are elements that have been found to be harmful to humans. They seem to be completely unnecessary to health. Cadmium, for example, interferes with the functions of iron, copper, and calcium, which are necessary for health. People exposed to large amounts of cadmium may suffer anemia, kidney damage, and bone deficiencies.

a Cadmium is harmful to humans. _____

b Lead, cadmium, and mercury are harmful to humans and are unnecessary for health. _____

c Lead is harmful to humans and has no beneficial properties.

_____

d Some minerals are harmful to human health. _____

4 With Lake Mead as its reservoir, Hoover Dam has proved very effective in the control of flooding. The dam controls not only the lesser flash floods that come anytime there is heavy rain but also the great flood-tide runoff that occurs each spring and summer.

a Hoover Dam has many benefits. _____

b Hoover Dam helps control spring flooding. _____

c Hoover Dam helps control flash floods. _____

5 One cheap and effective way of advertising your home is to place a sign in your front yard. The sign should be placed so that it can be seen easily from the street. The lettering should be large enough so it can be read easily. It is especially important that the telephone numbers are bright and easy to read. Block out your spacing before you start so your sign looks well balanced. A well-made lawn sign should put you in contact with many prospective customers.

a When selling your home it is important to advertise. _____

b A well-made lawn sign can help you sell your house. _____

c Selling your home can be a lot of work. _____

d The letters on your lawn sign should be easy to read from the street.

_____

6 Varicose veins can be very uncomfortable. Some sufferers experience a feeling of heaviness in the legs. Other common symptoms are tenderness and soreness, itching at the ankles, swelling, aches or stabbing pains in the leg, and cramps.

a People suffering from varicose veins sometimes experience a great deal of discomfort. _____

b Leg cramps are a symptom of varicose veins. _____

   c   Problems that involve the legs can be very uncomfortable.

   d   Varicose veins can be very uncomfortable. _____

7   Lenses for eyeglasses and sunglasses are more expensive if they are impact-resistant. They cost more because of the special processing necessary to make them impact-resistant. They are well worth the extra cost, however, since it is hard to put a price on one's eyesight.

   a   Eyesight is priceless. _____

   b   Impact-resistant lenses are well worth their extra cost. _____

   c   Impact-resistant lenses are more expensive than regular lenses.

8   In the course of growing up, children touch, taste, and smell many things. Unfortunately, many things we commonly have around the house, such as cleaners, medicines, and laundry products, can be poisonous or fatal when swallowed or inhaled.

   a   Many substances around the house can be poisonous to children.

   b   Children encounter many dangerous substances as they grow up.

   c   Laundry products can be poisonous to children. _____

9   When the weather is clear, pilots use their eyes to keep the airplane flying straight and level. In low-visibility situations, however, the eye and other orientation senses, such as our sense of balance, are not only useless, they may be totally misleading. The only safe way to fly an airplane in low-visibility conditions is to use instruments which indicate the attitude of the airplane.

   a   In bad weather, the senses can be misleading.

   b   Flying an airplane can be very difficult.

   c   When visibility is low the only safe way to fly an airplane is by using flight instruments. _____

   d   When the weather is clear, pilots use their eyes to keep the airplane flying straight and level. _____

10   Any advertisement that claims a product will result in dramatic changes in your body in a short time should be viewed with suspicion. Often such claims are designed to make the promoter rich at your expense. In some cases these products do nothing at all. In other cases they are positively dangerous.

a   Products which are claimed to make dramatic and rapid changes in the body may be useless or dangerous. _____

b   Many products which claim to change your body rapidly do nothing at all.

_____

c   Many products which make dramatic claims about changing your body in a short time are dangerous. _____

Exercise 4: Avoiding Irrelevant Ideas

Another common mistake readers make in trying to find the main idea of a reading passage is to come up with an irrelevant idea and think it is the main idea. Often we already know something about the topic the author is covering. If we think too much about the things we already know about the topic and don't pay enough attention to what the author is trying to say we can easily come up with a main idea which, although true, has nothing to do with the author's point.

In the following exercise read the paragraphs and decide whether each of the possible main ideas presented is relevant or irrelevant to the author's point.

1   Movies are actually separate still pictures shown so fast that the human eye cannot detect the break between them. When successive images are presented rapidly enough, we fuse them into a single moving image.

a   Movies are extremely popular. _____

b   Modern movies make much use of slow motion. _____

c   Motion pictures are separate pictures shown so fast that we see no break between them. _____

d   Motion pictures require an expensive camera, capable of making very rapid multiple exposures. _____

2   Blue dye is only one of the many chemicals that are changed by light. Any chemical which is changed by light is said to be "sensitive to light." If there were no light-sensitive chemicals, we would not be able to make photographs.

a   Light-sensitive chemicals are always blue. _____

b   If a chemical such as blue dye is changed by light, it is said to be "sensitive to light." _____

c   Blue dye is the only chemical which is changed by light.

_____

d   Without blue dye, there would be no photography. _____

3   Spelling skills are very important in modern life. People often form an impression of us based on what we have written. If what we have written is full of misspellings, their impression of us suffers. Some of us may have difficulty learning the principles of good spelling, but if we are to make a favorable impression on our teachers, associates, employers, and other people we communicate with in writing, these principles must be learned.

    a Spelling skills are not very important for some people. _____

    b Spelling skills are very important. _____

    c Some words are harder to spell than others. _____

    d Spelling principles are very easy to learn. _____

4 Shampoos that are medicated, whether sold by prescription or not, are classified as drugs rather than cosmetics. They contain drug ingredients designed to cure or help certain conditions such as dandruff. The manufacturers of these products are required to comply with the FDA's drug regulations or, if it is a new drug, to show that it is both safe and effective in meeting the claims on the label.

    a Some shampoos are designed only to clean hair. _____

    b Some shampoos are classed as drugs. _____

    c Some shampoos are fairly expensive. _____

    d Shampoos that are classed as drugs tend to be more expensive.

5 There is increasing concern about the effect of lead shot on waterfowl. Some evidence suggests that in areas where hunting pressure is great, ducks and other waterfowl are accidentally eating spent lead shot with their meals. If the amount of lead eaten is great enough, it can result in lead poisoning. Concern about this problem has resulted in efforts to require hunters to use steel shot in waterfowl hunting.

    a Lead shot can result in lead poisoning in waterfowl. _____

    b Efforts are being made to require hunters to use steel shot in hunting waterfowl. _____

    c Steel shot is less effective in knocking down waterfowl than lead shot.

    d Many waterfowl are crippled but not retrieved in waterfowl hunting.

6 The human eye is a miraculous piece of equipment. It adjusts to a wide variety of lighting conditions. It allows us to see clearly objects which may be very close or very far away by adjusting the lens of the eye to focus a clear image on the retina. It allows us to recognize colors, faces, words, and many other features that enable us to interpret everything we see.

    a The eyes are very delicate and should be protected.

b The eyes allow us to recognize faces, colors, and words.

_____

c We can see better in bright light than in dim light.

_____

d The eyes adjust to a wide variety of lighting conditions.

_____

7 Your stereo system is a chain, and the sound you get out of it will be only as good as its weakest link. Because of this, you should choose your speakers to match the rest of your system. In considering speakers you should take into account power-handling capabilities, frequency-response characteristics, impedance ratings, and the type of sound you prefer.

a Stereo systems can be very expensive. _____

b Your stereo speakers should be matched to the rest of your stereo.

_____

c Speakers can be very expensive. _____

d Most people like to have very attractive speaker cabinets.

_____

8 Sharks are classified as meat-eating fish. There are about 250 species of sharks in the world's oceans. Most sharks eat live fish. Although they are thought of as dangerous to people, there are fewer than 100 shark attacks in the world each year. Most shark species will not attack humans.

a Sharks have very poor eyesight. _____

b Sharks are not as dangerous to humans as most people think.

_____

c In some parts of the world sharks are eaten as food. _____

d Shark skeletons are made of cartilage rather than bone. _____

9 The various parts of the body grow at different rates and reach their full size at different times. The most rapid growth of the head occurs before birth. The rest of its major growth occurs soon after birth. During childhood it grows very slowly and reaches its final size when the child is between the ages of 9 and 15. In sharp contrast, the long bones of the arms and legs are very short at birth and remain relatively short throughout childhood. The trunk is fairly long at birth and grows very little until the person approaches adulthood. These different rates of growth of the various parts of the body help make it possible to guess a person's age by looking at a silhouette.

a Different parts of the body grow at different rates. _____

b Parts of the body grow faster at some times than at others.

_____

c Adults have body parts that are much larger than those of children.

_____

d Adults have larger heads than children. _____

10 In the early 1800s a ship's captain was completely in control of all the events on his ship. Sailors were often beaten, whipped, or dragged through the water as punishment. Flogging and keelhauling were usually reserved for serious offenses, but a cruel captain could punish his sailors in any way he saw fit.

In modern times there are numerous regulations governing the behavior of both sailors and captains on the seven seas. As a result, the captain of a ship is no longer an absolute dictator, and the life of a sailor is much more pleasant than it once was.

    a Ship captains are almost always men. _____

    b Ship captains were once absolute dictators on board their ships.

_____

    c Ship captains are no longer absolute dictators on board their ships.

_____

    d Sea voyages can last for months at a time. _____

Reading for Details

In all writing, authors use details to express and defend the point they are trying to make. To read effectively, the reader must be able to recognize and remember the important details of a passage.

A detail is a piece of information or fact in a paragraph which either proves, defines, or provides an example of the main idea of the paragraph. Some facts are whole sentences, while others are brief phrases. One way of deciding if something is a detail is to ask yourself, Is this a fact I could tell someone? For example, "Dogs have fleas" and "He was ill" are facts; "of the city" and "putting on a hat" are not facts because they contain no information you could tell someone.

When you have completed the exercises, check your answers in the back of the book.

Comprehension Exercises for Unit 32

Exercise 1: Recognizing Details
In the following selections look at the underlined parts and decide whether each is a detail or not. If the underlined part is a detail, put a check mark (✔) in the blank at the end of the line.

1 Standard grade beef has a high proportion of lean meat and very little fat. Because it comes from young animals it is fairly tender. _____

2 The climate of this area is typical of desert conditions. Summer temperatures often do not vary <u>widely from day to night.</u> _____

3 Farming was the main occupation of the people of this area; using irrigation <u>they grew corn</u>, beans, and squash. _____

4 Church records are frequently helpful because they contain information about births, baptisms, deaths, burials, and marriages. Church records can also help you find out about the movement of people <u>from one community to another.</u> _____

5 If you have already made a verbal agreement with a buyer, and <u>both of you want to consult lawyers</u> before signing a formal agreement to buy and sell, you can suggest a deposit. _____

6 <u>Ferns love moisture</u> and shade. If at all possible avoid putting them in full sun. _____

7 The best thing to do <u>the night before a big test</u> is get a good night's rest.

_____

8 The <u>function of the carburetor</u> in an automobile engine is to mix air and gasoline in the proper proportion. If the mixture is in the right proportion it will be very explosive. _____

9 All of the <u>drugs classed as opiates are physically addicting</u>, and when they are taken regularly the user develops a tolerance for them, so that larger and larger doses are necessary to achieve the same results. _____

10 People all over the world dream about the same amount each night. <u>People vary, however, in how well they remember their dreams.</u> _____

Exercise 2: Judging the Importance of Details
Often it is not enough just to recognize details. In many cases you must also be able to tell important from unimportant details or major details from minor ones. It is impossible to remember all of the details, so it is wise to pick out the important details as you read and attempt to remember them.

In the following exercise read each paragraph and decide which of the underlined facts is most important. Circle the letter next to the most important fact.

1 Madame Curie and her husband discovered that a piece of pitchblend produced a darkening of photographic plates out of all proportion to its uranium content. This meant to them that the pitchblend contained some other element. (a) <u>The Curies decided to try and isolate this new element.</u> (b) <u>The task took all their time for two years.</u> (c) <u>When they were through, the Curies had discovered not one but two new elements.</u> (d) <u>The first to be</u>

discovered was called polonium, after Madame Curie's native Poland; the other element was the famous metal radium.

2   (a) Only Congress can declare war. (b) A declaration of war cannot be made by the president alone. (c) Usually the declaration is a joint resolution adopted by at least a majority of both houses and signed by the president.

3   (a) Children are very curious by nature. (b) They often like to smell, touch, and taste things while exploring their environments. (c) Your home contains many products that are beneficial if used properly but may be dangerous or even fatal to children. (d) Children are often unaware of the dangers of these products.

4   (a) Standing or sitting for long periods of time is hard on anyone's circulation. (b) This is because blood accumulates in the lower legs and around the ankles, (c) and distends the veins in these areas. (d) This is especially harmful for people suffering from varicose veins.

5   (a) In 1978 a federal law was passed to prohibit abusive, deceptive, or unfair practices by debt collectors. (b) This law was designed to help consumers. (c) It provides new rights under the law for consumers who owe money. (d) Some people never have to deal with debt collectors; this law was designed to help those who do.

6   (a) There are a large number of lotions and oils available that claim to give protection from the sun. (b) Some provide much more protection than others. (c) Some are little more than moisturizers. (d) One study found para-aminobenzoic acid (PABA) to be the most effective in preventing sunburn.

7   (a) Trout farming is becoming a popular way for farmers and ranchers to increase their incomes. (b) For some, trout farming is a sideline and does not provide a major source of income. (c) For others it is a full-time job, providing their entire income. Whether it is a sideline or a main source of income, (d) trout farming is a very demanding business and requires intensive management.

8   (a) French psychologist Alfred Binet was asked by the French government to develop a test that would help find out which school children were not intelligent enough to profit from regular schooling. (b) Binet thought that intelligence should be measured by tests that required problem solving and reasoning. (c) Binet did a great deal of research with children of various ages. (d) As a result of his work, Binet developed the concept of the IQ, or intelligence quotient, which is the basis for much modern intelligence testing.

9   Saturated fats often raise the level of cholesterol in blood. (a) Increased cholesterol levels have been associated with heart attacks. (b) Saturated fats usually harden at room temperature. (c) They are found in many animal

products including dairy products and meats. (d) They are also found in co-
conut oil and palm oil.

10 (a) Some rain fell on drought areas of northern Mexico this week.
(b) Area residents have been coping with severe drought conditions for several months. (c) Weather bureau officials said that the rainfall was not
enough to provide significant relief from the drought. (d) The drought has
had deterimental effects on both crops and livestock.

Exercise 3: Remembering Facts from Reading
Obviously, facts are no good to you if you don't remember them. The following exercises are designed to improve your ability to retain facts you have
read.

Try to recognize and remember the facts in the following paragraphs.
Try to answer the questions without looking back at the paragraph.

You may deduct the full amount of certain medical and dental expenses you
paid for yourself, your spouse, and any person who is your dependent. You
may not deduct amounts paid for you by insurance.

1 What amount of medical expenses can you deduct?
- **a** Half of the amount you paid
- **b** The full amount you paid
- **c** 20 percent of the amount you paid
- **d** 75 percent of the amount you paid

2 You may *not* deduct medical expenses you paid for
- **a** Yourself
- **b** Your spouse
- **c** One of your dependents
- **d** Someone who is not your dependent

3 You may deduct
- **a** Dental expenses but not medical expenses
- **b** Medical expenses but not dental expenses
- **c** Only dental expenses you paid for yourself
- **d** Both medical and dental expenses

Owing to the large areas of open water between Oak Point and Silver Beach,
canoe trips downstream from Oak Point should only be undertaken by people experienced in open-water canoeing. When planning the trip, allowances
should be made for delays because of strong winds and rough water. Each
group of canoes should be accompanied by a power boat.

4 This passage contains information important to
- **a** Swimmers

    b Power boaters
    c Canoeists
    d Hikers

5 You may be delayed by
    a Strong currents
    b Delays at the border
    c Engine failure
    d Wind and rough water

6 Each group of canoes should be accompanied by
    a A power boat
    b A law enforcement official
    c A motorized raft
    d A licensed guide

7 Between Oak Point and Silver Beach there are
    a Dangerous rapids
    b Strong currents
    c Dangerous rocks
    d Large areas of open water

Magnesium can be found in all the tissues of the body but is mainly located in the bones. Magnesium deficiency is uncommon in humans but is sometimes seen in alcoholics and in some patients recovering from surgery.

8 The paragraph is about
    a Copper
    b Phosphorus
    c Calcium
    d Magnesium

9 Magnesium deficiency in humans is
    a Uncommon
    b A major health risk in the United States
    c Related to heart attacks
    d Extremely common but not dangerous

10 Magnesium deficiency is sometimes seen in
    a Children
    b Alcoholics
    c Adults over 65 years old
    d People with German measles

11 Most of the body's magnesium is located in
    a Hair
    b Bones
    c Skin
    d Muscle tissue

When selling your house, you may think of yourself as a potential lender. As such you have a right to expect information from the buyer about his or her financial condition. One thing you should get is a statement of income and current obligations. You want to be sure that the buyer can afford to make the payments on your house. As a rule of thumb, the cost of home ownership, including payments, utilities, maintenance, taxes, and insurance, should not come to more than 35 percent of the buyer's take-home pay.

12   According to the passage, when selling your house you may think of yourself as

    a   A potential lender
    b   A real estate agent
    c   A professional salesperson
    d   A prospective buyer

13   You have a right to expect buyers to tell you about their

    a   Job history
    b   Education
    c   Financial condition
    d   Religion

14   The cost of home ownership should not come to more than _____ of the buyer's take-home pay.

    a   10 percent
    b   15 percent
    c   40 percent
    d   35 percent

Thunderstorms and tornadoes struck the middle portion of the United States on Thursday, knocking out power to more than 50,000 Chicago residents, killing one man, and injuring 25 people.

15   A power outage was experienced by residents of

    a   Detroit
    b   Minneapolis
    c   Toledo
    d   Chicago

16   What part of the country did the bad weather strike?

    a   East
    b   West
    c   South
    d   Central

17   The power outage knocked out power for more than

    a   10,000 people
    b   12,000 people
    c   30,000 people
    d   50,000 people

18   How many people were injured?

   a 25

   b 19

   c 15

   d 10

19   On what day of the week did the storm hit?

   a Monday

   b Saturday

   c Thursday

   d Friday

The drainage basin of the Colorado River covers 240,000 square miles of the United States. This equals one-twelfth of the total land area of the country. Over 1400 miles long, it is one of the longest rivers in the nation.

20   What river is the selection about?

   a The Mississippi

   b The Ohio

   c The Colorado

   d The Missouri

21   What part of the country does the drainage basin of the river cover?

   a One-fourth

   b One-twelfth

   c One-twentieth

   d One-fortieth

22   The river is over _____ miles long.

   a 1400

   b 11,000

   c 1900

   d 800

23   The river's drainage basin covers about _____ square miles.

   a 150,000

   b 240,000

   c 125,000

   d 290,000

We may be seeing a new breed of trolleys carrying passengers in American cities. Trolleys were widely used in the 1920s when about 50,000 trolleys ran on over 26,000 miles of track in various cities. Modern trolleys are significantly quieter than the trolleys of the 1920s.

24   The passage is about

   a Buses

   b Taxis

   c Commuter trains

   d Trolleys

25   In the 1920s there were about _____ trolleys.

    a   50,000
    b   25,000
    c   22,000
    d   75,000

26   The trolleys of the 1920s ran on over _____ miles of track.

    a   21,000
    b   26,000
    c   50,000
    d   62,000

27   Modern trolleys differ from their ancestors mainly by being

    a   Noisier
    b   Safer
    c   Quieter
    d   Faster

An attractive commemorative stamp honors Helen Keller and her teacher, Anne Sullivan. It was first released in the city of Tuscumbia, Alabama, where Helen Keller was born in 1880.

28   Helen Keller was born in

    a   1874
    b   1910
    c   1890
    d   1880

29   Helen Keller's teacher was

    a   Mary Williams
    b   Anne Sullivan
    c   Laurie Taylor
    d   Louise Tuscumbia

30   Helen Keller was born in the state of

    a   Alabama
    b   Missouri
    c   Georgia
    d   Tennessee

31   Helen Keller has been honored by

    a   A bronze statue
    b   A national holiday
    c   A commemorative stamp
    d   A Pulitzer Prize

32   Helen Keller was born in the city of

    a   Tuskeegee
    b   Biloxi
    c   Atlanta
    d   Tuscumbia

Most of the mint grown in the United States is peppermint. It is produced mainly by commercial growers in large quantities. It usually yields about 50 pounds of oil per acre of peppermint. It is most often planted from roots or cuttings rather than seeds.

33   Most of the mint grown in the United States is
   a   Spearmint
   b   Peppermint
   c   Catnip
   d   Virginia mint

34   Most peppermint is grown by
   a   Amateurs
   b   Commercial growers
   c   Home gardeners
   d   Laboratory technicians

35   Peppermint yields about _____ pounds of oil per acre.
   a   50
   b   25
   c   30
   d   15

36   Peppermint is usually planted from
   a   Seeds
   b   Leaves
   c   Air layering
   d   Roots and cuttings

An $11.5 million lawsuit has been brought against three companies involved in designing and installing materials for the Metropolis City Hall. The roof of the six-year-old building has been leaking badly.

37   The lawsuit is for
   a $9.5 million
   b $3.8 million
   c $11.5 million
   d $13.5 million

38   The roof of the building is
   a   Collapsing
   b   Sagging
   c   Flaking
   d   Leaking

39   The building is _____ years old.
   a   Four
   b   Three
   c   Two
   d   Six

40   How many companies are named in the suit?
  a   Two
  b   Three
  c   Four
  d   Five

Reading for Organization

Time and time again, research has shown that to understand and remember what you read you must be reading actively. Too many readers think of reading as a passive task in which they move their eyes across the page and somehow soak up the words. They feel that it is the author's job to make them understand and remember the material. People who use this approach can be in for a sad surprise if they are tested on the material they have read. Successful reading is a very active process, and to be a successful reader you must learn to read actively.

One major step toward being an active reader is to be aware of the organization of a reading passage. The following exercises are designed to help you develop the ability to recognize the means used by authors in presenting and explaining their ideas.

How Parts of a Paragraph Are Related

There are many ways of describing the parts of a paragraph. For our purposes we will consider only four kinds of things in paragraphs: (1) the main idea, (2) supporting ideas, (3) the introduction, and (4) the conclusion. The main idea, of course, is the main point the author is trying to make, as you have learned in Unit 31. Supporting ideas are the facts, reasons, or arguments the author uses to explain, prove, or defend the main idea. The introduction and conclusion are devices used by the author to start and finish the topic.

When you have completed the following exercises, check your answers in the back of the book.

Comprehension Exercises for Unit 33

Exercise 1: Recognizing Paragraph Structure

In the following exercise label each sentence as: introduction, main idea, supporting idea, or conclusion.

Throughout history, moonlight has been the subject of a great deal of study. Moonlight is actually sunlight bouncing off the moon and striking the earth. Looking at a landscape lit by the full moon, we often feel that it is as bright as a cloudy day. Actually, however, the moonlight is extremely weak compared to sunlight. Measurements show that moonlight is only 1/400,000 as bright as sunlight. Because of its irregular surface the moon makes a poor reflector. The full moon looks bright in the night sky, but when we see it during the day we realize how dim it really is. The weakness of the moon's light, however, does not detract from our appreciation of it.

1 Throughout history, moonlight has been the subject of a great deal of study. _____

2 Moonlight is actually sunlight bouncing off the moon and striking the earth. Looking at a landscape lit by the full moon, we often feel that it is as bright as a cloudy day. Actually, however, the moonlight is extremely weak compared to sunlight. _____

3 Measurements show that moonlight is only 1/400,000 as bright as sunlight. _____

4 Because of its irregular surface the moon makes a poor reflector. _____

5 The full moon looks bright in the night sky, but when we see it during the day we realize how dim it really is. _____

6 The weakness of the moon's light, however, does not detract from our appreciation of it. _____

The correct answers can be found in the answer key at the back of the book.

Hound dogs are among the oldest dog breeds. The name refers to two groups of dogs. One type of hound hunts by smell. They follow the scent of the quarry. The other type of hound hunts by sight. The hounds that hunt by scent include the bloodhound, basset hound, coonhound, foxhound, beagle, and dachshund. Sight-hunting hounds include the greyhound, Afghan, Irish wolfhound, Scottish deerhound, and the borzoi. Typical hounds have long ears, long tails, and strong legs. Hounds have long been important in literature and history, as well as in hunting.

7 Hound dogs are among the oldest dog breeds. _____

8 The name refers to two groups of dogs. _____

9 One type of hound hunts by smell. They follow the scent of the quarry.
_____

10 The other type of hound hunts by sight. _____

11 The hounds that hunt by scent include the bloodhound, basset hound, coonhound, foxhound, beagle, and dachshund. _____

12 Sight-hunting hounds include the greyhound, Afghan, Irish wolfhound, Scottish deerhound, and the borzoi. _____

13 Typical hounds have long ears, long tails, and strong legs. _____

14 Hounds have long been important in literature and history, as well as in hunting. _____

Exercise 2: Identifying Details

In order to organize ideas in your head, you must be able to associate details with the topics they support. Authors do not always put the details for specific topics all in one place. Sometimes they sprinkle the details associated with several topics together throughout a paragraph. In these cases it is necessary for the active reader to sort out the details and mentally place them under the correct topic headings.

In the following exercise read each selection, and write the letters of the details that are associated with the topic headings listed.

Plants closely reflect climatic environments. A good classification of climatic regions has been based on the plants that naturally grow in different climates. Temperature and water supply are the most important climatic factors that affect plants. (a) The banana and mahogany flourish in the rainy tropics. (b) The drought-resistant olive is adapted to the dry summers and somewhat humid winters of the Mediterranean climate. (c) Many cacti are able to withstand the extreme heat of the desert, and (d) lichens and sphagnum moss do not wither in the bitter cold of the tundra. (e) Similarly, vines in the rain forest and cypress trees in dense swamps are designed to live with extremely high moisture levels.

1 Temperature: _____

2 Water: _____

(a) The liver can renew or regenerate itself if it is not too badly damaged. (b) Cirrhosis is scars on the liver. (c) If there are too many scars, the areas that are scarred cannot regenerate. (d) The extent to which the liver can heal itself depends on the extent of the scars. (e) The liver's function is to make protein, store carbohydrates, and reclaim many substances broken down by the body's metabolism. (f) If the liver becomes unable to make enough protein, the person becomes emaciated. (g) Low blood sugar results from a lack of stored carbohydrates. (h) If the liver's reclamation function is disturbed, that person may become mentally confused.

3 Regeneration: _____

4 Liver function: _____

Exercise 3: Summarizing the Author's Message
One way to be sure you are getting the author's main message is to try to summarize the ideas presented in a brief statement. In the passages which follow, try to pick out the statement that best summarizes what the author has said.

Impact Resistant Lenses

A Federal Ruling
On January 1, 1972 a Food and Drug Administration ruling of extraordinary significance became effective in all 50 states. This commendable rule—which requires eyeglass and sunglass lenses for use by the general public to be *impact-resistant*—was issued under FDA's authority to regulate medical devices, as spectacles are characterized.

The FDA ruling specifies that *impact-resistant* eyeglass and sunglass lenses must be capable of resisting an impact from a 5/8" diameter steel ball dropped from a height of 50 inches. Industrial strength safety lenses are verified by being struck with an even larger, heavier, steel ball. Most lenses previously available to the general public could not pass such tests.

Safeguarding eyesight cannot be accomplished with *impact-resistant* lenses alone! All such lenses function best when supported by frames that hold them securely, and which are made of flame-retardant materials.

1   The best summary statement is:
   a   The Food and Drug Administration has made up rules for eyeglass lenses.
   b   As of January 1972, the Food and Drug Administration rules require eyeglass lenses to be impact-resistant.
   c   Impact lenses must be able to resist a 5/8-inch steel ball falling 50 inches.
   d   Frames for impact-resistant lenses must be flame-retardant.

UPC. These letters do not stand for a new government agency, a new chemical, or a new football league. They are shorthand for "Universal Product Code." Supermarket shoppers across the Nation are seeing the UPC symbol on the packages of all kinds of products, from food to paper towels to detergents to over-the-counter (nonprescription) drugs. The symbol consists of many closely spaced lines, bars, and numbers and will be popping up on more and more items as time goes by.

   The lines and bars in the code symbol are unique to that product and can be read by a computer.

2   The best summary statement is:
   a   UPC is a new way to mark prices on products.
   b   UPC is a product code that consists of lines and bars that can be read by a computer.
   c   UPC can be used on many packages.
   d   UPC will be used on many packages.

Exercise 4: Outlining
Although it is possible to understand and remember an author's message without outlining, many readers find outlining extremely helpful in their reading. Some readers like to do the outlining in their heads as they read. Others prefer to make a written outline of the material to use later as a study aid. The following exercises are designed to acquaint you with the basic elements of a good outline and to improve your skill at outlining reading passages.

   Read the selection which follows, then try to complete the outline with a brief word, phrase, or sentence.

Credit can cost you pennies or dollars. It depends on your character, your capital and your capability to repay, the money market, and other economic factors.

   Two choices you frequently have are closed-end and revolving transactions. Under the closed-end plans you ordinarily sign a promissory note, if you are borrowing cash, or a retail installment contract, if you are using sales credit. You agree in advance on the specific amount to borrow, the number and size of weekly or monthly payments, and a due date.

On the other hand, the revolving charge plan is open-ended. A top limit is agreed upon, but purchases are added as they are made and finance charges are figured on the unpaid balance each month.

I Outline for credit cost
    A Credit cost depends on
        1 Character
        2 Capital
        3 Ability to pay
        4 Money market
        5 Other economic factors
    B Two choices for credit include
        1 Closed-end plans
            a Sign note on contract
            b Specific amount borrowed
            c Fixed payments
        2 Open-ended plans
            a Credit limit
            b _____

1 Choose the phrase that completes the outline:
    a Two kinds of credit
    b Charges on unpaid balance
    c Promissory note
    d Retail sale

Read the selection which follows. Then complete the outline that is started for you following the selection. The main heading and one sub-statement have been provided.

To help make forecasts more meaningful, the weather service has provided the following definitions of forecast terms they use:

Snow: when used without a qualifying word such as occasional or inter-mittent, means the fall of snow is of a steady nature and will probably continue for several hours.

Snow flurries: snow falling for short durations off and on, with small accumulations.

Snow squalls: brief intense fall of snow accompanied by gusty winds.

Blizzard: strong winds bearing large amounts of snow. Most of the snow is in the form of fine, powdery particles which are whipped in such great quantities that at times visibility is only a few yards.

Freezing rain and freezing drizzle: rain that freezes as it strikes the ground and other exposed surfaces forming a coating of ice.

2 Meanings of forecast words

a   "snow"—steady, several hours _____

b   _____

c   _____

d   _____

e   _____

Check the key on page 318 for the correct answers.

Using Reference Materials

Ready Sources of Information

The good reader not only knows how to read well but where to read for specific purposes. The incredible array of facts that exist in print would be almost useless if there were no way to locate them. Imagine what it would be like if your telephone book did not have an alphabetical listing and simply gave names and numbers in random order! Some readers are not familiar with how information is organized and reported. To them, much of the information they could use is not available simply because they do not know how and where to find it.

Exercise 1: Using the Newspaper

An example of the use of reference material is your daily newspaper. You may not have thought about it, but you probably understand how to use it quite well. Let's try an exercise to see how well you know the parts of your newspaper. On the left are kinds of information to be sought in a newspaper. On the right are the parts of the newspaper. Write the letter that corresponds to where you would look for each kind of information.

_____ 1 Used cars for sale   **a** Sports page

_____ 2 A late-night television   **b** Society page
movie

_____ **3** Expected temperature tomorrow

c Comics

_____ **4** Current price of hamburger

d Local news

_____ **5** A report on a recent local social event

e Food ads

_____ **6** Score in last Saturday's football game

f Classified section

_____ **7** Report on an event in Egypt

g National news

_____ **8** The local newspaper's stand on a current event

h TV and radio listings

_____ **9** A report on a burglary in your neighborhood

i Weather report

_____ **10** Little Orphan Annie's latest problems

j Editorial page

Exercise 2: Using Library Reference Materials

Unlike the daily newspaper, which comes into your home every day, most reference materials are printed less frequently and are available only in libraries. You should be familiar with at least the most common ones. In addition, it is important to know how to use the staff of the library to locate other sources of information. We will discuss the library and staff more in the next section, but for now let's see how well you can identify and use some of the most valuable references. Some of the references named in this exercise will probably be ones you have never used. However, try to guess which of the references in the right-hand column would be most likely to have the information sought in the left-hand column.

_____ **1** In which issue of the New York Times was Michener's book _South Pacific_ reviewed?

a _Encyclopedia Americana_

_____ **2** What is the name of the current president of Uganda?

b _International Encyclopedia of the Social Sciences_

_____ **3** Who paid Paul Revere for his expenses?

c _Readers' Guide to Periodical Literature_

_____ **4** What was the average family income in the United States last year?

d _Book Review Digest_

_____ **5** What major advances were made in the social sciences last year?

e *Statesman's Year-book*

_____ **6** Where would the best discussion of the topic "communication" be found?

f *Current Biography*

_____ **7** What is the chief product exported by Peru?

g *Dictionary of American History*

_____ **8** How old was the American author, Herman Melville, when he died?

h *Webster's New Geographical Dictionary*

_____ **9** In what magazine did an article on new electronic surgical techniques appear.

i *Statistical Abstracts of the United States*

_____ **10** How many Catholic voters are there in Turkey?

j *Dictionary of American Biography*

We could give a long list with descriptions of all the possible reference materials you might use. However, it would not be very interesting and/or meet any immediate need. Instead, we suggest that you make a visit to your school or community library. Go to the reference section and look around. You will find most or all of the references mentioned in the above exercise and a lot more. A few minutes paging through the materials there will be more revealing to you than anything we can say here. We will give some general information on the contents and use of the library in the next section.

The Library

Libraries are in some ways the best evidence we have of civilization. In them is the accumulated knowledge of the ages. The core of a college or university is its library. Schools are appraised and evaluated on the size and effectiveness of their libraries. Since libraries go on indefinitely and survive even the oldest teachers, they are full of very old books.

It is easy to think of a library as a place where a lot of musty old books sit unused on the shelf. On the other hand, libraries can be thought of as extremely timely and up to date. They have current books, magazines, newspapers, and other materials that would be very expensive and space-consuming if you were to subscribe to them all. Many libraries have extensive collections of nonbook materials as well, including large recorded-music collections.

The best way to use a library is to have some idea of how it is organized. Then you can use the *people* in the library as efficiently as possible. It is the staff of the library that really make it work. They know where to find the information you need.

You should be aware that different people in the library have different jobs. They range from highly trained reference librarians to part-time clerical help who probably don't know much beyond their specific job. The first thing to do if you are looking for information on a particular topic is to find the right person to help you.

Approach one of the library staff members (preferably one behind the desk in the reference section), and say, "Are you a reference librarian?" If you get an affirmative answer, then explain what you are looking for and, if appropriate, why you are looking for it. The reference librarian can then make a professional judgment about what materials to lead you to. People differ, of course, but generally reference librarians are eager to demonstrate the special training and knowledge they have. Many will really go all out to help you.

Parts of the Library

All libraries have some things in common. A librarian can move from one library to another and be quite sure that there will be such things as a circulation desk, a card catalog, a reference desk, a set of reserve materials, a periodicals section, and probably other special collections of materials.

The circulation desk (sometimes called the *loan desk*) is the one you will get to know. It is where books are checked out. Usually you go through the *card catalog* and make out a call slip for the book you want. Then you present it at the circulation desk to get the book. Sometimes, in an open-shelf library, you go to the shelf, pick out the book, and take it to the desk.

The *reference desk* is near the general reference materials, such as encyclopedias, dictionaries, yearbooks, and other materials that must be used in the library. The person behind the reference desk is usually a reference librarian and can be counted on to help you find information in the reference section.

The *reserve section* of the library contains materials that are being held for use by a lot of people. For example, teachers put certain books on reserve, so they can be used by all of the students in a class. Materials on reserve usually do not go out of the library, except for brief periods, such as overnight.

The *periodical section* of the library is where magazines are kept. The typical large library subscribes to hundreds of professional journals, newsletters, and popular magazines. All are called periodicals. A reference librarian can lead you to some special ways to locate articles in periodicals. The best-known of such special aids is the *Readers' Guide to Periodical Literature,* but there are many others. Some are specific to a field of study, such as the *Art Index* or *Psychological Abstracts.* Ask the reference librarian!

Special collections are typically materials on a special topic or large collections that some well-known person has donated. They are not usually of special interest to the general public or to an undergraduate student, unless they happen to relate to a special area of study.

Books

The problem most students have in a library is how to find books. The library has thousands of them! The answer is to have some idea how books are organized and how to use the *card catalog* to find them.

The card catalog is a list of all of the books in a library. It is an alphabetic file that is usually on cards. In some new systems, computer listings have begun to replace actual cards, but the idea is the same. Most books have three cards in the file: one by author, one by title, and one by subject. You can locate the book if you look up any one of the three. Sometimes you don't have any authors or titles in mind, and simply go to the file looking for the subject. All of the books on that topic will be listed. There may also be some "see also" suggestions for looking up other related topics.

Books in the library are given a call number using one of two major classification systems. Most libraries use the Dewey decimal system. It has the following classifications:

000   General works

100   Philosophy and psychology

200   Religion

300   Social sciences, including sociology, law, government, and education

400   Philology (languages)

500   Pure sciences

600   Useful arts or applied sciences, including agriculture and various technological fields

700   Fine arts

800   Literature

900   History, including biography, geography, and travel

The other classification system, the Library of Congress system, has the following divisions.

A	General works
B	Philosophy and religion
C	History and auxiliary sciences
D	History and topography (not including America)
E, F	America
G	Geography and anthropology
H	Social sciences
J	Political science
K	Law
L	Education
M	Music
N	Fine arts
P	Language and literature
Q	Science
R	Medicine
S	Agriculture
T	Technology
U	Military science
V	Naval science
Z	Bibliography and library science

The Library of Congress system is used primarily in very large libraries. It allows for a larger number of subdivisions than the Dewey decimal system.

When you look up a book in either of the above systems, you get much more than just the title, author, and subject. You get information regarding the publisher, the date of publication, the number of pages, the size of the book, and several other things.

The following is a typical card from the card catalog of a college library. As you can see, it has a lot of information on it. You may want to know if a book is a large one or just a small pamphlet. You will probably want to know how old it is. Sometimes the fact that a book has an extensive bibliography will be useful to you.

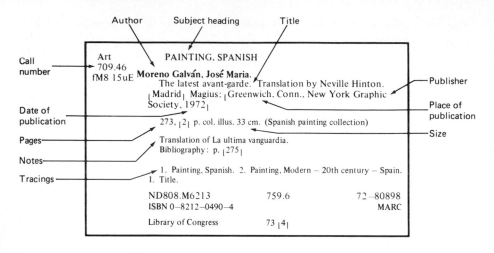

Other Library Materials and Services

In addition to books and periodicals, libraries have government documents, maps, newspapers, and other materials. Many libraries loan pictures and recorded music on tapes and platters. Most modern libraries also have a very efficient photocopy service.

To summarize this discussion of libraries, we suggest that you become acquainted with the library nearest you and seek the help of the reference librarian when you want to find things. It will save a lot of time and trouble.

Locating Information in Books

Often a student must find a particular topic or piece of information in a book. Some skill in dealing with tables of contents and indexes can save you a great deal of time when this happens. If a book has an index (most textbooks do), it will usually be the best guide to locating the information you seek. The index is an alphabetical listing of topics covered in the book and the page number for each topic. Sometimes your topic will appear as a subtopic under some other larger heading. If, for example, you want to look up the topic "dry skin" and do not find anything under that heading in the index, you may find it under "skin, dry." Some books have more than one index. Usually one will be a subject index, and the other will be an author or name index, covering the people mentioned in the text. If the book does not have an index, you should turn to the table of contents at the beginning of the book and search for your topic. Tables of contents are not alphabetical; rather the topics appear in outline form and in the same order they appear in the book. To find your topic, you must first decide which main section of the book it will be in. Then search for your topic. Remember that your specific topic may not be mentioned explicitly in the table of contents; you may have to determine which *section* of the book it is in and then search that section for your topic.

The following exercises are designed to give you practice in finding topics in an index or table of contents. Answers to the questions can be found in the key at the back of the book.

Exercise 3: Using the Table of Contents

In the following exercises parts of the table of contents from a number of different books are presented. Read the contents and answer the questions that follow.

A Book on Adolescence

Chapter 1   Introduction

Chapter 2   Physical growth

Chapter 3   Emotional growth

Chapter 4   Emotional problems

Chapter 5   Suicide

Chapter 6   Growth of intelligence

1 In what chapter would you expect to find a discussion of suicide prevention?

2 In what chapter would you expect to find a table of how height changes with age? _____

3 In what chapter would you expect to find information on depression? _____

4 In what chapter would you expect to find information on IQ? _____

5 In what chapter would you expect to find a general discussion of the book's topic? _____

A Cookbook

Chapter 1   Cooking methods

Chapter 2   Appetizers

Chapter 3   Vegetables

Chapter 4   Soups

Chapter 5   Main courses

Chapter 6   Desserts

6 In what chapter would you expect to find a discussion of broiling?
_____

7 In what chapter would you expect to find out how to make pie?
_____

8 In what chapter would you expect to find a recipe for green beans?
_____

9 In what chapter would you expect to find a recipe for onion soup?
_____

10 In what chapter would you expect to find a recipe for cheese spread?
_____

A Book on Houseplants

Chapter 1   Introduction

Chapter 2   Light

Chapter 3   Soil

Chapter 4   Fertilizer

Chapter 5   Diseases

Chapter 6   Insect pests

11 In what chapter would you expect to find a discussion about using artificial lights to help your plants grow? _____

12 In what chapter would you look to find out what to do about red spider mites on your plants? _____

13 If your plants' leaves are turning white and you don't see any insects, what chapter would you consult? _____

14 What chapter would tell you how to feed your plants? _____

15 In what chapter would you expect to find out what kind of dirt to use for each plant? _____

A Book on Coin Collecting

Chapter 1   Judging the condition of a coin, or "grading"

Chapter 2   How coins are made

Chapter 3   How to store coins

Chapter 4   Coins as an investment

Chapter 5   Coins with mistakes on them, or "mint errors"

Chapter 6   Coin auctions

Chapter 7   Price list of valuable coins

16 In what chapter would you look to find the value of a particular coin?

_____

17 What chapter would you read to find out about the minting of coins?

_____

18 What chapter would be likely to tell you which coins might make the best investments? _____

19 In which chapter would you expect to find information about how to safely keep your coins? _____

20 Which chapter would tell you how to "grade" a coin? _____

A Book on Poker

Chapter 1   The history of poker

Chapter 2   The rules of poker

Chapter 3   Poker etiquette

Chapter 4   Playing the odds

Chapter 5   Judging your opponent's hand

Chapter 6   Making your money

Chapter 7   Organizing a poker game

21 Which chapter would be likely to contain information on how to deal five-card-stud poker? _____

22 Where would you look to find out when poker was invented?

_____

23 What chapter would tell you the odds against improving a four-card flush? _____

24 What chapter would you read to find out how to tell how good another player's hand is? _____

25 Which chapter would be likely to contain information on how many players to invite to a poker game? _____

A Book on Flying

CONTENTS

26 On what page would you find information about fire in the air? _____

27 On what page would you look for information about preflight operations? _____

28 On what page would you look for information about wake turbulence? _____

29 Which chapter would contain the most information about load factors in steep turns? _____

30 On what page would you look for information about downwind turns? _____

A Book on Real Estate

CONTENTS

31 In what chapter would you expect to find a discussion of the things that need to be included in a sales agreement? _____

32 In what chapter would you expect to find sample advertisements for houses? _____

33 What chapter will tell you what types of appraisals are used to set prices for houses? _____

34 If you encounter terms that are new to you, where would you look to find their meanings? _____

35 You are trying to decide whether to sell your home yourself or use an agent. What part of the book would be most helpful? _____

Exercise 4: Using the Index
In the following exercises parts of indexes from a number of different books are presented. Use these indexes to answer the questions that follow.

1 On what page would you expect to find information about systolic pressure? _____

2 On what page would you look for information about sterile procedures? _____

3 Where would you look for information about dry skin? _____

4 On what pages would you expect to find information about sounds made while breathing? _____

5 Where would you look for a description of the Valsalva maneuver? _____

Nursing Index

Child Psychology Index

6 On what page would you expect to find information on sex-linked genes? _____

7 On what page would you look for information on S. B. Simon? _____

8 What page would you look on to find out about sociograms? _____

9 Where would you look for information about adolescent sexuality? _____

10 What page would you check to find out the life span of spermatozoa? _____

Geography Index

11   What page would you check to find out what a syncline was?

_____

12   What page would you look on to find out about the resources of sub-tropical dry-summer climates? _____

13   What page would you check for information about intermittent streams?

_____

14   On what page would you expect to find information about time zones?

_____

15   On what page would you expect to find information about the uses of surface water? _____

Reading Graphs and Tables

Research shows that a very large number of students lack skill in reading graphs and tables. A graph or table is like a paragraph of writing. It contains information which is usually important and often cannot be found anywhere else.

Most graphs describe the relationship between two things, one listed along the bottom of the graph and the other along the left side. For example, if a car-wash owner keeps a record of how many cars were washed each day, the record might look like the following graph:

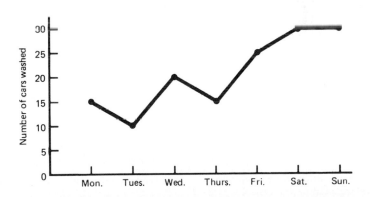

A glance at the graph will tell us that 15 cars were washed on Monday and Thursday, 10 on Tuesday, 20 on Wednesday, 25 on Friday, and 30 on Saturday and Sunday. We can also see that business is better over the weekend.

When looking at a graph, the first thing to do is determine exactly what is being measured along the bottom and left side of the graph. Then look for general relationships or trends in the graph.

In a table, what is in each column is listed along the top of the table and what is in each row is listed along the left side. A sales firm might represent monthly sales for each employee in a table similar to Table 34-1.

TABLE 34-1   SALES PER MONTH IN DOLLARS

	January	February	March	April	May
Joe	334	245	213	534	122
Mary	345	234	243	654	132
Tom	354	243	241	598	112

By looking at the table we can determine many things. For one thing we can see what each salesperson sold in any month listed. We can also see that April was a good month for the company and that May was a slow month.

Exercise 5: Using Graphs
In the exercises below, examine each graph presented and then answer the questions that follow it. Refer back to the graph as you answer the questions.

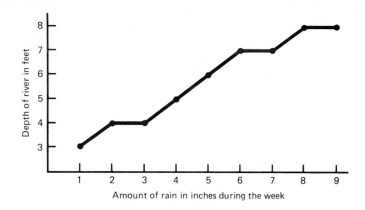

1   In Figure 34-3 the two things related are
  a   Temperature and rainfall
  b   Rainfall and depth of the river
  c   Depth of the river on consecutive days
  d   Temperature and depth of the river

2   In general, the greater the rainfall,
  a   The shallower the river
  b   The narrower the river
  c   The deeper the river
  d   The slower the river's rate of flow

3   When the rainfall was 6 inches the depth of the river was
    a   3 feet
    b   6 feet
    c   7 feet
    d   5 feet

4   How many inches of rainfall does it take to make the river 6 feet deep?
    a   4
    b   6
    c   3
    d   5

5   The deepest the river ever gets is
    a   4 feet
    b   6 feet
    c   8 feet
    d   9 feet

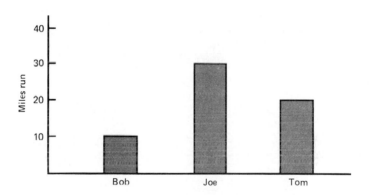

6   According to the graph, how far did Joe run?
    a   10 miles
    b   20 miles
    c   30 miles
    d   40 miles

7   How far did Tom run?
    a   10 miles
    b   20 miles
    c   30 miles
    d   40 miles

8   How far did Bob run?
    a   10 miles
    b   20 miles
    c   30 miles
    d   40 miles

9 Who ran the most miles?
  a   Bob
  b   Joe
  c   Tom

10 Who ran the fewest miles?
  a   Bob
  b   Joe
  c   Tom

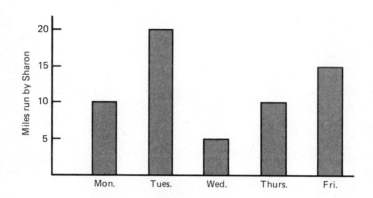

11 According to the graph, how many miles did Sharon run on Wednesday?
  a   5
  b   15
  c   20
  d   10

12 How many miles did Sharon run on Friday?
  a   5
  b   15
  c   20
  d   10

13 What day did Sharon run the most miles?
  a   Monday
  b   Thursday
  c   Tuesday
  d   Friday

14 What day did Sharon run the fewest miles?
  a   Monday
  b   Wednesday
  c   Friday
  d   Tuesday

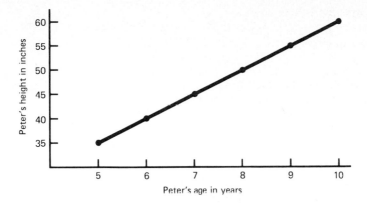

15 What two days did Sharon run the same number of miles?

a Monday and Tuesday
b Thursday and Friday
c Monday and Friday
d Monday and Thursday

16 This graph shows the relationship between

a Height and weight for one child
b Age and height for all children
c Weight and age for one child
d Height and age for one child

17 How tall was Peter when he was 8 years old?

a 40 inches
b 45 inches
c 50 inches
d 55 inches

18 How tall was Peter when he was 10 years old?

a 60 inches
b 35 inches
c 45 inches
d 50 inches

19 How old was Peter when he was 40 inches tall?

a 5 years old
b 6 years old
c 7 years old
d 8 years old

20 How old was Peter when he was 50 inches tall?

a 5 years old
b 6 years old
c 7 years old
d 8 years old

Exercise 6: Using Tables

Examine each table and answer the questions. Refer back to the table as you answer the questions.

TABLE 34-2   PERCENT AND TYPE OF CLASS MEMBERSHIP

Class	Membership	Percent
Upper upper	Aristocracy	0.5
Lower upper	New rich	1.5
Upper middle	Professionals and managers	10.0
Lower middle	White-collar workers	33.0
Upper lower	Blue-collar workers	40.0
Lower lower	Unskilled workers	15.0

1   According to Table 34-2, the lower middle class is made up of
   a   New rich
   b   Unskilled workers
   c   White-collar workers
   d   Blue-collar workers

2   What percent of the population are in the lower-upper class?
   a   0.5
   b   33.0
   c   15.0
   d   1.5

3   Into what class do 10.0 percent of the population fall?
   a   Upper middle
   b   Lower middle
   c   Lower lower
   d   Upper lower

4   The smallest percentage of the population falls into the
   a   Lower upper class
   b   Lower lower class
   c   Upper lower class
   d   Upper upper class

5   The largest percentage of the population falls into the
   a   Upper lower class
   b   Lower upper class
   c   Upper upper class
   d   Lower lower class

TABLE 34-3   CONTENTS OF 12-OUNCE CAN OF BEER

Calories	106
Carbohydrates	3.2 grams
Protein	0.64 grams
Fat	0.0 grams

6   According to Table 34-3, how many calories are in the beer?
  a   94
  b   106
  c   102
  d   108

7   How many grams of protein are in the beer?
  a   10.6
  b   3.2
  c   0.64
  d   106

8   The beer contains no
  a   Calories
  b   Fat
  c   Protein
  d   Carbohydrates

9   The beer contains 3.2 grams of
  a   Protein
  b   Water
  c   Carbohydrates
  d   Fat

10   How many grams of fat are in the beer?
  a   0.0
  b   3.2
  c   0.64
  d   10.5

TABLE 34-4   TOTAL ARREST FOR VIOLENT CRIMES

Crime	Percent Increase	
	Males	Females
Murder	120	118
Robbery	162	293
Auto theft	60	155
Burglary	72	187

11 The right-hand columns of Table 34-4 report
   a The number of crimes committed by men and women
   b The increase in the number of crimes committed by men and women
   c The decrease in crimes committed by men and women
   d The percent increase in crimes committed by men and women

12 For which crime is the percent increase greater for men than women?
   a Murder
   b Auto theft
   c Robbery
   d Burglary

13 What is the percent increase in robbery for women?
   a 162
   b 293
   c 72
   d 60

14 What is the percent increase in auto theft for men?
   a 155
   b 293
   c 60
   d 72

15 In what crime did men have a 120 percent increase?
   a Burglary
   b Auto theft
   c Robbery
   d Murder

TABLE 34-5   APPROXIMATE ANNUAL INCOME OF BLUE-COLLAR AND WHITE-COLLAR WORKERS, 1972

	Sales workers	Craftsworkers and Supervisors	Clerical	Operatives
Male	$11,500	$9,500	$10,500	$8,500
Female	$4,500	$6,000	$ 5,500	$5,000

16 According to Table 34-5, in what occupation do females earn more than males?
   a Sales
   b Craftsworkers and supervisors
   c Clerical
   d None of the occupations listed

17 What is the income listed for male operatives?
   a $10,000
   b $6,000
   c $8,500
   d $11,500

18 What is the difference in listed income between male and female operatives?
  a $500
  b $1,000
  c $3,000
  d $3,500

19 What is the difference between the listed salaries of female clerical
workers and female operatives?
  a $500
  b $1,000
  c $1,500
  d $2,000

20 What is the listed income for female sales workers?
  a $6,000
  b $5,500
  c $4,500
  d $11,500

TABLE 34-6 PULSE RATE AT VARIOUS AGES

Age	Pulse rate in beats per minute
Infancy	130–140
First year	115–130
Second year	100–115
Third year	90–100
4–8 years	85–90
8–15 years	80–85
Adult	70–80
Old age	60–70

21 According to Table 34-6 a pulse rate of 120 for a child in its third year
would be
  a Above normal
  b Below normal
  c Normal
  d Way below normal

22 For an adult a pulse rate of 75 would be
  a Above normal
  b Below normal
  c Normal
  d Way below normal

23 You would expect a person with a pulse rate of 95 to be
  a An infant
  b An adult
  c In old age
  d In his or her third year

24   A normal adult would have a pulse rate of
   a   130–140
   b   70–80
   c   60–70
   d   90–100

25   As people grow older their pulse rate
   a   Goes up
   b   Goes down
   c   Goes up and then down
   d   Goes down and then up

TABLE 34-7   TAX COMPUTATION

If Form 1040, line 34, is—		And the total number of exemptions claimed on line 7 is—		
Over	But not over	1	2	3
		Your tax is—		
17,100	17,150	2,943	2,643	2,378
17,150	17,200	2,958	2,658	2,391
17,200	17,250	2,973	2,673	2,404
17,250	17,300	2,988	2,688	2,417
17,300	17,350	3,003	2,703	2,430
17,350	17,400	3,018	2,718	2,443
17,400	17,450	3,033	2,733	2,456
17,450	17,500	3,048	2,748	2,469
17,500	17,550	3,063	2,763	2,482
17,550	17,600	3,078	2,778	2,495
17,600	17,650	3,093	2,793	2,508
17,650	17,700	3,108	2,808	2,521
17,700	17,750	3,123	2,823	2,534
17,750	17,800	3,138	2,838	2,547
17,800	17,850	3,153	2,853	2,560
17,850	17,900	3,168	2,868	2,573
17,900	17,950	3,183	2,883	2,586
17,950	18,000	3,198	2,898	2,599
18,000	18,050	3,213	2,913	2,613
18,050	18,100	3,228	2,928	2,628
18,100	18,150	3,243	2,943	2,643
18,150	18,200	3,258	2,958	2,658
18,200	18,250	3,273	2,973	2,673
18,250	18,300	3,288	2,988	2,688

26   If Table 34-7 shows that Form 1040, line 34, is $17,834 and you claim two exemptions, your tax is

   a $3,750
   b $2,430
   c $3,245
   d $2,853

27   If Form 1040, line 34, is $18,101 and you claim one exemption, your tax is

   a $2,489
   b $3,203
   c $3,243
   d $2,688

28   If Form 1040, line 34, is $17,300 and you claim three exemptions, your tax is

   a $2,417
   b $2,688
   c $3,453
   d $2,943

29   If Form 1040, line 34, is $17,749 and you claim two exemptions, your tax is

   a $2,823
   b $3,543
   c $3,458
   d $2,645

30   If Form 1040, line 34, is $17,801 and you claim three exemptions, your tax is

   a $2,345
   b $2,560
   c $3,435
   d $2,456

Critical Reading

Back in an earlier part of this book we commented that it is important to remember that everything you read was written by someone. In this section we will be paying more attention to that someone—the author. The essence of critical reading is to consider what, why, and for whom the author has written.

What is Critical Reading?

It might seem that you could summarize the idea of critical reading by simply saying, "Don't believe everything you read." However, there is much more to it than that. The good reader not only doesn't believe everything but also does a lot of other things as well:

1 Considers the source of information given

2 Considers the intended audience for the material

3 Determines the author's purpose

4 Recognizes propaganda techniques

5 Questions ideas that are presented

6   Questions material that is illogical or confused

7   Recognizes that the author may write only that which supports his or her point of view

8   Recognizes conflicting, contradictory, or inconsistent ideas

9   Discounts arguments that are not sound

10   Recognizes the use of literary devices such as metaphors, idioms, figures of speech, and slang

11   Recognizes that the author's choice of words determines the tone of the material and can have the effect of slanting it toward a particular point of view

12   Distinguishes between fact and opinion

13   Distinguishes among humor, satire, sarcasm, irony, and straightforward writing

14   Recognizes implicit assumptions or inferences the author is making

15   Considers the reliability of the author as an expert or informed writer

Knowing *when* to pay particular attention to the need for critical reading is just as important as knowing *how* to read critically. Some reading material is designed simply to inform, without any particular point of view expressed. For example, a book on auto mechanics contains instructions on such things as repairing or replacing parts of the engine. Usually the author's intention is clear, and the material presented is not biased, opinionated, or false.

On the other hand, you know immediately when you begin reading some advertising material that the author has carefully presented only the positive characteristics of the product. The purpose is clear. The idea is to get you to buy the product.

Sometimes the purpose of advertising is less obvious. There is a type of advertising, called "image" advertising, that is designed to promote the general good name of the company. The assumption is that the image will cause people to believe that the company is reliable, public-spirited, trustworthy, progressive, inventive, or whatever the image involves. Examples of slogans used in image advertising are, "Our best product is progress," "Better things for better living through chemistry," "Like a good neighbor," or "Research is the key to tomorrow."

Not only business people use advertising or other techniques to get you to do things. Politicians, teachers, priests, ministers, doctors, dentists, safety engineers, and others are constantly trying to get you to alter your behavior in some way. You might say that they all use "propaganda" techniques. There is an important difference between those who use persuasion to bring about useful changes and those who simply want to sell you their product. It has to do with who will benefit if you do what is suggested. The manufacturer who advertises a product will benefit directly if you buy. The doctors who put out health information through free pamphlets on various medical problems will not directly benefit from your increased good health.

A good question to ask yourself when you begin reading anything that involves persuading you to do something is, Will I benefit from doing this, or will this author (or the company or political party) benefit?

In the exercises which follow, we will give you some information and practice in two areas which seem to give students the most trouble. One is the process of distinguishing between fact and opinion. The other is recognizing the role of the author in the communication process.

Separating Fact from Opinion

Many authors intermingle statements of fact and opinion in such a way that it is sometimes hard to tell them apart. Part of effective critical reading involves being able to tell the difference between fact and opinion. A fact, as we are using the term here, is a statement about which there could be no argument. Opinions are statements which could be denied or argued against, even though you may agree with them. Many readers make the mistake of reading opinions they agree with as facts. If, for example, an author writes, "Most teachers are more interested in educating children than in making a lot of money," and does not support this statement with concrete evidence, it is a statement of opinion no matter how much you or anyone else agree with it.

In the following exercises write the words "fact" and "opinion" next to each statement as appropriate. Then check your answers in the back of the book.

Exercise 1: Fact or Opinion
A recent poll has shown that 47 percent of the students at our local high school admit to having experimented with drugs. _____(1) This figure is surprisingly high. _____(2) It is important for us, as parents, to do something about this. _____(3) Many parents feel that the odds against their children experimenting with drugs are at least 100 to 1. Obviously this is not the case. _____(4) If our children spent less money on drugs they would have more money to spend in other ways. _____(5) The use of drugs is a threat to our self-respect as parents. _____(6) Since the use

of many drugs is prohibited by law _____(7) our community will benefit from attempts to stamp out drug use altogether. _____(8)

Exercise 2: Fact or Opinion
To the Editor:

The mail carriers of Metropolis should be embarrassed by their outrageous salary demands. _____(1) As a road worker on the city's freeway system, I know quite a lot about how much some people should make for a living. _____(2) At present we road workers make about $2,000 less per year than the average mail carrier. _____(3) We have to work on the roads in all kinds of weather, _____(4) with people whizzing by in cars who usually don't care whether they hit us or not. _____(5) Obviously we deserve to be paid more than someone with a safe job like carrying the mail. _____(6)

Exercise 3: Fact or Opinion?
There are various ways of thinking about social differentiation. One common one is based on differences in sex roles. _____(1) There is no society on earth where males and females have identical roles. _____(2) Some people think this is due to biological differences between men and women. _____(3) Others think it is the result of cultural influences. _____(4)

Exercise 4: Fact or Opinion?
To the Editor:

I can't imagine why the police chief has directed his officers not to shoot looters. These people are breaking the law. _____(1) Most of us are not looters. _____(2) We work for a living. _____(3) We pay taxes. _____(4) We have a right to see those who break the law punished as severely as the law allows. _____(5)

Exercise 5: Fact or Opinion?
Most people are not aware of the details of recent research on the effects of marijuana. _____(1) Marijuana has been shown to be harmful in several ways. _____(2) What the studies do not show, however, is marijuana's effect on the spirit of the user. _____(3) It seems clear to me that marijuana users are giving up all willpower by using the drug _____(4) and making a statement that they don't care what happens to their body or their mind. _____(5) Therefore, it is obvious that the

penalties for marijuana use and possession should be increased. _____(6)

The Role of the Author

Every author has certain opinions about the topic he or she is writing on. These opinions will be reflected in the intent, attitude, tone, and bias. These four characteristics can be expressed in the form of the following four questions:

Intent What does the author hope to accomplish by writing this?

Attitude How does the author feel about this topic?

Tone How does this passage appear to the reader (serious, humorous, bitter, objective, emotional, etc.)?

Bias Does the author have a strong opinion about the topic which may affect the choice of facts presented and language used?

Often the answers to these questions are not stated explicitly in the passage but have to be guessed at, or "inferred." This is called reading for inferences and is an important part of critical reading.

Exercise 6: Identifying the Author's Role
In the following passages practice your critical reading ability by answering the questions concerning the author's intent, attitude, tone, and bias.

To the Editor:

I pay a good amount of my income in taxes. I think I have a right to be able to get out of my driveway the day after a snowstorm. Why pay taxes if you can't depend on getting decent service from them?

1   This author's tone would be best described as
   a   Angry
   b   Amused
   c   Bored
   d   Happy

To the Editor:

When are the police of this city going to do something about organized crime? They seem to be too busy giving out parking tickets to bother with a multimillion-dollar crime racket.

2 This author would best be described as
   a Apologetic
   b Disgusted
   c Bored
   d Amused

Dear Bob,

I'm sorry I haven't written you sooner. The new job has kept me really busy, and everyone around here has been sick lately.

3 This author's purpose is mainly to
   a Complain
   b Express anger
   c Apologize
   d Ask for money

To the Editor:

Why isn't your newspaper reporting any good news? All I read about is murder and death. Frankly, I'm sick of all this bad news.

4 This author's purpose is mainly to
   a Complain
   b Apologize
   c Amuse
   d Inform

Let the bread rest for ten minutes. Then shape it into two long loaves by rolling it back and forth on a bread board. Place the loaves in well-greased bread pans and bake in a 350° F oven for 40 minutes.

5 The author's purpose is mainly to
   a Complain
   b Amuse
   c Express anger
   d Inform

Daylight savings time is just another bureaucratic boondoggle. It doesn't really do anyone any good, and it creates countless problems. I say, let's get rid of it.

6 This author
   a Doesn't feel very strongly about daylight savings time
   b Wonders if daylight savings time will be of benefit to farmers
   c Is strongly in favor of daylight savings time
   d Is strongly opposed to daylight savings time

Never leave your automatic transmission running when the shift indicator is in Park or Neutral, unless you are in the driver's seat. There is a chance the transmission might slip into gear, and serious damage or injury might result.

7 This author's purpose is mainly to
 a Amuse
 b Warn
 c Express anger
 d Ask for information

Please send me your packet of information about local bicycle trails.

8 This author's purpose is mainly to
 a Amuse
 b Ask for money
 c Express anger
 d Request information

I suggest that there is an easy way to solve the housing problem we are facing. Let's move the state legislature into tents and let needy families move into the capitol building. At least that way we might get something for our tax money.

9 This author's purpose is mainly to
 a Make a serious proposal
 b Ask for information
 c Amuse the reader
 d Warn the reader

Dear Mary,

It's been a busy month around here. The kids have been sick and my back has been acting up again. Bobby won a prize for a story he wrote in school, and Becky won a record in a radio contest, so there has been some excitement as well as illness . . .

10 This author's purpose is mainly to
 a Express anger
 b Complain
 c Ask for information
 d Inform

Reading in Content Areas

Reading the Social Sciences

One common problem that students have with reading social science material such as psychology or sociology is their tendency to see the information
presented as nothing more than common sense translated into scientific
jargon. This is an easy mistake to make, as we all think we know a lot about
people—after all, we've been observing them all our lives. Unfortunately,
students who make this mistake are often in for a terrible shock when it
comes time to take a test and they find that common sense does not give
them the answers to the questions. Although social science material seems
very "sensible" when we read it, it usually contains a great deal of information—information that a student will be expected to know.

In the following exercises, the passages have been taken from social science textbooks. As you read them, try to ask yourself, What information
from this passage might I be tested on? Often it is a good idea to try to make
up actual test items in your head as you go along. As you answer the questions for each selection, think again about the information in the passage. If
you are not able to answer the questions, try to see what you are doing
wrong as you read.

Exercise 1: Reading the Social Sciences

Several theories have been presented about why we forget things. Common
sense tells us that our memories simply wear out if we don't use them. This

is called the "decay through disuse" theory. In spite of the commonsense appeal of this theory there is virtually no experimental evidence to support it. Displacement theory, another way of looking at forgetting, suggests that every new item we put into our memory knocks out some old memory. Like decay theory, displacement theory has little or no experimental evidence to support it. Two more popular theories are interference theory and loss of access theory. Interference theory argues that memories interfere with each other and that we forget because our memories sometimes damage each other to the point that they are not usable. Loss of access theory says that we actually don't forget anything. that all our memories are still "up there," it's just that some are buried so deeply that we can't find them. This theory is currently the most popular with memory theorists.

1   The theory that says we must forget something to learn something is called
    a   Displacement theory
    b   Interference theory
    c   Loss of access theory
    d   Decay through disuse theory

2   The theory that says that our memories wear out over time is called
    a   Displacement theory
    b   Interference theory
    c   Loss of access theory
    d   Decay through disuse theory

3   The theory that says that some of our memories mess up other memories is
    a   Displacement theory
    b   Interference theory
    c   Loss of access theory
    d   Decay through disuse theory

4   The theory that says that we don't forget things but that our memories become harder and harder to locate is called
    a   Displacement theory
    b   Interference theory
    c   Loss of access theory
    d   Decay through disuse theory

5   The theory that is currently the most popular with memory theorists is
    a   Displacement theory
    b   Interference theory
    c   Loss of access theory
    d   Decay through disuse theory

When infants suffer severe malnutrition they may experience retarded mental development. Infants who die of marasmus, a protein deficiency disease, have been found to have fewer brain cells than normal babies of the same age. Also, brains of malnourished children have been found to weigh less than those of normal children. These effects can be severe and are almost always irreversible.

6 This passage is about
   a Children in general
   b Marasmus
   c Brain weight of children
   d The effects of malnutrition

7 The passage discusses the effects of malnutrition on
   a Adults
   b Laboratory animals
   c Humans and animals
   d Infants

8 The effects of severe malnutrition in infants are
   a Usually not very serious
   b Usually irreversible
   c Often corrected by medication
   d Restricted to physical development

9 Marasmus is
   a Never fatal
   b The result of overeating
   c The result of vitamin deficiency
   d The result of a protein deficiency

10 Compared to normal children, malnourished children were found to have
   a Larger brains
   b Lighter brains
   c More brain cells
   d Deformed brain cells

How warm parents are with their children has a strong influence on the children's personalities. Boys who are highly masculine, for example, tend to see their fathers as very warm and regarding. The warmth of both parents tends to lead to more femininity in girls. The influence of the fathers seems to be more important, since fathers generally treat male and female children differently as compared to mothers who treat male and female children in a more similar manner.

11   The passage is mainly about
   a   Male children and how they develop a sex role
   b   Female children and how they develop a sex role
   c   Babies and how they are affected by their parents
   d   Parental warmth and its effects

12   Boys with warm fathers tend to be
   a   Confused
   b   Retarded
   c   More feminine
   d   More masculine

13   How feminine girls are seems to depend on the warmth of
   a   Their brothers
   b   Both parents
   c   Their sisters
   d   Their brothers and sisters

14   Which of the following tend to treat male and female children more alike?
   a   Fathers
   b   Mothers
   c   Sisters
   d   Brothers

15   In determining the personality of the child, the most important factor seems to be the warmth of
   a   Sisters
   b   Brothers
   c   The mother
   d   The father

Free access to information about what the government is doing is a primary feature of an open society. In closed societies it may be hard to obtain *any* information about government operations. In the U.S.S.R., for example, it is nearly impossible to obtain accurate information about agriculture, industry, finance, or living standards. In contrast, the United States and Britain provide tons of such information. In the United States information is readily available except in the areas of national defense and foreign affairs; and even in these areas the level of information is much higher than in the U.S.S.R. and other closed societies.

16   This passage is mainly about
   a   The U.S.S.R.
   b   The United States

   c   Living standards in various countries
   d   Freedom of access to information in various countries.

17   In the U.S.S.R. information about agriculture and finance is
   a   Printed in daily newspapers
   b   Available in the government section of popular magazines
   c   Available only by written request
   d   Nearly impossible to obtain

18   According to this passage, open societies, as compared with closed societies,
   a   Have much higher costs of living
   b   Have more restrictions on access to information
   c   Have more freedom of access to information
   d   Have much lower standards of living

19   The passage suggests that the United States
   a   Has less freedom of access to information than the U.S.S.R.
   b   Has much less freedom of access to information than Britain
   c   Has much more freedom of access to information than Britain
   d   Has about the same freedom of access to information as Britain

20   In the United States information is *not* readily available in the area of
   a   Agriculture
   b   National defense
   c   Finance
   d   Living standards

There is reason to believe that when teachers feel that a certain child will do well in school, that child will in fact do well. The self-fulfilling prophecy—a phenomenon by which people act as they are expected to—has been documented in many different situations (Rosenthal & Jacobson, 1968).

In the Oak School experiment, some teachers in the California elementary school were told at the beginning of the term that some of their pupils had shown unusual potential for intellectual growth. Actually, the children identified as potential "bloomers" had been chosen at random. There was absolutely no basis for thinking that their IQs would rise anymore than would those of any other children. But on subsequent tests several months or more later, many of the selected children—especially the first and second graders—showed unusual gains in IQ scores. Furthermore, the teachers seemed to like the "bloomers" better.

21   The self-fulfilling prophecy has been documented by
   a   Rosenthal and Jacobson
   b   Smith and Rutland
   c   Vincent and Gardenia
   d   Olson and Wertheimer

22 The children named as having potential for intellectual growth were chosen
  a On the basis of their IQ scores
  b On the basis of teachers' reports
  c At random
  d On the basis of their work in school

23 These "gifted" children were called
  a "Spurters"
  b "Gifted students"
  c "High-potential students"
  d "Bloomers"

24 According to the passage, these children experienced
  a Periodic depressions
  b Actual increases in IQ scores
  c Abuse from the other children
  d No change in their IQ scores

25 The gains of the "bloomers" were greatest if they were in
  a Third or fourth grade
  b Sixth or seventh grade
  c Eighth or ninth grade
  d First or second grade

Reading the Natural Sciences

Students who are not used to studying natural science material are often surprised and dismayed by the amount of material they are expected to know. Natural science texts are often very dense; that is, the facts are packed into the text so that on any page there may be a very large amount of information to be learned.

Students often panic and are tempted to give up when they are faced with so much material all at once. Obviously, one way of dealing with this problem is to break up the assignments into smaller units, sections, pages, or even single paragraphs. Learn one small group of facts at a time, but don't forget to review ones learned earlier. Notes and flashcards can be very helpful with this kind of material.

Another problem students sometimes have with natural science assignments is that they don't realize that they must slow down their usual reading speed to cover this kind of material. If you are used to reading novels, newspapers, or other kinds of materials that can be read at fairly rapid rates, your normal reading speed may be much too rapid for studying natural science. Because of this, cramming or putting off your reading until the last minute can be particularly disastrous in natural science courses. Be sure to allow yourself plenty of time to read and review your assignments and read them slowly enough to get everything out of them that is expected of you. As with all kinds of studying it is a good idea to make up test questions in your head as you read. Read the following passages and see if you can answer the questions.

Exercise 2: Reading the Natural Sciences

Aristotle felt that when a body is in motion, it will come to rest unless it has some force acting on it continuously. Of course, this meant that the planets must have some force acting on them all the time to keep them from stopping. Since no such force could be observed, scientists began to wonder about Aristotle's theory.

Galileo (1564–1642) performed a number of experiments on the motions of various bodies. The equations of kinematics are largely based on his work. Galileo observed that when there was very little friction, a ball would roll for a great distance on a horizontal plane. He formed the opinion that on a perfectly frictionless horizontal plane a ball would roll forever without changing speed once set in motion.

Isaac Newton (1642–1727) accepted Galileo's ideas and incorporated them into his first law of motion: "A body at rest remains at rest and a body in motion remains in motion with constant velocity along the same straight line unless acted upon by an outside force."

1 Aristotle believed that
   a Objects only appear to move
   b Objects will normally come to a stop unless some force keeps them going
   c Objects remain moving forever unless something stops them
   d It is impossible to explain the motion of bodies

2 The equations of kinematics are based on
   a Aristotle's experiments
   b Galileo's experiments
   c Newton's laws of motion
   d The theories of Einstein

3 Which of the following puts the three famous scientists in their proper order?
   a Aristotle, Galileo, Newton
   b Galileo, Newton, Aristotle
   c Aristotle, Newton, Galileo
   d Newton, Aristotle, Galileo

4 Galileo believed that a ball rolling on a frictionless plane
   a Would wander because of the forces acting on it
   b Would slow down and stop, since no force was pushing it

    c   Would speed up owing to the force of gravity
    d   Would roll forever at a constant speed

5 "A body at rest remains at rest and a body in motion remains in motion" is a partial statement of
    a   Newton's second law of motion
    b   Galileo's first kinematic equation
    c   Newton's first law of motion
    d   One of Aristotle's theories

There are a number of stars whose brightness continually varies. Some of these variable stars show wholly irregular fluctuations, but the greater number repeat a fairly definite cycle of change. A typical variable grows brighter for a time, then fainter, then brighter once more, with irregular minor fluctuations during the cycle. Periods separating times of maximum brightness range all the way from a few hours to several years. Maximum brightness for some variables is only slightly greater than minimum brightness, but for others it is several hundred times as great. Since the sun's radiation changes slightly during the sunspot cycle, we may consider it a variable star with an extremely small range in brightness (a few per cent at most) and a long period (about 11 years).

    The light changes in a few variable stars are simply explained; the stars are actually double stars whose orbits we see edgewise, so that one component periodically eclipses the other. But the fluctuations in most variables cannot be accounted for so easily. In some the appearance of numerous spots at regular intervals may dim their light; others might be pulsating, expanding and contracting so that their surface areas change periodically.

6 Most variable stars
    a   Fluctuate irregularly
    b   Have a fairly definite motion pattern
    c   Shift patterns over a number of years
    d   Have a generally consistent fluctuation cycle

7 Times for the cycle of different variable stars
    a   Are fairly uniform
    b   Range from a few seconds to many hours
    c   Range from a few days to infinity
    d   Range from a few hours to several years

8 The sun is a variable star with
    a   A small range in brightness and long period
    b   An unusually short period
    c   An irregular fluctuation cycle
    d   A small range in brightness and a short period

9 One usual explanation of the change in brightness is that
   a The star is consuming its fuel
   b The distance is changing
   c Spots dim the brightness
   d The star is eclipsed by its satellites

10 Another possible explanation of most changes in brightness is that
   a The star is dying
   b Pulsation causes surface area change
   c The star is actually a double star
   d Changes in the earth's atmosphere affect perception

The outside air in most urban communities is grossly polluted by smoke, dust, and gases. In some large cities tons of dust and dirt are deposited in downtown districts. Much of this comes from incinerators; from automobiles, trucks, and buses; from various industries; and from the incomplete combustion of coal. In addition to this solid material, such air contains large amounts of ammonia, chlorine, carbon monoxide, sulfur dioxide, and other gases. In January 1960 the fall of dirt averaged 53 tons per square mile in the city of Chicago but totaled 102 tons in the "Chicago Loop." In New York in 1962 a monthly average of 89 tons of soot and dirt fell on each square mile of the city. In the summer dust is blown into the air from streets, playgrounds, parking lots, or distant farms.

11 The air in urban areas is polluted by
   a Smoke, dust, and gases
   b Fumes, gases, and water
   c Smoke and fire fumes
   d Gas and large particles of dirt

12 Incinerators, transportation vehicles, and industries often
   a Cause tons of gases to be deposited in urban districts
   b Cause very little dust and dirt to be deposited in downtown districts
   c Cause tons of dirt and dust to be deposited in downtown districts
   d Cause much dust and dirt to be deposited in rural areas

13 The primary gases which cause air pollution are
   a Ammonia, chlorine, carbon dioxide, and sulfur monoxide
   b Ammonia, carbon monoxide, chlorine, and sulfur dioxide
   c Ammonia, chlorophyll, carbon dioxide, and sulfur monoxide
   d Sulfur monoxide, chlorine, carbon monoxide, and ammonia monoxide

14 In 1962 New York averaged a monthly accumulation of
   a 98 tons per square mile of soot and dirt
   b 89 pounds per square mile of soot and dirt
   c 89 tons per square mile of soot and dirt
   d 89 tons per square foot of soot and dirt

15 Much of the dust is brought in various areas by the
  a Rain in the summer
  b Wind in winter months
  c Floods during spring
  d Winds in the summer months

In liquids the molecules move freely with respect to each other but are held together by attractive forces. Not only do the molecules of a liquid cling to each other, but they also cling to the molecules of other substances, as may be seen when a piece of glass is dipped into a vessel of water. The molecules of water adhere to the glass and form a thin film over its surface. The attraction of like molecules for one another is called cohesion; the attraction of unlike molecules for one another is called adhesion. It is cohesive forces which hold together so firmly the molecules of iron, copper, and other solid substances.

If the molecules of a liquid have less attraction for each other than for the molecules of the solid with which they are in contact, the liquid adheres to the solid and wets it. Here adhesive forces are greater than the cohesive. When the cohesive forces are greater than the adhesive, the solid is not wet by the liquid. Such is the case when mercury is in contact with glass. If a drop of mercury and a drop of distilled water are placed on a clean glass surface, the water spreads over the glass in a thin layer, while the mercury forms a distorted ball.

16 The molecules in a liquid
  a Move freely with respect to one another but are held together by attractive forces
  b Are bound with respect to one another and do not move freely
  c Are held together by adhesion
  d Involve no attractive forces

17 The attraction of like molecules for one another
  a Is called cohesion
  b Seldom happens in nature
  c Does not occur in solids
  d Is called adhesion

18 The attraction of unlike molecules to one another
  a Operates when mercury is placed on glass
  b Is called cohesion
  c Is called adhesion
  d Does not occur in nature

19 If the molecules of a liquid have less attraction for each other than for those of a solid
  a The solid will stay dry
  b The solid will break in half

 c The solid will cohere
 d The solid will become wet

20 When mercury is placed on glass
 a It acts as a glue
 b The glass may break
 c It penetrates the surface of the glass
 d Cohesion is greater than adhesion

One of the most serious respiratory diseases is influenza, for it is able to attack people of all ages throughout the world. Incidence frequently is highest in young adults. It is an example of a disease that has increased in virulence throughout the years, although since 1942 it seems to have become milder again. Influenza periodically has been epidemic in the United States from 1918 to the present time. Several tragic world-wide pandemics have occurred. One of the most dreadful was the 1918–1919 outbreak, in which there were some 20 million cases of influenza and pneumonia and approximately 850,000 deaths occurred.

  Influenza is an acute disease of the respiratory tract that affects the whole body. It is characterized by a sudden onset, with chills, fever around 102° that may rise to 104°, headache, muscular pains, prostration, sore throat, and cough. Like the common cold, it paves the way for secondary infections caused by hemolytic streptococci and pneumonia. Most deaths are due to complications from pneumonia. Recovery is usual in four or five days.

21 Influenza deserves attention as an important respiratory disease because it
 a Usually results in pneumonia or death
 b Has a long recovery period
 c Attacks all age groups in all countries
 d Occurs most frequently among young adults

22 Influenza is a disease which
 a Has generally increased in virulence
 b Was unknown in the United States
 c Has remained constant in its toxicity
 d Is not difficult to control

23 In the 1918–1919 world influenza outbreak,
 a There were 5,000 deaths
 b There were 2 million deaths
 c A count of deaths was impossible to take
 d There were 850,000 deaths

24 Influenza is a serious disease because
 a It frequently leads to heart disease
 b High fevers usually accompany it

    c It confers no immunity

    d Quarantine is the only really effective control

25 Most deaths from influenza are due to

    a Parainfluenza

    b Faulty diagnosis

    c Complications due to pneumonia

    d Complications leading to hepatitis

Reading Mathematics

Many people have difficulty in studying mathematics. Sometimes their difficulty stems from the psychological idea that they are "no good at math." It has been demonstrated many times that it is often this idea that is causing their problems rather than any lack of skill in mathematics. The best way to deal with this problem is to tell yourself that math involves using the same numbers you have been using all your life and that you know them as well as anyone else. Then set your mind to learning how they are used in the particular part of mathematics you are studying. Many schools offer "math anxiety" courses which are designed to help people overcome their fear of math. These courses have proved very successful, and if you can't overcome your fear by yourself, by all means seek out one of these courses.

Another problem many people encounter is that in mathematics, unlike some other subjects you may have studied, the material has a very important sequence or order. If you don't understand a section of a mathematics text, it is no use going on to the next section. Many sections of math books are based on information presented earlier, so it is essential that you understand a section before going on to the next.

Sometimes students in mathematics courses do not read the written material in the text but assume that the instructor will tell them what they need to know. This can cause them serious problems, since many instructors assume that students have read the text before coming to class. The written sections of mathematics textbooks contain much valuable information. Read the passages in the following exercises and try to answer the questions that follow them.

Exercise 3: Mathematics

A fraction such as A/B where A and B are integers (whole numbers) indicates division: A divided by B or $A \div B$

The number below the line is called the *denominator*. It can also be thought of as the divisor of the division problem presented. The number above the line, which is the dividend of the division problem, is called the *numerator.*

1   An integer is the same as a
   a   Denominator
   b   Whole number
   c   Numerator
   d   Dividend

2   The number below the line in a fraction is called
   a   Numerator
   b   Dividend
   c   Addend
   d   Denominator

3   In the fraction 3/4, the 3 is the
   a   Numerator
   b   Denominator
   c   Divisor
   d   Addend

4   The number above the line in a fraction is called the
   a   Numerator
   b   Denominator
   c   Divisor
   d   Addend

5   If you are dividing A by B and express this division as a fraction, B is the
   _____ of the fraction.
   a   Numerator
   b   Dividend
   c   Denominator
   d   Addend

If the numerator, or top number, of a fraction is less than the denominator, or bottom number, then the value of the fraction must be less than 1. If the numerator is equal to the denominator, then the fraction must be equal to 1. If the numerator is greater than the denominator, then the value of the fraction must be greater than 1.

6   The number above the line in a fraction is called the
   a   Addend
   b   Numerator
   c   Denominator
   d   Divisor

7   If the value of a fraction is equal to 1, then the numerator
   a   Must be 1
   b   Must be equal to the denominator
   c   Must be greater than the denominator
   d   Must be less than the denominator

8   If the value of a fraction is greater than 1, then the numerator must be
   a   Equal to 1
   b   Equal to the denominator
   c   Greater than the denominator
   d   Less than the denominator

9   If the value of a fraction is less than 1, then the numerator must be
   a   Equal to 1
   b   Equal to the denominator
   c   Greater than the denominator
   d   Less than the denominator

10   The fraction 4/3
   a   Has a denominator greater than the numerator
   b   Is equal to 1
   c   Has a value greater than 1
   d   Has a value less than 1

Fractions in which the numerator is equal to the denominator are equal to 1. Fractions in which the numerator is less than the denominator are called *proper* fractions and have a value of less than 1. Fractions in which the numerator is greater than the denominator are called *improper* fractions and have a value greater than 1. A number made up of both a whole number and a fraction such as 2 3/4 is called a *mixed* number.

11   Fractions in which the numerator is less than the denominator are called
   a   Proper fractions
   b   Improper fractions
   c   Correct fractions
   d   Mixed numbers

12   If the value of a fraction is 1, the numerator must be
   a   Equal to 1
   b   Equal to the denominator
   c   Greater than the denominator
   d   Less than the denominator

13   3/4 is an example of
   a   An improper fraction
   b   A proper fraction
   c   A fraction in which the numerator is greater than the denominator
   d   A mixed number

14 7/5 is an example of
  a   A mixed number
  b   A proper fraction
  c   An improper fraction
  d   A whole number

15 3 5/8 is an example of
  a   A whole number
  b   A mixed number
  c   A proper fraction
  d   An improper fraction

Fractions are usually reduced to their lowest terms. A fraction is said to be in its lowest terms when there is no number that will divide evenly into both the numerator and the denominator. For example, 2/4 is not in its lowest terms, since both the numerator and the denominator can be divided evenly by 2. If we divide both the numerator and denominator of 2/4 by 2 the result is 1/2. Therefore 2/4 reduced to its lowest terms is 1/2. Similarly, 3/6 may be reduced to its lowest terms by dividing both the numerator and the denominator by 3. Therefore, 3/6 reduced to its lowest terms is 1/2. A fraction like 3/4 is already reduced to its lowest terms, since there is no number which will go evenly into both the numerator and the denominator.

16 To reduce 3/9 to its lowest terms the numerator and denominator should be divided by
  a   2
  b   3
  c   4
  d   0

17 3/9 reduced to its lowest terms is
  a   1/2
  b   1/3
  c   2/3
  d   3/4

18 Which of the following fractions is already reduced to its lowest terms?
  a   2/6
  b   3/5
  c   4/6
  d   2/8

19 To reduce 5/10 to its lowest terms the numerator and denominator should be divided by
  a   10
  b   2
  c   3
  d   5

20 4/12 reduced to its lowest terms is
   a 2/3
   b 1/5
   c 1/3
   d 3/4

Answer the following questions based on what you have learned about fractions.

21 4/5 is an example of
   a A mixed number
   b A whole number
   c A proper fraction
   d An improper fraction

22 6/5 is an example of
   a A mixed number
   b An improper fraction
   c A whole number
   d A proper fraction

23 1 4/5 is an example of
   a A mixed number
   b A whole number
   c A proper fraction
   d An improper fraction

24 6/9 reduced to its lowest terms is
   a 1/3
   b 2/3
   c 1/4
   d 3/4

25 Which of the following fractions is already reduced to its lowest terms?
   a 2/4
   b 3/9
   c 2/6
   d 7/8

Reading the Humanities

Reading in the humanities is somewhat different than in other content areas. In the humanities, which include literature, fine arts, and philosophy, the author's ideas are usually more important than the facts presented.

The author's ideas may be more or less hidden in the humanities. Sometimes you may have to be something of a detective to find out what they are.

Literature is divided into poetry and prose, although the difference is not always clear. Usually any writing which goes all the way across the page and has a normal flow of words in complete sentences (like what you're reading now) is prose. Any writing that is not prose can be called poetry.

In poetry, the writer's ideas may be extremely well hidden. In fact, in some poetry the author's ideas are so well hidden that the author is not aware of them. When reading poetry for a class, there are a number of things to keep in mind.

1   Has the instructor given you any clues about what to look for in the poem? Consult your notes or, if necessary, ask the instructor for help.

2   Notice the sound of the poem. Read it aloud to yourself or to someone else. Does the sound have anything to do with what is going on in the poem? If it's a love poem, is the sound soft and friendly? If terrible things are happening in the poem, is the sound harsh or frightening? Does the sound of the poem change at different points? If so, why?

3   If there are characters in the poem, what are they like? Make a list of adjectives to describe them (for example, mean, selfish, nasty, greedy, etc.). Do you like them? How does the author tell you what they are like?

4   If the poem is written in the first person, remember that the author may not agree with what the poem says. Does the speaker in the poem speak for the author? How do you know?

5   Even if the poem is not in the first person, it may contain many statements the author does not agree with. Watch out for this. Try to find out what the author really thinks. Then try to find out what it is in the poem that tells you how the author feels.

6   Try to see beyond the obvious meaning of the things in the poem. If the poem talks about fall and winter, for example, perhaps it is really about growing old and dying. If a character in the poem talks about leaving, maybe they are considering suicide. If it rains in the poem, maybe this is a reference to crying. Many ideas in poetry are hidden in this symbolic form. Try to watch for them.

7   Many poems attempt to create a mood in the reader. Try to see what mood the author wants to create and then try to see *how* the author attempts to create this mood. Look at the author's use of sound and color, and think about why the author has used the exact words in the poem rather than other words which might have a similar meaning.

8   What is the author trying to say about life? Many poems contain a message. Try and find the message in this poem. Is the author saying that we have to get used to the idea of death? That love is worth the pain it causes (or isn't worth the pain it causes)? That people are basically good (or evil)? That there is life after death?

In prose, many of the above hints apply as well, but the ideas are usually not quite as well hidden. As in poetry, the big question is, Why is the author writing this? What does the author have to say?

In prose there is more likely to be a story or plot. Think about what happens to the characters. Do they get what they deserve? Why? Try to remember the details of the plot, since some instructors will test you on them to make sure you've done the reading. But go beyond the plot to consider the ideas the author is trying to express. Consider the points above about word choice, color, symbols, sound, etc. Another thing to look for in prose is the setting (when and where the action takes place). Why has the author chosen this particular setting?

In philosophy, the ideas are usually very complex thoughts about broad topics. Philosophers try to deal with the nature of life and the universe. They usually have something to say about the world or about how people ought to behave.

They deal with issues like the existence of God. They like questions. What is God like? What kinds of acts are right and wrong? What is the mind? What is the universe like? In philosophy you must first understand what the philosopher is trying to say. But, more important, you must learn what arguments the philosopher has presented to support the position taken. You must also think about what implications their ideas have. For example, a philosopher might say that killing another person is wrong. What does this say about capital punishment? What about defending your home and family by force? What about defending your country? What arguments does the philosopher present to back up a statement? In studying philosophy, try not to let your own opinions get in the way of understanding what the philosopher is trying to say. You may not agree that it is wrong to kill in defense of your country, but put your opinion aside if you can, at least long enough to understand why the philosopher has taken another position on this subject.

As you can see, studying the humanities requires a lot of thought on your part. You have to go beyond the words and facts of the author. You have to look for the author's ideas. Once you find them, you must try to see why the author has a particular idea and be able to say how you know the idea is there.

A Final Note To Students

You are to be congratulated! You have now finished all of the book. By now you should have learned to read much more rapidly. In addition you should be able to skim and scan material when it is appropriate to do so. Most important of all, you should now be an efficient, flexible reader, with good comprehension skills.

We said earlier that reading improvement as largely a matter of habit change. You have now probably changed your reading habits in addition to gaining a lot of information. For the habit of rapid reading to continue to develop, you need to practice over a longer period than the one you have spent on this book. We suggest that you continue to try to read faster. You can improve much more than you already have if you stick with it.

Over the long run, you will begin to lose some of the reading-rate improvement you have made if you don't do anything to keep these new skills growing. We suggest that you schedule some time for future practice on rapid reading.

One way to remind yourself to pay some attention to your reading rate is to take a calendar that you use a lot and circle one day in each month for the next few months. Then when that day comes, try to do some practice.

One good way to practice is to pick out a nice long, interesting book that you have always wanted to read. Count the words on a few pages to get a word count. Then set up a certain number of pages, and time yourself on them. If you know about how many words you have read, you can divide by the number of minutes it takes to get a reading rate. Try to keep your rate at least as high as the top rate you managed in this book. In time you will find that it is very easy for you to maintain a high rate. Like any other skill, the secret is practice.

Comprehension skills also must be practiced if they are to continue to improve. We suggest that you pay attention to the skills we have worked on in this book. Think about the need to get main ideas and details as you look at new material. Make an effort to see how it is organized, what reference materials are included, and what point of view is being taken by the author.

Time and effort spent to continue improving your reading skills will pay off for the rest of your life.

We wish you the best of success.

Answer Keys

	Unit 2	Unit 3	Unit 4	Unit 5	Unit 6
1	d	d	b	c	c
2	b	b	a	b	d
3	c	d	d	b	a
4	b	a	b	b	c
5	a	c	b	c	d
6	b	a	d	c	a
7	b	c	d	c	b
8	c	b	d	a	a
9	a	d	d	c	c
10	d	d	a	c	d

	Unit 7	Unit 8	Unit 9	Unit 10	Unit 11
1	a	c	b	c	b
2	d	b	d	b	c
3	a	d	c	b	a
4	d	d	b	a	c
5	c	d	a	d	d
6	d	b	d	b	b
7	c	a	d	a	b
8	d	a	b	c	c
9	c	c	d	c	a
10	a	c	b	a	d

Part 2

Unit 13
1. 1410 River Drive **2.** $72,500 **3.** 6 **4.** 2791 Bayside Drive **5.** 781 Tartan Drive **6.** Dishwasher, disposal **7.** 10 **8.** 781 Tartan Drive **9.** 744 Biltmore Drive **10.** 721 Canterbury Drive

Unit 14
1. 7 **2.** 12 **3.** 133–134 **4.** 368–374 **5.** 353 **6.** 61 **7.** 363 **8.** 340 **9.** 55 **10.** 379

Unit 15
1. 11,000 **2.** Start early in the day **3.** Build up speed early **4.** Once **5.** Stop during peak traffic periods **6.** Smooth **7.** 33 percent **8.** 2 **9.** Not necessary or should be avoided **10.** One which allows you to travel at a steady speed

Unit 16
1. a **2.** c **3.** b **4.** a **5.** d

Unit 17
199–211, Chapter on food service; 190–191, Constipation; 327, Nutrition, preoperative; 52, Food, serving of, to isolation patients; 39–40. Pasteurization, milk; 76, Stomach

	Unit 18	Unit 19	Unit 20	Unit 21	Unit 22	Unit 23
1	b	a	d	b	d	c
2	c	b	b	d	d	d
3	d	b	c	a	b	d
4	b	c	d	b	c	b
5	a	b	c	b	b	a
6	b	d	d	a	b	d
7	d	c	c	d	a	a
8	b	b	d	c	a	b
9	a	a	d	b	c	d
10	a	c	c	d	b	c

Part 3

	Unit 26	Unit 27	Unit 28	Unit 29
1	d	c	a	a
2	a	c	a	d
3	c	c	b	a
4	b	a	d	c
5	c	d	c	c
6	d	d	d	b
7	c	c	c	c
8	d	b	a	d
9	c	d	b	b
10	b	c	d	d

Part 4

Unit 31

Exercise 1
1. Rocks 2. Heiroglyphics 3. Van Gogh 4. Water 5. Alcohol 6. Jacket 7. Parole 8. Car cards 9. Pork 10. Spine

Exercise 2
1 The vampire is probably the most frightening of the legendary monsters.

2 Then compressed air came into use as a means of speeding up the movement of mail from place to place.

3 The risk of premature death from all causes is much greater among cigarette smokers than among nonsmokers.

4 To get the best bargain, you need to carefully weigh the advantages and disadvantages of each deal before making your final selection.

5 The class of drugs known as depressants act to slow down the functioning of the central nervous system.

6 Poultry, ground meat, and seafood become unsafe to eat when they start to spoil.

7 If your car is stopped in a blizzard, by all means stay in it.

8 Poison oak and poison ivy can usually be destroyed with herbicides with little or no danger.

9 Encouraging good behavior is always more rewarding for everyone involved than punishing bad behavior.

10 Today's consumers are more aware of the need for vitamins and minerals in the human body than any previous generation.

Exercise 3

1   **a** main idea **b** too specific **c** too general

2   **a** too general **b** main idea **c** too general **d** too specific

3   **a** too specific **b** main idea **c** too specific **d** too general

4   **a** too general **b** too specific **c** too specific

5   **a** too general **b** main idea **c** too general **d** too specific

6   **a** main idea **b** too specific **c** too general **d** main idea

7   **a** too general **b** main idea **c** too specific

8   **a** main idea **b** too general **c** too specific

9   **a** too specific **b** too general **c** main idea **d** too specific

10   **a** main idea **b** too specific **c** too specific

Exercise 4

1   **a** irrelevant **b** irrelevant **c** relevant **d** irrelevant

2   **a** irrelevant **b** relevant **c** irrelevant **d** irrelevant

3   **a** irrelevant **b** relevant **c** irrelevant **d** irrelevant

4   **a** irrelevant **b** relevant **c** irrelevant **d** irrelevant

5   **a** relevant **b** relevant **c** irrelevant **d** irrelevant

6   **a** irrelevant **b** relevant **c** irrelevant **d** relevant

7   **a** irrelevant **b** relevant **c** irrelevant **d** irrelevant

8   **a** irrelevant **b** relevant **c** irrelevant **d** irrelevant

9   **a** relevant **b** relevant **c** irrelevant **d** irrelevant

10   **a** irrelevant **b** relevant **c** relevant **d** irrelevant

Unit 32

Exercise 1
Check marks should occur after numbers 1, 3, 6, 9, and 10.

Exercise 2
1. d 2. a 3. c 4. d 5. a 6. d 7. d 8. d 9. a 10. c

Exercise 3
1. b 2. d 3. d 4. c 5. d 6. a 7. d 8. d 9. a 10. b 11. b 12. a 13. c 14. d 15. d 16. d 17. d 18. a 19. c 20. c 21. b 22. a 23. b 24. d 25. a 26. b 27. c 28. d 29. b 30. a 31. c 32. d 33. b 34. b 35. a 36. d 37. c 38. d 39. d 40. b

Unit 33

Exercise 1
1. Introduction **2.** Main **3.** Supporting **4.** Supporting **5.** Supporting **6.** Conclusion **7.** Introduction **8.** Main idea **9.** Supporting **10.** Supporting **11.** Supporting **12.** Supporting **13.** Supporting **14.** Conclusion

Exercise 2
1. c, d **2.** a, b, e **3.** a, b, c, d **4.** e, f, g, h

Exercise 3
1. b **2.** b

Exercise 4
1. b **2.b.** "snow flurries"—short time, on and off; **c.** "snow squalls"—brief, intense, gusty; **d.** "blizzard"—strong winds, large amounts, low visibility; **e.** "freezing rain" or "freezing drizzle"—freezes on ground, coats with ice

Unit 34

Exercise 1
1. f **2.** h **3.** i **4.** e **5.** b **6.** a **7.** g **8.** j **9.** d **10.** c

Exercise 2
1. d **2.** f **3.** g **4.** i **5.** b **6.** a **7.** h **8.** j **9.** c **10.** e

Exercise 3
1. 5 **2.** 2 **3.** 4 **4.** 6 **5.** 1 **6.** 1 **7.** 6 **8.** 3 **9.** 4 **10.** 2 **11.** 2 **12.** 6 **13.** 5 **14.** 4 **15.** 3 **16.** 7 **17.** 2 **18.** 4 **19.** 3 **20.** 1 **21.** 2 **22.** 1 **23.** 4 **24.** 5 **25.** 7 **26.** 12 **27.** 24 **28.** 34 **29.** 2 **30.** 17 **31.** 8 **32.** 4 **33.** 2 **34.** Glossary **35.** 1

Exercise 4
1. 397 **2.** 251 **3.** 498 **4.** 451–452 **5.** 329–330 **6.** 77 **7.** 309, 436 **8.** 499 **9.** 583–592 **10.** 37 **11.** 203 **12.** 119 **13.** 166 **14.** 22–23 **15.** 164

Exercise 5
1. b **2.** c **3.** c **4.** d **5.** c **6.** c **7.** b **8.** a **9.** b **10.** a **11.** a **12.** b **13.** c **14.** b **15.** d **16.** d **17.** c **18.** a **19.** b **20.** d

Exercise 6
1. c **2.** d **3.** a **4.** d **5.** a **6.** b **7.** c **8.** b **9.** c **10.** a **11.** d **12.** a **13.** b **14.** c **15.** d **16.** d **17.** c **18.** d **19.** a **20.** c **21.** a **22.** c **23.** d **24.** b **25.** b **26.** d **27.** c **28.** a **29.** a **30.** b

Unit 35

Exercise 1
1. Fact 2. Opinion 3. Opinion 4. Fact 5. Fact 6. Opinion 7. Fact 8. Opinion

Exercise 2
1. Opinion 2. Opinion 3. Fact 4. Fact 5. Opinion 6. Opinion

Exercise 3
1. Fact 2. Fact 3. Opinion 4. Opinion

Exercise 4
1. Fact 2. Fact 3. Fact 4. Fact 5. Opinion

Exercise 5
1. Fact 2. Fact 3. Fact 4. Opinion 5. Opinion 6. Opinion

Exercise 6
1. a 2. b 3. c 4. a 5. d 6. d 7. b 8. d 9. c 10. d

Unit 36

Exercise 1
1. a 2. d 3. b 4. c 5. c 6. d 7. d 8. b 9. d 10. b 11. d 12. d 13. b 14. b 15. d 16. d 17. d 18. c 19. d 20. b 21. a 22. c 23. d 24. b 25. d

Exercise 2
1. b 2. b 3. a 4. d 5. c 6. d 7. d 8. a 9. c 10. b 11. a 12. c 13. b 14. c 15. d 16. a 17. a 18. c 19. d 20. d 21. c 22. a 23. d 24. b 25. c

Exercise 3
1. b 2. d 3. a 4. a 5. c 6. b 7. b 8. c 9. d 10. c 11. a 12. b 13. b 14. c 15. b 16. b 17. b 18. b 19. d 20. c 21. c 22. b 23. a 24. b 25. d

Progress Chart

Rate

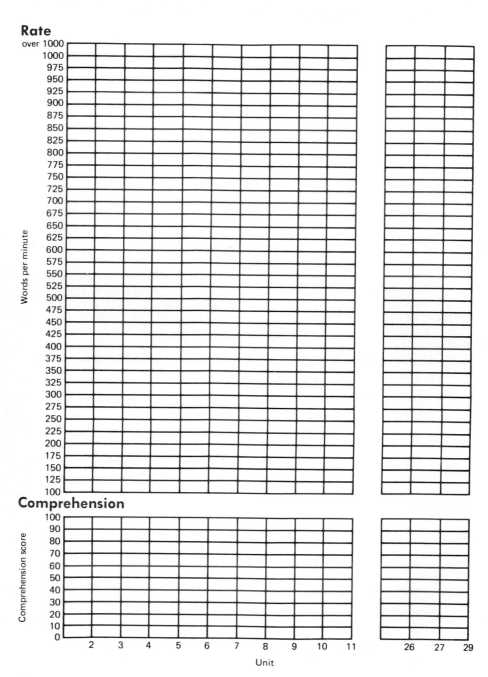

Words per minute

over 1000
1000
975
950
925
900
875
850
825
800
775
750
725
700
675
650
625
600
575
550
525
500
475
450
425
400
375
350
325
300
275
250
225
200
175
150
125
100

Comprehension

Comprehension score

100
90
80
70
60
50
40
30
20
10
0

2 3 4 5 6 7 8 9 10 11   26 27 29

Unit

Acknowledgments

Clover, Marian: "The Last of the Copper Kettle Makers," by permission, *Early American Life*.

Davidoff: *Introduction To Psychology,* pages 356–364. New York: Mc-Graw-Hill.

Donovan, Belsjoe & Dillon: *The Nurse Assistant,* title page, pages iii, v, vii, 393–404. New York: McGraw-Hill.

Horton & Hunt: *Sociology,* pages vii–xiv. New York: McGraw-Hill.

Kraske, Robert: "Okay, So How Fast Does a Chipmunk Run?", by permission, *The Minnesota Volunteer*.

Mitchell: *Concepts Basic To Nursing,* page 574. New York: McGraw-Hill.

Trewartha, et al: *Fundamentals of Physical Geography,* page 374. New York: McGraw-Hill.

Papalia & Olds: *A Child's World,* page 665. New York: McGraw-Hill.